The Spirit of Ruchel Leah

The Spirit of Ruchel Leah

Lester Blum
Preface by Elaine A. Blum

Printed in the United States of America

ISBN Print: 978-0-578-29071-3
ISBN Ebook: 978-0-578-29072-0

Book Cover and Interior Design: Creative Publishing Book Design

"For the dead and the living, we must bear witness."
—Elie Wiesel

Dedicated to the memory of:

Ruchel Leah Taus
Anschel Taus
Elka Taus
Surcha Taus
Moshe Blum
&
the millions who perished
those who survived
and their families

All were victims of the Holocaust
We must never forget!

"The spirits of evil are emerging in a new guise, presenting their anti-Semitic, racist, authoritarian thinking as an answer for the future, a new solution to the problems of our age. And I wish I could say that we Germans have learnt from history once and for all. But I cannot say that when hatred is spreading (throughout the world)*…"*—Frank-Walter Steinmeier, President of Germany – World Holocaust Forum 2020

Contents

Acknowledgements

Over twenty years ago, while perusing one letter from a stack of letters and postcards written in 1939 by his sister, Ruchel Leah, from Poland, Abraham I. Blum felt compelled to bring her Holocaust story to the world. We owe it to his determination that the struggles and courage of Ruchel Leah, his brother-in-law, Anschel, nieces – Elka and Surcha, and his brother, Moshe would always be remembered. The letters were to remind the world of the ravages of the Holocaust. Never Forget! Never Again!

In his later years, Abraham spent countless hours sorting, dating and translating the correspondence from multiple languages – Yiddish, Polish, and French. He annotated many of the letters and documents so that future generations would have a clearer comprehension of their contents. The accomplished task was arduous and emotional. It was difficult for him as he recalled the family's heartfelt reaction to receiving each letter – not knowing if the family in Poland was still alive or dead.

It was the legacy of my sister, Elaine A. Blum, and me to collate his work into a book for today and future generations to understand the struggles our family and many individuals endured during and after the Holocaust.

"How will our children know who they are if they don't know where they came from?" John Steinbeck, author (1902-1968).

As with most significant endeavors, it takes a team to achieve monumental results. *"No man is an island, no man stands alone..."*. John Donne, poet (1572-1631). I have been fortunate to have worked with a stellar collaborative team to execute *The Spirit of Ruchel Leah*.

Infused with our family history since childhood, Elaine worked diligently researching data to establish both the accuracy of the content and to broaden the scope of the book. She engaged in extensive historical and family research thus placing the letters into their proper context; directed avenues of exploration; studied and analyzed the United States immigration policy which resulted in the concise, understandable explanation found in the Preface; and read / re-read the drafts editing them into a cohesive final manuscript. The comprehensive details contained within the letter commentaries would not have been possible without her scholastic guidance. One cannot adequately express one's indebtedness for the scope of her contributions. *The Spirit of Ruchel Leah* has been enriched by her dedication to the legacy.

The letters are filled with a wide range of emotions and attributes – hope, courage, perseverance, resiliency, and despair. To bring these feelings into the letter commentaries required a special understanding of human nature. I am grateful for the continuous contributions of Vladimir Rios. Thankfully, with his life experiences and educational background in the social sciences, he was able to guide us in the editing process. The results are a unique blend of facts coupled with a full range of emotions bringing humanity into the story. I am grateful for his advice, critique, and suggestions during the development and final editing stages of the book. Words, alone, cannot express my gratitude for his many contributions in bringing *The Spirit of Ruchel Leah* to life.

A major obstacle in writing the letter commentaries was the passage of time. Many records were either destroyed or lost during and after the Holocaust; memories have faded into the past; and most of the individuals mentioned in the letters are now deceased. Yet, with the support and assistance of many individuals and organizations, we have been able to reconstruct the history and comprehension of various events. We thank each individual for their contributions.

We wish to acknowledge the scholarly insights into the history of Poland, specifically the Holocaust, afforded us by Dr. Tomasz Cebulski.

On a journey to Poland, Jakub Kuba Lysiak led us shtetl (village) to shtetl on the road of discovery. As I was writing and became mired at different road junctures, he along with Pawel Lukaszewicz and Dr. Kamil Kijek – Department of Jewish Studies, Wroclaw University, acted as directional signs, clarifying the path.

Walking down the dark road of research, one often believes one has reached a roadblock. When faced with these situations, I contacted Slawomir Monik who illuminated the path around the blockage by identifying locations, communicating with various Polish resources, and translating documents. We thank him for his valuable assistance.

When the project was originally conceived, our aunts Nettie Blum Berliner and Norma Blum Hoffman contributed profound recollections of their life in Poland prior to immigrating to the United States in 1930 and of the family who remained in Poland during the war years. We thank them, posthumously, for the information they shared.

We are grateful for the information and photographs furnished by Aunt Sylvia Blum Rubin's children, Nathan Rubin and Marilyn Rubin Goldstein as well as that supplied by Aunt Norma's sons, Bruce and Charles Hoffman.

We thank Evelyn and Harold Gregg for their support in honor of Evelyn's stepfather, Abraham I. Blum's dedication to insure that the family story would not be lost in the annals of time.

Our gratitude is extended to the Israeli descendants of Feige Taus Frydman – her granddaughter-in-law, Betty Vievorka and grandson, Sandro Gilboa, for providing information pertaining to Feige and her children, Chaim and Shoshana.

Perhaps the biggest surprise was becoming acquainted with Michael Chorev, a distant cousin, who facilitated our communication with Shabatai Chrynovizky, Abraham's 1st cousin. Prior to his death in Israel in 2022 at 105, Shabatai, z"l, granted permission to incorporate his poem, *Goworowo* in the book. We are truly honored.

In small shtetls, friendships lasted a lifetime. Abraham remained friends with Reuben and Abe Schmeltz and their niece, Shirley Schmeltz Freedman even after they were all living in New York and his subsequent migration in 1950 to Texas. We thank Reuben's son, Ralph Schmeltz, for information he was able to submit as well as for connecting us with his cousin, Michel Goldflus (whose grandfather was Anschel's brother, Zisket) in Brazil. We appreciate that Michel was able to furnish pertinent information regarding his grandparents. At 100, Shirley contributed early memories of life in Goworowo as well as information and photographs of the Schmeltz/Taus family in Brazil. *May her memory be for a blessing.* We are indebted to the Schmeltz family for their contributions to *The Spirit of Ruchel Leah.*

With minimal clues contained within the letters, the French connection to our story remained an enigma. We wish to express our gratitude and appreciation to Valerie Kleinknecht, Archives Department of the Mémorial de la Shoah, Paris for researching not only identities but also the events pertaining to each individual. The information gleaned allowed for the completion and amplification of that portion of the book.

Family life was often centered on the kitchen where, in spite of limited resources, all meals were seasoned with love. We thank June Hersh, author of *Recipes Remembered, a Celebration of Survival*, for lending her research and expertise to provide us with appropriate recipes for inclusion in the book.

Often when translating, certain words or phrases could be interpreted differently. There were sections in various letters that we felt needed further clarification. Sandra Chiritescu tackled the challenge which resulted in a clearer understanding. To saturate the book with the character of the individuals and flavor of life in the shtetl, we enlisted Sandra's assistance to translate from Yiddish "A Walk Through the Shtetl" from the *Goworowo Memorial Book* (1966) as well as an eyewitness account, "The Tragedy of the Shtetl Goworowo". Information gleaned from both these resources infused the book with compassionate reality. We are sincerely appreciative of the results she presented.

Last, and certainly not least, we would like to acknowledge Olga Guillet for translating the Russian letters written by Ruchel Leah. These previously untranslated letters added an impact to the year that the family was residing in Soviet Russian territory prior to their disappearance. We thank her for also translating the German documents we received from the Wiener Holocaust Library in London.

We wish to thank all individuals and organizations/agencies such as Yad Vashem, United States Holocaust Memorial Museum, History Hub, Imperial War Museum London, Jewish Historical Institute of Warsaw, Jersey City Free Public Library, YIVO, Atlit Detention Center, Magen David Adom, New York Public Library, Arolsen Archives – International Center on Nazi Persecution, Ancestry, Jewish Gen, the Wiener Holocaust Library, and JDC Archives for information and guidance.

The Spirit of Ruchel Leah would not have been possible without the contributions of all of you. For that, we express our gratitude.

Thank You!

Preface

To understand the conundrum addressed in Ruchel Leah Taus' correspondence, it is imperative to focus on the social, political, and economic situation in the United States that fueled the Reed-Johnson Act of 1924 which continued through the 1930s and 1940s. An additional pillar to comprehend is the various provisions in this restrictive first permanent United States immigration law to which her daughter, Elka Taus, and all perspective immigrants in the 1930s needed to adhere. A third component to our understanding was the broad and varied interpretations of this law as imposed by the Foreign Service Officers (Consular Officers) as suggested by Breck-inridge Long, the Assistant Secretary of State (1940-1944). Lastly, it is important to understand President Franklin Delano Roosevelt's position on immigration throughout the Depression and War Years.

The new immigration legislation marks a complete reversal of our previous policy—a landmark in our national history. We no longer are to be a haven, refuge for oppressed the whole world over. We found we could not be, and now we definitely abandon that theory. America will cease to be the melting pot. David A. Reed, Sponsor of the Johnson-Reed Act of 1924

By the 1920s, America was the destination of choice for over 60% of all the world's immigrants which caused a shift in attitude regarding the definition of an "American". Should society be a pluralistic one or a homogeneous one that would conform to the white, Anglo-Saxon, Protestant mold? The prevailing attitude of the 1920s was one of xenophobia, isolationism, nativism, and anti-Semitism.

Xenophobia, a fear or hatred of what is foreign or strange, was expanded to include a dislike of people from other countries due to social and cultural differences; it is a type of nativism that focused on expanding the population base only with the same type of people (from the same geographic areas – Anglo-Saxons and Scandinavians from Northern Europe) as had previously come to the United States. From 1920-1921, in contrast to those who had proceeded them, over 119,000 arriving immigrants were from Central and Eastern Europe. These new arrivals were culturally different as well as more inclined to be urban dwellers rather than from an agrarian society. There were numerous anti-immigration groups such as the American Protective Association and the Immigration Restriction League which had been established in the late 1800s. These groups warned America that these new immigrants would contribute to the power of crooked bosses due to their preference to living in an urban environment and their radical ideas. *"It was not that nativists believed assimilation was impossible, but they did believe that the melting pot of America was suffering from 'alien indigestion'."* President Warren Harding *"called for legislation to allow only people whose racial background proved they could embrace American values to immigrate".* Increasing xenophobia and fear of diluting the American culture gave rise to many opponents of immigration. Senator David Reed, one of the writers of the 1924 Immigration Act, affirmed that earlier legislation *"disregards entirely those of the US who are interested in keeping American stock up to the highest standards—that is, the people who were born here"*.

During his first campaign for a seat in the House of Representatives from the state of Washington in 1912, Albert Johnson proposed, in March 1924, a new bill, the Johnson-Reed Act, stated, *"the greatest menace to the Republic today is the open door it affords to the ignorant hordes from Eastern and Southern Europe, whose lawlessness flourishes and civilization is ebbing into barbarism"*. Johnson remained a Congressman from 1913-1933; between 1913 and 1918 he served as a member of the House Immigration Committee and was appointed Chairman of the committee in 1919. While Chairman, in 1919, he tried to suspend all immigration, but the proposal was rejected by the House of Representatives. In 1921, the House acquiesced to a two-year moratorium on all immigration though this bill was not supported by the Senate. Senator LeBaron Colt of Rhode Island, chaired the United States Senate Committee on Immigration and also supported restricting immigration.

Secretary of Labor from 1921-1930 under three Presidents (Warren Harding, Calvin Coolidge, and Herbert Hoover) James J. Davis, was also an ardent opponent of immigration. He stated his doubt, *"Whether such vast throngs could be assimilated and Americanized or would eventually submerge and absorb the American people, as the old Roman civilization was completely submerged by the hordes which once migrated into that fair land for peaceful purposes"*. Since the Immigration and Naturalization Bureau was originally under the jurisdiction of the Department of Labor, James Davis exerted enormous influence in directing the policies regulating immigration. Under Davis, the Bureau was reorganized and streamlined to meet the demands of changing immigration policy of the United States during the 1920s.

Eugenics, which was the study of how to rearrange reproduction within human populations to maximize the occurrence of desirable characteristics, was a very popular "scientific" movement in the United States beginning in the late 1800s. It emphasized the idea that among Homo sapiens there were superior and inferior genetic types. The study of eugenics served as justification for the fears and paranoia regarding the new immigrant populations and gave these attitudes a modicum of legitimacy. It also formed a foundation for racial prejudice and anti-Semitism. The 1917 immigration statute which excluded "all idiots, imbeciles, feebleminded persons, epileptics and insane persons" from immigrating to the United States was implemented for eugenicist purposes. James J. Davis supported the eugenics movement. He believed that Americans, under the rubric of the eugenics movement, could discern between *bad stock and good stock, weak blood and strong blood, sound heredity and sickly human stuff*". Albert Johnson advocated these beliefs among his Congressional colleagues which aided his crusade against immigrants and radicals; he was appointed president of the Eugenics Research Association of America and used data gathered by the organization to campaign for a change in immigration policies.

There was a period of escalating racial unrest and violence after World War I—most notably the Tulsa, Oklahoma race riot of May 1921 in which thirty-five blocks of the Greenwood District, a black neighborhood, were destroyed. Between thirty-nine and seventy-five people were killed, eight hundred injured, and over 6,000 interned.

Other riots had occurred in 1919 in Chicago and Washington D.C. Madison Grant, the author of *The Passing of the Great Race*, wrote,

> *"We Americans must realize that the altruistic ideas that have controlled our social development during the past century and maudlin sentimentalism that has made America 'an asylum for the oppressed' are sweeping the nation towards a racial abyss".*

During this period, the Klu Klux Klan membership, with its virulent anti-immigrant, anti-Jew, anti-Catholic and anti-Black attitudes, proliferated so, that by 1924, it had over four million members. New York State, alone, had over 200,000 members in 1923.

Notable figures such as Henry Ford through his newspaper, the *Dearborn Independent*, Charles Lindbergh through his organization, the America First Society, Father Coughlin through his radio broadcasts which began in 1926, and the Daughters of the American Revolution became known for their anti-Semitic sentiments which were sometimes couched in diatribes against socialism and communism. Religion did not officially play a role in the formation of the immigration policy as Jews were considered "white", however, Albert Johnson called Jews *"unassimilable, filthy, un-American and often dangerous in their habits"*, and *"a stream of alien blood".*

In 1922, Harvard University imposed a 15% Jewish admission quota to offset the "Jewish problem" of a 20% Jewish component to the student body. The American Jewish community was reticent in light of these verbal attacks as they had no cohesion and feared to disrupt the status quo as well as exacerbate the anti-Semitism.

After the massive industrial effort that powered World War I ended, the United States fell into a state of economic depression, post-war inflation and ultimately a stock market crash, known as the "forgotten depression", in 1920 that lasted through July 1921. With the returning troops and the crash, unemployment in 1920 reached 12% and the populace feared that new immigrants would take their jobs which caused labor unrest. Samuel Gompers, President of the American Federation of Labor, posited that unrestricted immigration would flood the country with unskilled as well as skilled labor for the "purposes of breaking down American standards", while restriction of immigration would "prevent disintegration of American economic standards". Unions were viewed as a product of foreign-inspired anarchists and Bolshevik agitators. Gompers also opined that those new immigrants would accept lower wages which would lead to lower wages for all workers. One goal of restricting immigration was to keep wages and living standards high for both the existing population and for any new arrivals.

The year 1919 witnessed a series of labor strikes and bombings which were blamed on socialist ideas brought from Europe by Russian and Eastern European immigrants—the Red Scare. As per Senator Miles Poindexter, the strikes were "a desire to overthrow our Government, destroy all authority and establish Communism." Numerous Red Flag parades in celebration of May Day, the worker's holiday, which ended in riots, also occurred in 1919. It was presumed that the celebrants were socialists, anarchists, communists, and unionists. Those involved were subsequently arrested and deported as radical aliens.

On April 29, 1920 Attorney General Alexander Palmer warned the nation that the Department of Justice had uncovered plots against the lives of more than twenty Federal and State officials as part of the May Day celebrations.

These events further supported the views promulgated by the afore-mentioned anti-immigration groups. At this time, 21% of the

American population believed that "most Jews were Communists". This sentiment also extended to the Italian population.

The effects of the Red Scare and the radical political agitation lingered into the 1920s as evidenced by the presumed guilt of two confessed anarchists in the Sacco-Vanzetti court case. In this case, two Italian immigrants, purported anarchists, were tried for robbery and murder in Massachusetts on April 15, 1920 and found guilty. It has been posited that anti-Italianism, anti-immigrant, and anti-anarchist sentiment and bias as well as fear of radicals influenced the verdict. The accused were executed in August 1927 though evidence of their innocence was produced during the appeals process. This case had national and international repercussions as well as continued to fuel the xenophobic and nativist sentiments of the times.

In 1913 the Department of Labor was established to regulate labor issues and enforce labor and occupational safety standards; additionally, it included the pre-existing Bureaus of Immigration and Naturalization. However, in 1918, the State Department was created and established a Visa Department. The State Department continued to have visa responsibilities throughout the Depression and the War Years (1929-1945).

Prior to 1921, no passports, visas, nor alien registration restricted immigration to the United States; the previous legislation was the Chinese Exclusion Act of 1882 and the 1917 Immigration Act. The 1917 act was the first widely restrictive immigration law which imposed a literacy test, an arrival tax, and gave officials more discretion and more categories regarding whom to exclude. The act also reaffirmed the ban on contracted labor and introduced the issue of "likely to become a public charge" as a basis for exclusion. Special provisions were established regarding those fleeing racial or religious persecution to evade the literacy test. It created an "Asiatic barred zone" which covered British India, most of Southeast Asia, and almost all of the Middle East. The only exceptions were the Japanese whose immigration had previously been limited in 1907 by a "Gentlemen's Agreement" and those born in the Philippines, a United States colony since 1898. Students and certain professionals with their wives and children from this zone such as teachers, government officers, lawyers, physicians, and chemists were exempted from the prohibition to immigrate. Under this act, entry decisions were made upon disembarking in the United States by the Immigration Officials at the Port of Entry.

In order to placate business needs for laborers in light of the impact of the Spanish flu pandemic during 1918/1919 and the unions' concerns regarding keeping foreign workers out of the country to maintain higher salaries, in 1921, Senator William Dillingham proposed an approach which would limit immigration by setting admission quotas based on nationality. Each nation would be allowed to send only 5% of its 1910 United States census population, i.e., foreign-born persons of that nationality, as immigrants to the United States. Albert Johnson reduced the quota to 3% with a total yearly limit of 350,000. Although Woodrow Wilson rejected the bill, Congress passed it as the Emergency Quota Act of 1921. Although the 1910 census extended the questionnaire to include the Hebrew race as a category, the Emergency Quota Act was only concerned with the country of birth to determine quotas.

The 1921 act did not include any immigration from Canada, Mexico, or other Western Hemisphere countries in this quota system; therefore, illegal immigration through Canada and Mexico increased. Relatives of American citizens (wives, children under 18, parents, brothers, and sisters) were exempt from this quota in order to preserve family unity. Quotas were opened at the beginning of the month. Ships filled with prospective immigrants were turned away and sent back to their places of origin if the quotas from their respective countries had been filled. With 1910 as the base year, "the southern and eastern European countries received 45% of the quotas while the northern and western European countries received 55%. This quota reduced the immigration from southern and eastern Europe by 20 percent from prewar levels. The annual quota for Poland in 1921 was 30,977. In May, 1922 the law was extended for another two years.

The nativists believed that the immigration reduction under the 1921 Emergency Act was insufficient, so, in keeping with his belief that "the greatest menace to the Republic today is the open door it affords to the ignorant hordes from Eastern and Southern Europe, where lawlessness flourishes and civilization is ebbing into barbarism", Albert Johnson proposed, in March 1924, a new bill, the Johnson-Reed Act which would further limit the influx from these areas. The purpose of the Act was "to preserve the ideal of US homogeneity" according to the United States Department of State's Office of the Historian. This Act used the 1890 census as a benchmark and lowered the quota percentage to 2% of those foreign-born of the **total** United States population. It also lowered the annual limit to 165,000 immigrants. As most immigration from Southern and Eastern Europe occurred after 1890, this basis would automatically limit immigration from those areas. The law also excluded from immigration all persons ineligible for citizenship; under the previous 1790 and 1870 laws those of Asian lineage were excluded from citizenship and now could no longer immigrate to the United States. In contrast to the 1917 act, this act gave no priority to refugees fleeing racial or political persecution. In an attempt to curtail illegal immigration through Canada and Mexico (non-quota countries) potential immigrants from those countries had to prove residency of at least two years prior to emigration to the United States. Token quotas of 100 were given to the independent African States of Ethiopia and Liberia along with the international protectorates of Palestine and Iraq. Only 12.4% of the quota went to Southern and Eastern European countries in contrast to 85.6% to the Northern and Western European countries. The annual quota for Poland was reduced from 30,977 to 5,982 in 1924.

In addition to lowering the existing quotas, changing the quota calculation method and excluding those ineligible for citizenship from immigrating, the 1924 Johnson-Reed Act or National Origins Act transferred the issuance of visas from Immigration Officers at the port of entry to the Foreign Service Officers of the Consulates of the countries of origin. The Foreign Service Officer had discretionary (final and unreviewable) authority to deny or grant visas. The Act also authorized the State Department to develop its own procedures and forms. A "consular control system of immigration", whereby the State Department and the Immigration and Naturalization Service evolved into a two-tier inspection system; that is, a valid visa issued by the State Department abroad did not guarantee admission as immigration officers in the United States could yet exclude the potential immigrant. This Act allowed the decrease of immigration without the necessity of any Congressional action and established a more permanent immigration law.

The transference of legal responsibility for visa issuance eliminated the need for ships to be returned to their ports of embarkation as the visas filling the quotas were issued prior to leaving the country of origin and an individual could not leave the country without a valid visa. The Foreign Service Officers could not issue more than 10% of the quota in visas per month (for Poland, this would be less than 600 visas monthly.) Unused quota slots were ineligible to be carried over to future years. The "quota year" was considered to be June to June. Per Alfred J. Hillier, the 1924 Bill was "the most important immigration law to be enacted in the history of the country". It was considered the high point of Alfred Johnson's career and was "*the culmination of decades of nativist agitation going back to the Know-Nothings of the 1850s*" (a political party officially known as the "Native American Party") Alan Dawley.

> "*At one level, the new immigration law differentiated Europeans according to nationality and ranked them in a hierarchy of desirability. At another level, the law constructed a white American race, in which persons of European descent shared a common whiteness distinct from those deemed to be not white.*" Historian Mae Ngai

Henry Laughlin, a eugenicist, stated that after the 1924 act, "*the immigrant to the United States was to be looked upon, not as a source of cheap or competitive labor, nor as one seeking asylum from foreign oppression, nor as a migrant hunting a less strenuous life, but as a parent of future-born American citizens. This means that the hereditary stuff out of which future immigrants were made would have to be compatible racially with American ideals.*"

On July 7, 1927, though not implemented until 1929, the annual quota calculation changed in that the two percent rule was replaced by an overall cap of 150,000 immigrants annually and quotas were to be determined by "national origins" as revealed in the 1920 census which did not include blacks, mulattos, or Asians.

This national origins quota system established in 1924 with few adjustments continued until the 1965 Immigration and Nationality Act, which admitted immigrants based on their relationship to a United States citizen, green card holder or United States employer, was established.

The procedures and protocols required by the 1924 act made the quest for a visa more difficult and a "new kind of misery". Prospective applicants were placed on a waiting list after first registering with the consulate. Until 1938, the waiting period was generally 3-4 months in Germany; however, after Kristallnacht (a massive anti-Jewish pogrom prompted by Gestapo Chief Heinrich Muller on November 9-10, 1938 in Germany, Austria, and the Free City of Danzig) the wait for an appointment extended to 2-3 years. Under the Act, the potential immigrant had to prove his eligibility by completing an application form, passing an interview with the Foreign Service Officer, acceptance of financial support documentation and passing a physical examination.

Section 7 (b) and (c) of the 1924 Act specifies the requirements for a visa application and the supporting documents required. The visa application consisted of 23 categories of questions on a 7-page document. The questions revolved around the following: the prior 5 years places of residence; place/date of birth; marital/family status; names and addresses of close family members in the United States, Europe, or North Africa; education/occupation; political activities and affiliations; basis of belief "may be endangered in country of present residence by reason of past political connections or activities"; names, addresses, nationality of all persons or organizations interested in the admission of the applicant; purpose of immigration; whether ever in prison or if applicant or parents were treated for mental issues.

Also 2 copies of a police dossier with criminal and military records along with a birth certificate and "all other available public records concerning him (the applicant) kept by the Government to which he owes allegiance" were required, if available. The potential immigrants used the waiting period for the Consulate interview to gather all the necessary documentation.

The two major barriers to this process were the individual's ability to produce the required documentation and the ability to satisfy the financial support stipulation that would confirm that the individual would not likely become a public charge.

Consular officials had no authority to waive the documentation request if it were obtainable; this issue was clarified in 1934 by an instruction that stated that if the documentation would be obtained with "serious inconvenience", "personal injury", "financial loss" or peculiar delay and embarrassment, the requirement for documentation could be exempted. Although Raymond Herman Geist, American Consul in Berlin, was greatly concerned regarding fraudulent documents being promulgated and urged Consular Officers to strictly uphold the requirements, he admitted that difficulties might exist in obtaining the necessary documents under the Nazi regime.

In 1929, President Herbert Hoover, in the face of the Great Depression ordered the State Department to make sure immigrants would not become economic burdens; therefore, it was established that any potential immigrant who would need to work to support himself was automatically designated as "likely to become a public charge". Under previous law, this designation referred only to those mentally or chronically ill. In order to avoid this designation, employers were not allowed to confirm employment prior to admittance to the United States.

Francis Perkins, the Secretary of Labor, was the only member of Roosevelt's Cabinet who advocated liberalizing immigration procedures. In 1933 she tried to revise the "likely to become a public charge" strict interpretation by suggesting that Section 21 of the 1917 immigration law allowed the Secretary of Labor to accept a bond as a guarantee for a potential immigrant which would have exempted applicants from being rejected under the "likely to become a public charge" clause. The State Department rejected this suggestion based on the fact that the 1917 act intended the bond to cover only hardship situations and was to operate only after the immigrant would arrive at a United States port. They also posited that the 1924 law invalidated the previous act. The Assistant Attorney General Office ruled in Labor's favor, although some discretion was still retained by the Foreign Service Officers. The Department of Labor prepared new regulations to disseminate to the Consuls which was done in the summer of 1935; however, the State Department never changed their position. Commissioner General of Immigration, David McCormack, said in 1937 that since visas were being favorably handled, there was no urgency to implement the bond measure. The Department of Labor failed to push the issue of bonds versus sponsors.

In 1936, the language of the order changed from "likelihood (possibility) to probability" to become a public charge. The interpretation of this provision varied among Consular Officers in different countries as well as within the same Embassy and from year to year. Two American sponsors were necessitated who had the financial resources and willingness to guarantee the potential immigrant's economic status. Close relatives of the prospective immigrants who were either American citizens or had permanent resident status were preferred, but were not required. For many immigrants, obtaining these financial sponsors was the most difficult part of the American visa process.

The sponsor needed to submit 6 notarized copies of an Affidavit of Support and Sponsorship that included a certified copy of the Federal tax return; a Dun and Bradstreet statement or certified account of business, income, and investments (if a businessman) or a notarized letter from the employer designating occupation, salary, and length of employment (if an employee); an affidavit from a bank about account and amounts sent abroad; the cash surrender value of insurance; notarized broker statements; real estate deeds; details of relationship or friendship with potential immigrant; letters of recommendation from businessmen or prominent citizens. No additional money was required if the credit on the affidavit was deemed to be sufficient. In 1934 George Warren, economic advisor to Franklin Roosevelt, stated that the documents requested from the American sponsors were "oppressive and illogical and so varied that no two Foreign Service Officers made the same stipulations".

The Foreign Service Officers also scrutinized the sponsors' affidavits rigorously and rejected them for the smallest error which required the entire application for a visa to be refiled. The Foreign Service Officers believed that the State Department expected them to restrict immigration, so 75% of the applicants were denied visas. The application failure could be a product of "unsatisfactory documents", political activities or affiliations raised in the interview process, medical issues including mental faculties as well as problems with the sponsors' affidavits.

In October 1939, the United States State Department issued three new visa requirements: confirmation that the applicant was not a member of the Communist Party or any other group working against American institutions; a loyalty certificate; proof of permission to leave Germany and German occupied territories; and proof of transportation to the United States. In 1939, journalists stated that "slamming shut the gates of immigration is admitting that American democracy has failed in the past and no longer exists today".

Although the Immigration and Naturalization Service was transferred from the Labor Department to the Justice Department in May 1940 due to concerns of national defense and to curtail sabotage and spying, the Visa Department was still the purview of the State Department.

Breckinridge Long, a long-time friend of Franklin Roosevelt and an avowed anti-Semite, was the Assistant Secretary of the State Department from 1940-1944 and, as such, the head of the Visa Department. By 1943 he supervised 23 out of the 42 divisions relating to immigration. He was the most vocal advocate against immigration during the 1930s and 1940s. While Ambassador to Italy from 1933-1936, he showed sympathy to the fascist leader, Benito Mussolini and advocated for long term accommodation with Hitler.

On June 26, 1940, just ten days after the surrender of France to Germany, Long issued a memorandum to the State Department officials which outlined ways to obstruct the granting of United States visas. *"We can delay and effectively stop for a temporary period of indefinite length the number of immigrants into the United States. We could do this by simply advising our consuls, to put every obstacle in the way and to require additional evidence and to resort to various administrative devices which would postpone and postpone and postpone the granting of the visas. However, this could only be temporary. In order to make it more definite it would have to be done by a suspension of the rules under the law by the issuance of a proclamation of emergency...."*

In response to this memo, Secretary of State Cordell Hull instructed all officials abroad to screen applicants more fully and to reject any applicant whose identification or intentions were doubtful even if the individuals had been recommended by the President's Advisory Committee on Political Refugees.

Long had the authority to remove Consuls who did not agree with his positions; *"when he pressed for Consuls in occupied countries to decide whether visas were accepted or rejected, it all but guaranteed that the visas would not be accepted".*

In June 1941, the Visa Department further restricted the process by denying visas to individuals who had close relatives in Nazi-occupied territory; the rationale was fear of 5th columnists, spies embedded in American society, and Nazi blackmail. In addition, the Visa Department began to require FBI background checks on all visa applicants.

All United States consulates in Nazi-occupied territories were closed in July 1941. Prospective immigrants would have to reach consulates in neutral countries, Southern France, or Portugal in order to complete their visa process.

Upon the close of the United States consulates, the visa control was transferred to an interdepartmental review committee (consisting of the State Department, Justice Department, FBI, and military intelligence) in Washington, D.C. This transfer required the submission of new paperwork on behalf of the potential immigrants.

By October 31, 1941, Nazi Germany no longer allowed immigration or the issuance of exit visas. The United States declared war on Nazi Germany on December 11, 1941.

President Franklin D. Roosevelt's role in the immigration and refugee crisis has been viewed as one of indecisiveness, obstructionist, non-humanitarian, and anti-Semitic which led to the loss of thousands of lives. He neither supported nor refuted restricting immigration. Roosevelt felt that to support less restrictive legislation would have been political suicide in light of his largely anti-immigrant Congress and public opinion. He also did not want to support any legislation that would have prematurely pulled the United States into another war with Germany. He believed that a military victory ultimately would solve the issues of immigration and refugees. He stressed that the refugee problem was a global issue not solely an American one; so, in 1938, he created the President's Advisory Committee on Political Refugees who would study the issue and propose solutions. He urged the State Department to reduce delays in screening and to listen to recommendations of the Advisory Committee; however, Breckinridge Long stated in his diary in October 1940 that Roosevelt "was whole-heartedly in support of the policy which would resolve in favor of the United States any doubts about admissibility of any individual". Ultimately, Roosevelt was a politician juggling the immediate needs of his country against a humanitarian worried about the salvation of a people.

"To sin by silence when they should protect makes cowards of men." Ella Wheeler Wilcox (1850-1919) Poet/Journalist

As it is apparent, Ruchel Leah and her quest for a visa for Elka, her eldest daughter, was derailed from the outset by the United States' attitude towards immigration and the unfortunate timing of her request in August 1938 for an interview with the Consulate. Ruchel Leah as well as her family in the United States were also stymied by misinformation, a lack of understanding of the requirements, the process, the obstacles that needed to be overcome and the quota system in general. The continually changing rules and requirements, and, the obstructionism of the State Department, also would have impacted the determination of Elka's eligibility for a visa.

Dorothy Thompson wrote in 1938 in *Refugees: Anarchy or Organization?*: *"It is a fantastic commentary on the inhumanity of our times that for thousands of people a piece of paper with a stamp on it is the difference between life and death."*

This proved to be the case for Elka Taus and countless others.

Elaine A. Blum

Map of Poland 1921-1938

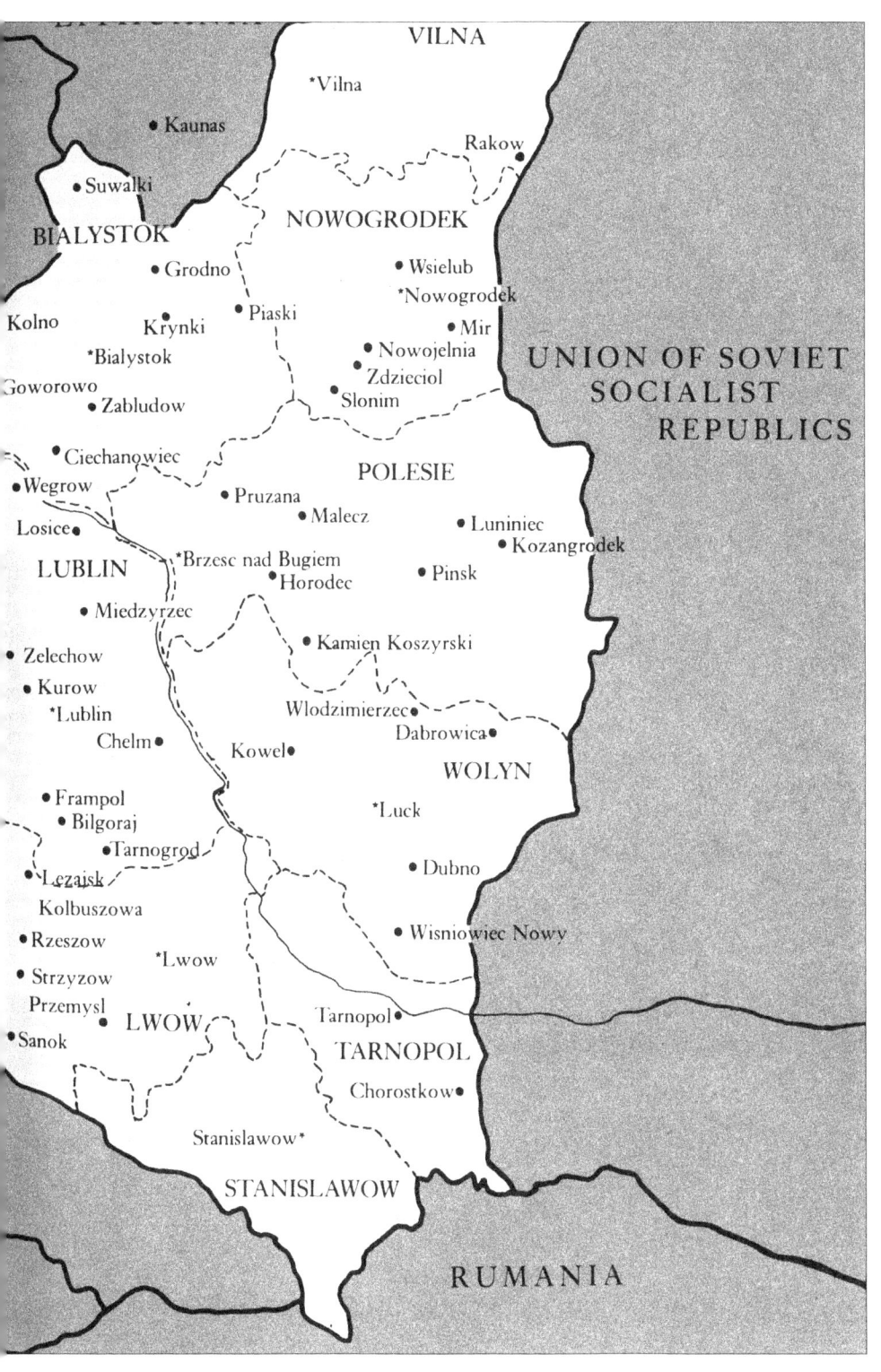

VILNA

*Vilna

• Kaunas

Rakow

• Suwalki

BIALYSTOK   NOWOGRODEK

• Grodno   • Wsielub

Kolno   *Nowogrodek

Krynki   • Piaski   • Mir

*Bialystok   • Nowojelnia

Goworowo   • Zdzieciol

• Zabludow   • Slonim

• Ciechanowiec   POLESIE

• Wegrow   • Pruzana

Losice•   • Malecz   • Luniniec

LUBLIN   *Brzesc nad Bugiem   • Kozangrodek

• Horodec   • Pinsk

• Miedzyrzec

• Zelechow

• Kurow   • Kamien Koszyrski

*Lublin

Chelm•   Wlodzimierzec•

Kowel•   Dabrowica•

• Frampol   WOLYN

• Bilgoraj   *Luck

•Tarnogrod

•Lezajsk   • Dubno

Kolbuszowa

• Rzeszow   • Wisniowiec Nowy

• Strzyzow   *Lwow

Przemysl   Tarnopol•

•Sanok   LWOW   TARNOPOL

Chorostkow•

Stanislawow*

STANISLAWOW

RUMANIA

UNION OF SOVIET
SOCIALIST
REPUBLICS

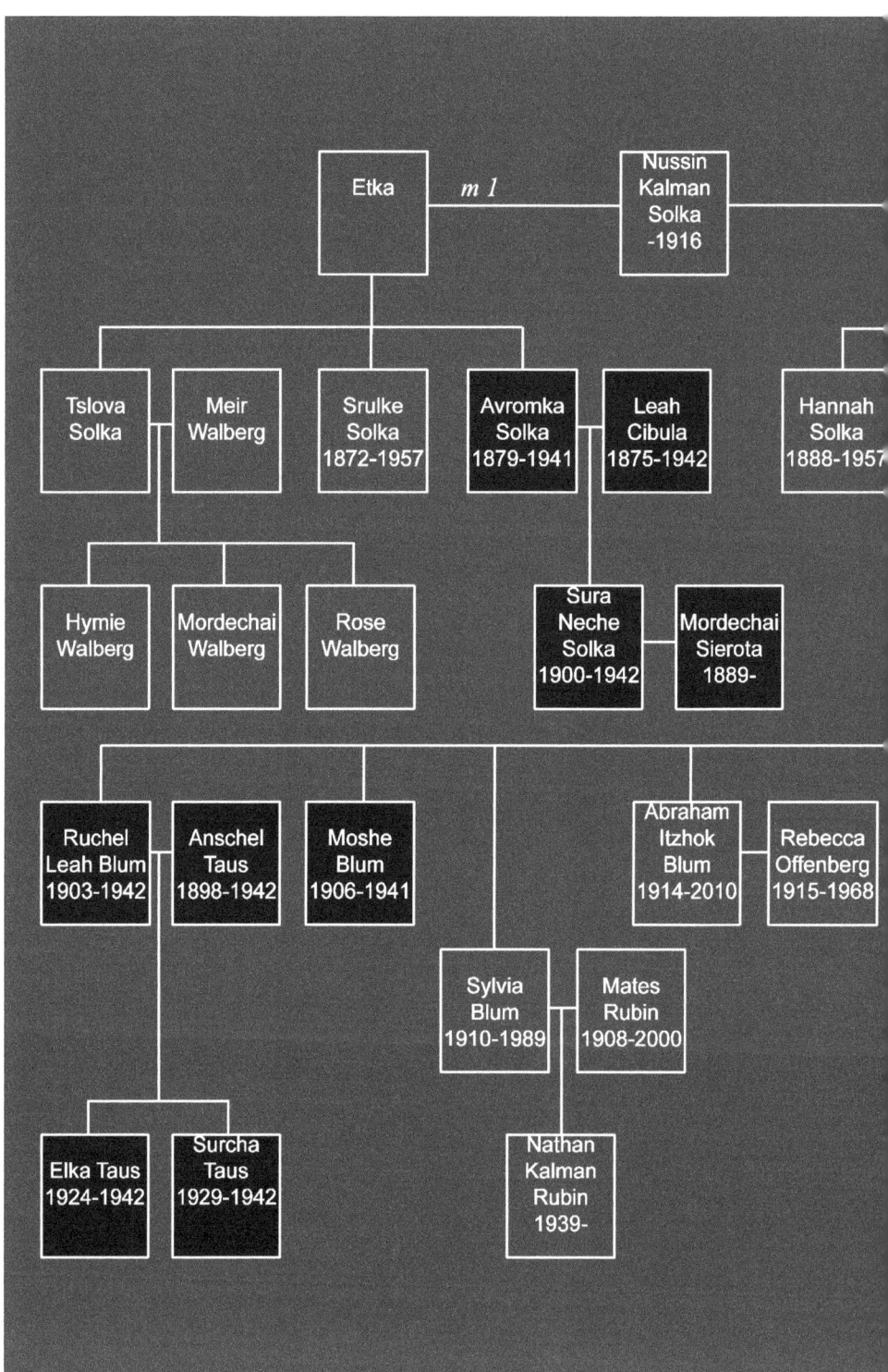

Solka/Blum Family Tree

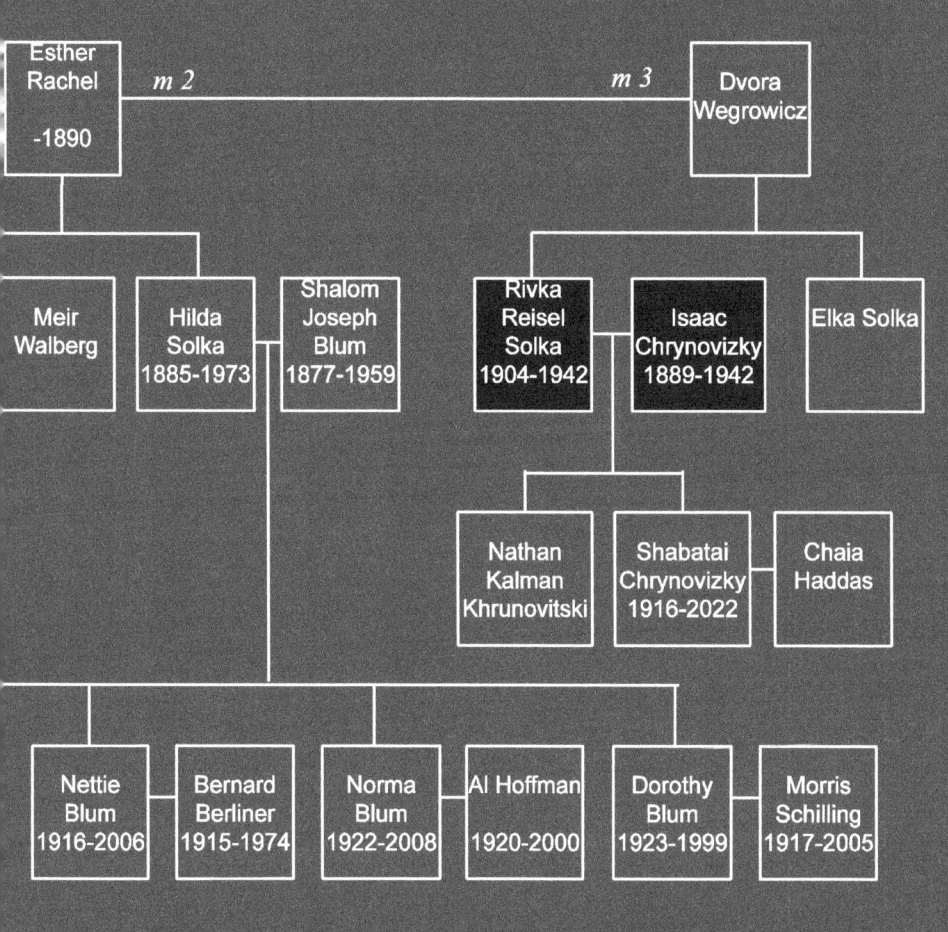

| Esther Rachel -1890 | *m 2* | | | | *m 3* | Dvora Wegrowicz | |

Meir Walberg

Hilda Solka 1885-1973

Shalom Joseph Blum 1877-1959

Rivka Reisel Solka 1904-1942

Isaac Chrynovizky 1889-1942

Elka Solka

Nathan Kalman Khrunovitski

Shabatai Chrynovizky 1916-2022

Chaia Haddas

Nettie Blum 1916-2006

Bernard Berliner 1915-1974

Norma Blum 1922-2008

Al Hoffman 1920-2000

Dorothy Blum 1923-1999

Morris Schilling 1917-2005

SOLKA / BLUM FAMILY

Perished in the Holocaust

Introduction

Goworowo   *23 January 1935*

My dear Bubbe (Grandmother, Hilda Solka Blum) *and Zeyde* (Grandfather, Shalom Joseph Blum) – *be well and in good health*

I am well, thank you. How are you both feeling? My longing for you is very great. I'll never forget you. I remember well when you left for America. We remained standing at the railroad station, lost and bewildered.

I never dreamed that it would be this long and still, we do not get to see you. It is already twelve years since Zeyde left for America. It is sad but I do not even know my Zeyde. Only God knows when I'll get to meet my Zeyde.

Dear Aunt Sylvia,

I thank you very much for your promise to send me dresses.

I close now with kisses to you, my dear Bubbele and Zeydele and heartfelt regards to Aunt Sylvia and Uncle Itzhok (Abraham), *they should live and be well. Heartfelt regards to*

1

(Aunts) *Nettie, Norma, and Dorothy. Please each one write to me. I, in turn, will answer each one of you.*
Elka Taus

Goworowo 23 January 1935
My beloved Nettie,

I received your dear letter and I am pleased to hear that you are healthy. I really like how Auntie is writing in English and would like to learn how to write in English.

I just hope that all of you strive to take me to America. Here, if you finish the 7th grade you can only learn to become a seamstress. Learning at the gymnasium is very expensive – one thousand zloty a year ($5,200 today).

Polish Letter from Elka
January 23, 1935

Right now I can let you know about my music studies. Last winter I had one lesson per week and last summer, four times a week. This winter, it was twice a week. My music teacher needs a job and we cannot pay him. I have a lot of sheet music so I am playing by myself. I hope…and right now I am playing as second chair violin.

I will try to write in every letter something from me.
Be well, healthy,
Elka

Plagued by political strife, poverty and pogroms, life in the small shtetls (villages) of Poland, in the early decades of the 20th century, was not the idyllic presentation of village life as seen in modern literature, movies, or plays. While men worked and studied Torah (the Old Testament) and Talmud (primary discourse of Jewish religious law and theology) or were craftsmen, women took care of the home, children, tended the vegetable garden, operated market stalls and businesses, dealt with family and financial matters, recited tkhines (supplications) and dreamt of a better world, and the children went to school, fought, and stole apples from the local orchards. Everyone visualized leaving the village for "die goldene medina" (the golden land) of America or to be a pioneer in Eretz Israel (Land of Israel).

Similar in size and structure to countless other Polish villages, Goworowo was located in the countryside – five miles along a forest road to Rozan and eleven miles to Ostroleka. Goworowo, during the 1930s had a total population of 500 families of which 300 were Jewish consisting of about 1000 individuals. The earliest known Jewish population in Goworowo dates from the 18th century. Many of the families were inter-related by marriage.

The majority of the town was composed of wooden structures. There were only a few brick buildings or buildings with brick foundations. In the interwar years (1919-1938), there was no sewer system, electricity or running water in the village. Water had to be carried, prior to the installation in 1927 of a city pump near the synagogue, from the Hirsh River (Orz River in Polish) on the banks of which Goworowo had been built.

After the town was burned during World War I, a temporary wooden synagogue was constructed. In 1922, under the initiative of Rabbi Moshe Burstein, plans for a new brick synagogue were submitted for approval to the authorities in Bialystok, the provincial capital. Construction funds were mostly raised with the active assistance of a Goworowo landsleit (townsmen) Sura Gitl Klass and her husband who were living in the United States.

City of Białystok,   *27. XI. 1922* (November 27, 1922)
Reconstruction of the Synagogue in Goworowo – Opinion

The design of the new synagogue is artistically part of the type of modern buildings, a large number of which were erected in Ostroleka, allegedly based on Kurpie's (an ethnographic group living in the Zagajnica and Biala Forests noted for wooden structures) *architectural themes.*

Plan Rendering for New Synagogue 1922

The roof lines of this type of buildings are harmonious only in the drawings and visible from a greater distance, but in short, seen up close, leave much to be desired.

Much more graceful to the eye, and to maintain the old Polish building traditions, are the roofs known from the reproductions of synagogues in Grodno, Wolpa, Zabludow, and in other Polish towns, ranking from Eastern Malopolska to Dzwina.

(Southeastern Poland to the Daugava River in the north which flows into the Baltic Sea)

However, the whole designed Synagogue looks quite impressive.

No objections are made regarding the erection of a new wooden Synagogue.

The interior was designed in a traditional manner – men prayed downstairs and the women, upstairs. There is no available information regarding the interior décor other than the building had two tiled stoves. On the eastern wall, a special plaque was placed to honor the contribution of the Klass family.

The new synagogue was built adjacent to the old wooden structure which was not demolished. It continued to serve as a hachnasat orchim (guest reception) for poor people who came from other villages to Goworowo for the Sabbath. Since they could not travel home on Saturday, they were fed a Sabbath meal by individual families and slept in the old synagogue.

Market Day in Goworowo was on Thursday. "Peasants came into town barefooted and walked along their wagons loaded with produce, grain, etc." (Nettie) Goworowo was a shtetl of shoemakers, tailors, carpenters, hatters, and coach drivers. People in the shtetl made their living from the products they produced and sold in the Goworowo market or in the markets of towns like Rozan, Ostroleka, or Dlugosiodlo. Other residents were retailers, brokers and shipping agents who eked out a living with difficulty. The financial support from relatives and friends in America contributed to the well-being of the general population.

On Fridays, everyone went to the mikvah (ritual bath) which along with the shvitz bod (sauna) was near the stream adjacent to the marketplace. Women went in the morning and men around 1-3 p.m. The mikvah was a pool of natural water in which observant Jews immersed themselves to restore a ritual purity. Natural bodies of water such as rivers, oceans and spring-fed lakes are considered mikvahs in the most primal form, however, since these waters are not always accessible or private, mikvahs were constructed according to specific Rabbinical regulations. Basically they had to be built into the ground or as an essential part of the building. They could only be filled with natural water – rainwater, snow or ice.

The ritual bath was not a monthly substitute for bathing. Jewish law stipulates that the person must be scrupulously clean prior to entering the mikvah. Married Orthodox Jewish women are required to use the mikvah once a month, seven days after the end of their menstrual cycle, in order to purify themselves. The men used the mikvah to ritualistically purify prior to attending the synagogue for the Sabbath or holiday services.

Goworowo was a microcosm of Poland. Side by side were Jews and Christians; Orthodox: five different Hasidic sects – Gerer, Aleksander, Otwocker, Amshinaver, Vurker, each adhering to its own hereditary leader, a Rebbe and Misnagdim – those who opposed the Hassidic movement; and secular Jews; tailors, shoemakers, saddlers, market vendors, peddlers, and businessmen; all political factions ranging from Zionists to Bundists to the illegal Communist party; political and non-political newspapers; and traditional chedars (primary religious day schools), Yeshivas (secondary religious schools), Beit Yaakov girls' school for religious education and a Polish public school.

Brimming with life, the shtetl was populated with personalities who deserved to have been immortalized by Yiddish authors such as

Sholem Aleichem, I.L. Peretz, and Sholem Asch.

A stereotypical cast of village residents – yentes (gossips), matchmakers, milkmen, butchers, bakers, a village simpleton, rabbis, tradesmen, and the backbone of shtetl life – the women – created the background of life in the village.

There was blind Efroyim Boynes who daily went, on his own, to study Talmud. On Rosh Hashanah (Jewish New Year) and Yom Kippur (Day of Atonement) he even, from memory, conducted prayer services.

Ruchel Leah and Friends

Although he was illiterate, partially paralyzed, Sholyme Klas volunteered as an assistant to the Polish Post Director, Rasul, to sort the mail. With a special ability, he could look at the letters and recognize to whom they belonged.

Shmuel Dzhize was a frequent visitor to the courthouse. He had an affinity to become involved in quarrels between Christians and Jews.

Tales from other villages were conveyed by Arn Aronson, an itinerate preacher/teacher who traveled around the country delivering sermons and telling stories and fables.

The only way Abale Likhtman was able to get his half dead mare to walk at a respectable pace pulling the coach along the Goworowo-Rozan line was to sing the Friday night prayer, Lecha Dodi, or other prayers.

The most lovable shtetl resident was the water carrier, Shloyme Akive Beserman, who was considered to be "simple" ever since he was a child. The wife of the tinsmith, Chaya Zelde Klempner ensured that he had clean clothes and food. Shloyme Akive was always happy, a melody on his lips, an excellent memory, along with a ferocious appetite. He attended every social event in the village, often helping with the food preparations. Yet, the women had to watch him as he had a tendency of consuming a large portion of the food as it was being prepared.

Shloyme Akive Beserman

Goworowo was rife with gossip, petty jealousies, financial woes, political and religious conflicts, hopes and dreams. There were political organizations, libraries, and cultural events. Every street was vibrant with life. This was the world of Goworowo.

Plans to immigrate to the United States began as early as 1910 when Shalom Joseph Blum left his growing family for the golden land only to return to Goworowo in 1913 due to health issues.

With the onset of World War I, eastern Poland, which was under the jurisdiction of Imperial Russia, was thrown into turmoil. In 1915, the Russian authorities accused the entire village of Goworowo of being German spies. Apparently the Russians misconstrued the wire enclosure strung from poles around the circumference of the village as a communication telephone line to the German enemy.

Shalom Joseph Blum

In reality, this enclosure was an "eruv" which, according to Jewish law, defines an area as an extension boundary of one's home whereby Orthodox Jews are then allowed to carry or push items within their "home" without violating any Sabbath observance restrictions.

It took an explanation and the intervention of Rabbi Itzhok Rubinstein (1880-1945) of Vilna, Lithuania for a special Czarist decree of annulment to be issued. In retaliation for the dismissal of charges, the withdrawing Russian forces burnt the entire village. The town inhabitants scattered in all directions but, most fled east, deeper into Imperial Russia.

Shalom Joseph, his wife, Hilda, and their children, Ruchel Leah, Sylvia, Moshe, Abraham Itzhok (known in Poland by his middle name, Itzhok), and Hilda's father, Nussin Kalman Solka joined the flight for safety; fleeing to Kozlov, Tambov Oblast (Region) in the Pale of Settlement of Russia. It was reasoned that the unknown of Russia was better than remaining in Poland to face the savagery of war.

Created by Catherine the Great by an Imperial decree in 1791, the Pale of Settlement was an area, with varying borders, in the western region of Czarist Russia in which the Jewish population was allowed to establish permanent residency. To live and work outside the Pale of Settlement was mostly prohibited.

Ruchel Leah, Moshe, Sylvia, Hilda

Russia, itself, was in political disorder during the war years (1914-1918). This culminated in the Bolshevik Revolution which demolished the reign of the Czars and established the Soviet government under Vladimir Lenin (1870-1924). With Germany's surrender ending World War I on November 11, 1918, Shalom Joseph decided it was time for the family to return to their home in Poland.

With an additional child, Nettie, the family embarked, in a freight car, on what turned out to be a sixteen week trek, rather than the anticipated normal 24 hour train trip. It was an arduous and, in some sectors, a dangerous journey. The route was a hot bed of conflict between the counter revolutionary White armies and the Bolshevik Red armies for control of Russia. At one point or another the train was stopped for inspection by one or the other of the armies. In many sections, the train tracks had been disabled. The family was in peril every time they disembarked from the train, but they had to continue at all costs.

White Russian Cossack soldiers arbitrarily pulled Jews off the trains or took them from various stations and simply, murdered them. The justification was that the victim was suspected of being a Bolshevik supporter because they were Jewish. Ruchel Leah was fluent in Russian having attended Russian primary school. There were several encounters, during the journey, where her ability to converse in Russian actually saved the family.

Prior to leaving Russia, Shalom Joseph, being a shoemaker, had secreted extra money in the hollow heels of everyone's shoes. He also placed money in the frontispiece page of each book of the Chumash (Five Books of Moses), sewing the page to the leather book cover. Shalom Joseph extracted money, as needed, from these hiding places to use as bribes to ensure the family's survival. Each time the train was unable to continue, Shalom Joseph rented a sled or cart to go to the nearest town that might have train service to enable a continuation of their journey.

Upon arrival in Goworowo, the family lived with Hilda's brother, Avromka Solka in his top floor apartment near the market while their home on Long Street, which had been one of the buildings destroyed by the Russian military fire years earlier, was being rebuilt on its original foundation.

Considered an important man, being an usher in Goworowo's rabbinic

Esther and Avromka Solka

11

court and the shamas (sexton) in the synagogue, Avromka was involved in the town's affairs. He was considered to be among the area's most capable matchmakers, knowing everyone's secrets.

With the completion of their house, Shalom Joseph re-established his shoe shop and life settled into a routine of relative tranquility in what had then become the Republic of Poland (Rzeczpospolita Polska).

Believing that the family was in a safe and secure position, Shalom Joseph decided that it was an opportune time for him to return to the United States. He borrowed money from his brothers-in-law, Srulke Solka in New York and Meir Walberg in Memphis to finance the journey. In 1923 he embarked for New York to forge the path for the family's eventual emigration.

The Emergency Quota Act of 1921 allowed admittance to

Shalom Joseph

the United States for those who had previously been in the country without regard to the national quota. Therefore, Shalom Joseph returned to the United States without any tribulations.

Having obtained his citizenship in September 1929, Shalom Joseph had no difficulty in sending for his wife and minor children. The children would automatically become citizens by virtue of derivative citizenship immediately upon landing on American soil. The law applied to all minors born to a foreign national who had become a United States citizen prior to the child becoming 18 years old.

By scrimping and scraping, enough money was finally accumulated to facilitate the exodus from Poland. With travel documents in hand, in June 1930, Hilda, along with her "minor" children – Sylvia, Abraham Itzhok, Nettie, Norma, and Dorothy left the only world they had known, aboard the United States Lines ship, SS *America*, sailing from Cherbourg, France to New York.

Abraham Itzhok Blum's Polish Passport

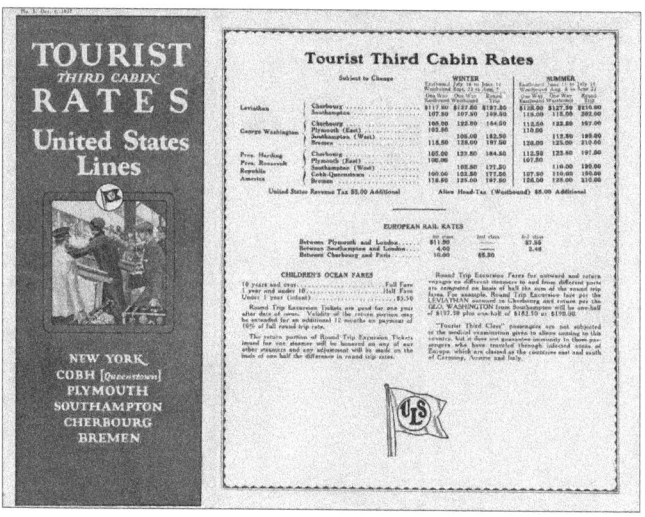

United States Lines Tourist Rate Card

SS America Manifest

Facing the unknown filled each of them with anticipation, apprehension, and sadness. They all expected a better life; "one filled with chocolate candy" (Norma). What actually awaited them? Were the streets paved with gold as they had dreamed? They were headed to a land filled with strangers, who spoke a different language, ate different food, and had different customs to be re-united with a father they hardly knew. Each wondered if they would ever see their brother, Moshe, sister, Ruchel Leah, her husband, Anschel Taus and their granddaughters/nieces, Elka and Surcha, ever again.

Ruchel Leah, Surcha, Anschel, Elka

Everyone believed and planned that, in a few years, when enough money had been saved, the remainder of the family would apply for their visas. The master plan was to bring everyone to the United States, one by one, beginning with each girl as she finished her education in Goworowo.

It was understood that Moshe's immigration would possibly pose a problem as he suffered from an unknown medical issue which could have made him ineligible for a visa. In anticipation of the family's eventual immigration to the United States, Hilda traveled with Moshe to Warsaw for medical treatment. Either the doctor did not have a diagnosis or, treatment for his "illness" or alternatively, the family simply did not have the resources for medication or continued medical visits; nothing was ever resolved regarding Moshe's health situation.

Based on family recollections of the symptoms he exhibited, it is assumed that he had a form of autism spectrum disorder (ASD). Typical of ASD, he had repetitive leg movements, was always hungry, and blurted out inappropriate and often incomprehensible statements. If his condition was revealed during the medical examination associated with the United States visa application, he most likely would have been denied an entry visa.

With the family's departure, Ruchel Leah assumed full responsibility for Moshe's well-being. Hilda was completely devastated about leaving her children and granddaughters behind. The sadness and guilt remained with her for her entire life. At that time, in her heart, she understood that Shalom Joseph's plan was the best for the wellbeing and future of the family.

On Friday night, June 13, 1930, prior to boarding the train bound for Warsaw to commence their journey, officials from Ostroleka, the county seat, turned the switch on the first incandescent street lamp in the center of the village square. This historic event was deemed a miracle. It was an omen of the modern world the family would be entering once they reached the shores of America.

Eight years later a different realization took place as the lights began to flicker. The early promise of brightness and a modern world for Poland had proved to be only illusionary.

The family, on both sides of the Atlantic, expressed feelings of hope and despair.

Plans for Elka's immigration were implemented by 1938. A saved series of correspondence which had commenced on August 14, 1938 primarily pertaining to Elka's immigration documents expressed hope and frustration.

A journey of remembrance ensued after the death of his mother, Hilda, on January 3, 1973 when Abraham gathered and translated Ruchel Leah's letters into English. "It is important for future generations…to understand what went on during the Holocaust years." (Abraham) The letters, as presented, are the exact translations without any grammatical adjustments.

Contained within the letters are a myriad of details and references to various individuals. Since time has obliterated the availability of witnesses and documented resources, conclusions have been presented based on available facts, documents, witness testimony and oral history. In instances of conflicting information, all possibilities are presented based on the accumulated data.

While all of the events annotated in the letter commentaries may not have directly involved the individuals in the book, they are actual occurrences which could have been experienced by them. Certain liberties were taken to further enhance the explanations of the letters, placing the events into a historical, social, and religious context giving the reader a more comprehensive foundation of the contents of the correspondence.

Hope – in the face of despair
Courage – in defiance of the dire situation
Resiliency – amidst the terror

The Spirit of Ruchel Leah

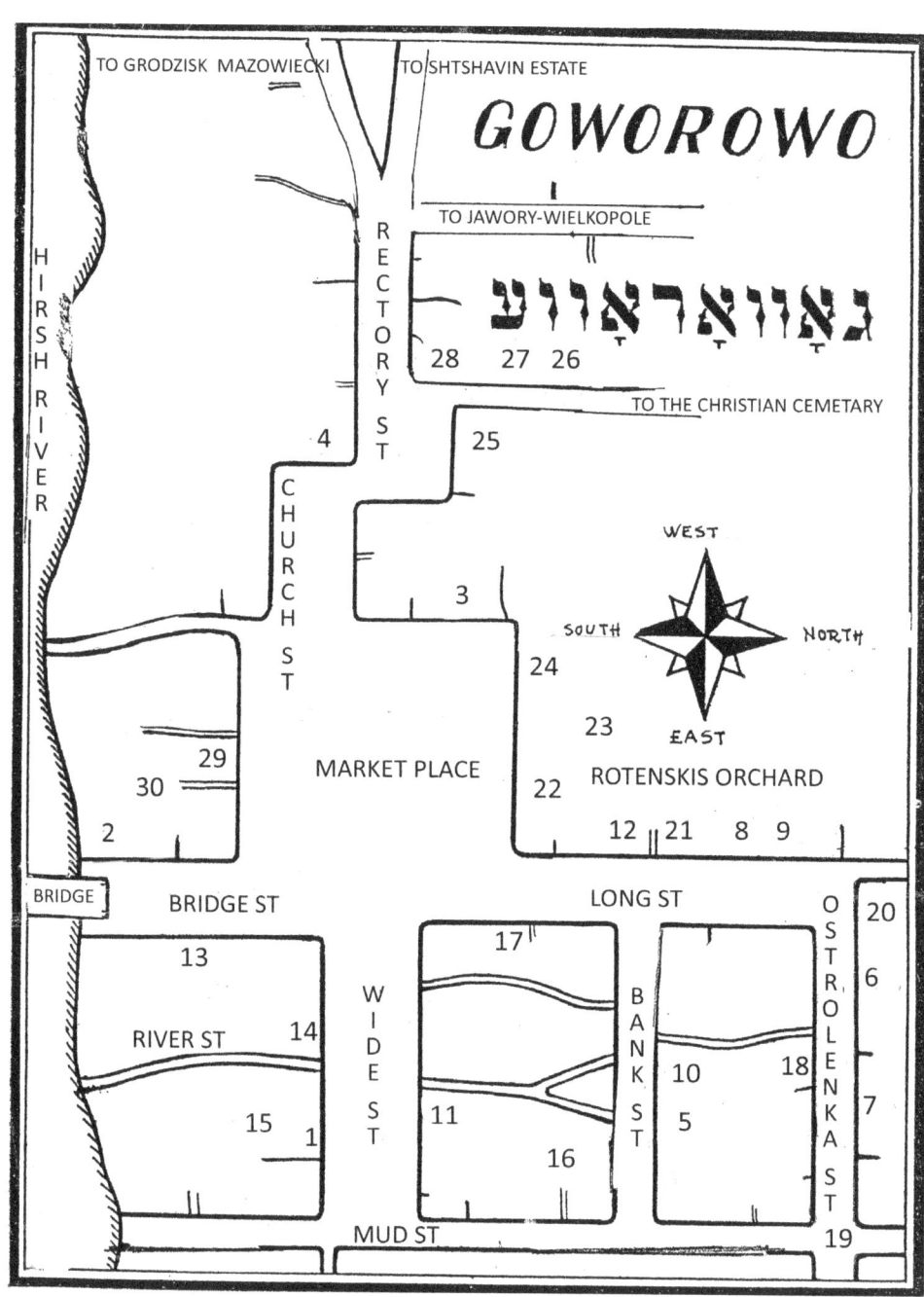

Goworowo Street Map

GOWOROWO

1 – Rabbi Alter Burstein Home

2 – Brick Synagogue built 1924/25

3 – Community Center

4 – Church of the Holy Cross

5 – Jewish Credit Bank

6 – Village Hall / Administrative Buildings / Prison

7 – Polish Public School

8 – Family Home occupied by Anschel & Ruchel Leah Taus

9 – Itche Yosel & Schwartza Dvora Taus Home Lazar & Feige Frydman Lived There

10 – The Merchant's Bank

11 – Mendel Chaim Rubin Home

12 – Mikhl (Max) Schmeltz Home

13 – Baruch Kuperman Home

14 – Chana Frydman Home

15 – Mikvah / Sauna Bath

16 – Avrom Meyer Schmeltz Home

17 – Bund & Peretz Library

18 – Village Slaughterhouse

19 – To the Goworowo Train Station

20 – Artisans and Retailers Bank

21 – Esther Shafran Colonial Store

22 – Kosher Restaurant

23 – Village Societal Hall

24 – Avromka Solka Home

25 – Christian Co-operative

26 – Post Office

27 – Police Headquarters

28 – Priest's Home

29 – Hotel & Restaurant

30 – Beit Yaakov School

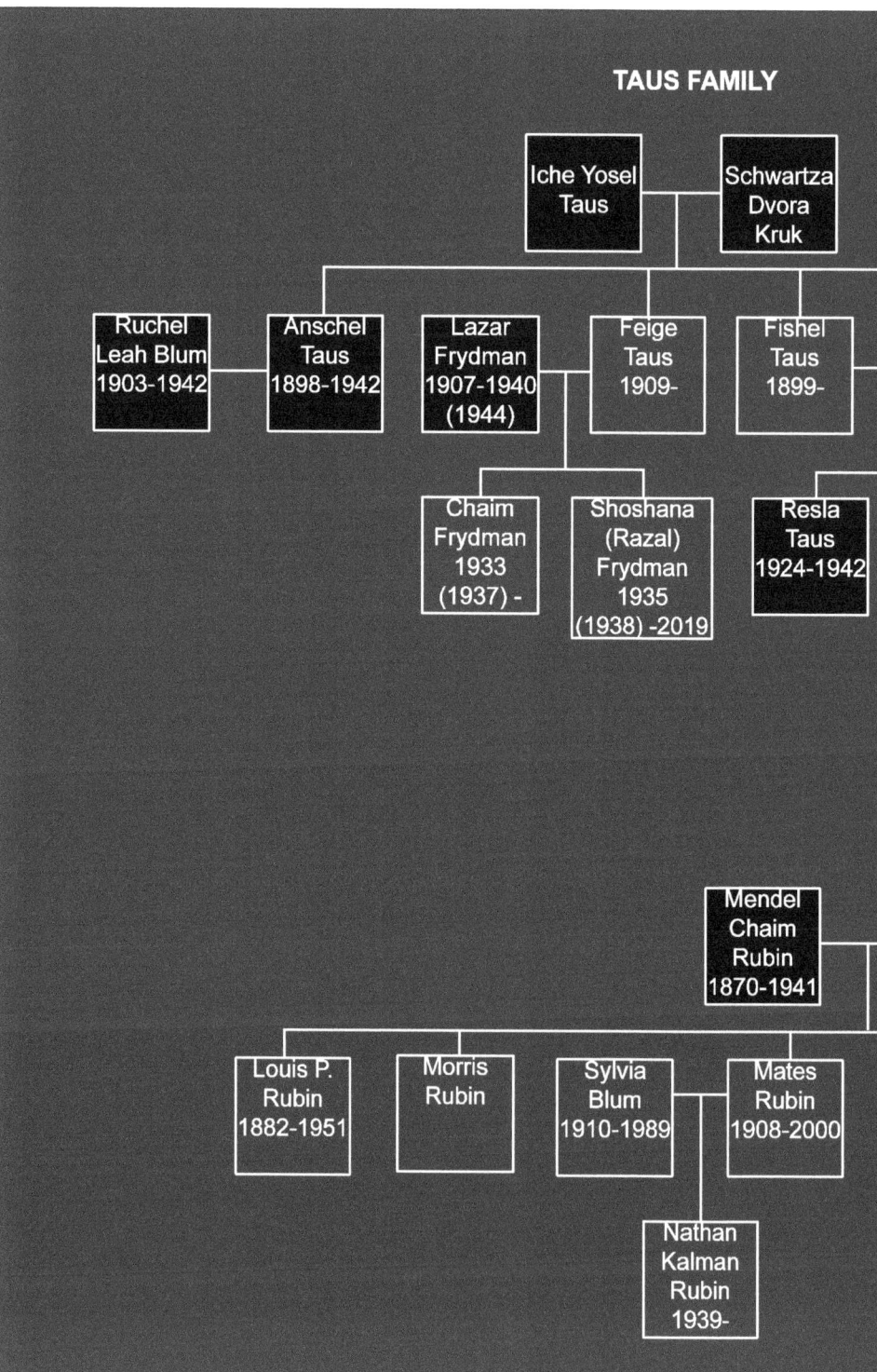

Taus Family Tree and Rubin Family Tree

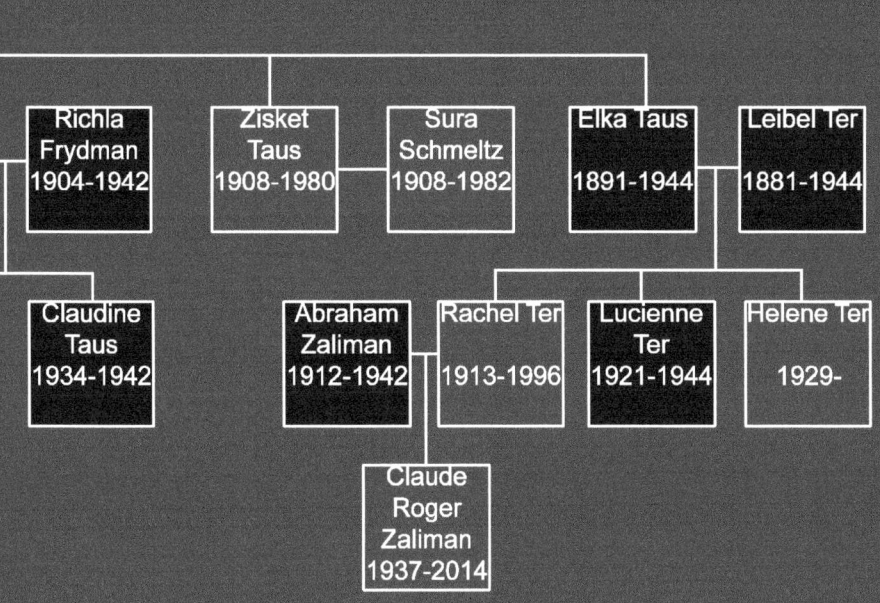

| Richla Frydman 1904-1942 | Zisket Taus 1908-1980 | Sura Schmeltz 1908-1982 | Elka Taus 1891-1944 | Leibel Ter 1881-1944 |

| Claudine Taus 1934-1942 | Abraham Zaliman 1912-1942 | Rachel Ter 1913-1996 | Lucienne Ter 1921-1944 | Helene Ter 1929- |

Claude Roger Zaliman 1937-2014

RUBIN FAMILY

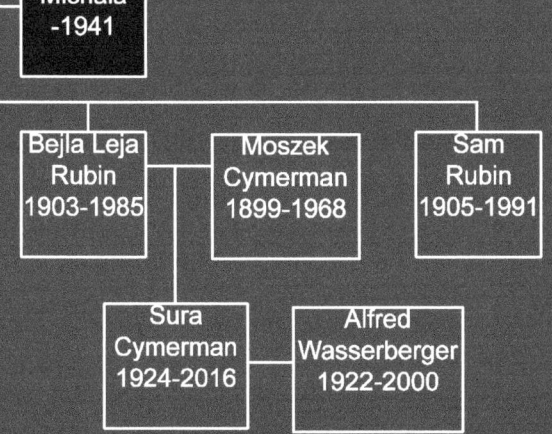

Michala -1941

| Bejla Leja Rubin 1903-1985 | Moszek Cymerman 1899-1968 | Sam Rubin 1905-1991 |

| Sura Cymerman 1924-2016 | Alfred Wasserberger 1922-2000 |

Perished in the Holocaust

Mirage of Hope

Goworowo   *14 August 1938*

Dear Parents, Sisters, Brother-in-law (Mates) *and Brother,*

This is to acknowledge that I received a letter from Mr. Linder including an English letter. I forwarded that English letter plus my own letter requesting (pleading) for the consul to send Elka a number for a visa. On August 13th, I received a reply. He requests that we should send him Elka's birth certificate and a few other papers. Tomorrow I will mail the consul the requested documents. Now the consul requests some information from you. I am forwarding those forms for you to fill out. Read the instructions carefully and answer all the questions. The first few questions pertain to us about her. I'll take care of them; however #5, 6, 7 and 8 are questions for you to answer. It refers to your earnings, money in the bank, etc. Answer all the questions otherwise it causes delays. Tomorrow Anschel will go to Ostroleka to verify the birth certificate getting the stamp on it and upon his return we will immediately forward it to the American consul. I would appreciate very much if you would let me know when you mail the documents to the consul.

Your Mr. Linder, in his letter, accuses me of not cooperating. It seems to me that the fault is yours, not mine, since you did not inform us about the request of the consul. Had we known about the request we would have taken care of it without delay. Let's hope that from now on everything will go smoothly.

Thank Mr. Linder for his letter. I did not send him an acknowledgement since I'm writing to you. You may forward the information to him.

I sent you two letters when I received the telegram so that you should have received them. A few days ago I mailed you a letter in which I acknowledge the receipt of the snapshots.

That is all for now.

Best and heartfelt regards to my parents, sister and brother-in-law. Best regards to my sisters Norma, Dorothy, and Nettie. A separate regards for my brother, Itzhok. From your daughter, son-in-law, son and grandchildren.
Ruchel Leah

Dear Parents,

When you complete the application please include a personal letter to the consul pleading with him to expedite the process and that you and your family are willing and capable of supporting Elka.

Who was Mr. Linder? Why was he so prominent in the quest for Elka's immigration visa? To truly understand this story of hope, courage, perseverance, resiliency, and despair, we have to understand why Abe Linder was engaged for his immigration expertise.

In the spring of 1938, the New York family began submitting the required immigration visa paperwork for Elka, age 14, to be the first of the family still residing in Poland to immigrate to the United States. Arrangements were made by Mates Rubin (Sylvia Blum's husband) to hire Abe Linder to facilitate the entire immigration process.

Abe Linder (1881-1954) was a known immigration "fixer". At that time he was President of the Hudson County Jewish Regular Republican Org. Inc. in Hoboken, New Jersey, having worked for over 20 years as a Republican Committeeman for Hoboken's First Ward and was also a clerk in the Hudson County Bureau of Elections.

The era was a high point of ethnic based "machine" politics. While the Democratic Party dominated Hudson County New Jersey, Republican organizations often acted as swing blocs in coalitions. They also served as de facto social organizations in distributing services and acting as intermediaries between the general population and larger government agencies.

With the restricted quota based Johnson-Reed Act of 1924, the immigration system required a great deal of expertise to navigate. Without the assistance of an immigration "expert" or a refugee organization to synchronize the required documents and transportation, there was a very slim chance that the immigrant would be successful in receiving his visa.

Linder had experience in obtaining the necessary visa. It was known that he had been engaged in immigration work since at least 1927 as evidenced from a court case from that year in which he was involved.

*"Judgment Awarded Man Who Paid To Cut Immigration '
Red Tape'*

*Suing in Hoboken District Court to recover $150 which
he said he gave to Abe Linder, 118 Garden St., Hoboken, to
'cut red tape' and bring his father to this country from Italy in
1927. Michael Totaro, 521 Jefferson St., Hoboken, yesterday
was awarded $210 by a jury. Judge Joseph Greenberg presided.*

*On the stand, Totaro said he went to Linder on April 12,
1927, and asked him to 'fix things' so that his father would have
no difficulty in coming to this country. Totaro further testified
Linder agreed without reservations to get the man in, but said
he required $350 for expenses. Totro (sic) gave him $150 on
account and received a receipt.*

*It was stated Linder agreed to refund the money if he was unable
to 'fix things.' Totaro asked for his money back and was refused.*

*Linder said that before he undertook to bring the man's father
in, he asked Totaro if his parent could get an Italian passport and,
upon being assured that the elder Totaro could, Linder said he
went to Washington and saw several officials, including Walter
Edge, who was U.S. Senator at the time. It was only after he had
done this, he said, that he learned that Totaro's father could not
get the Italian passport and, assuming he had fulfilled his part
of the agreement while Totaro had fallen down on his, he said,
he kept the money.*

*Totaro insisted there was no mention made of an Italian
passport when they made the original agreement in 1927. Linder
contended his failure to bring the father into this country was
only due to Totaro's lie about the Italian passport." THE JERSEY
JOURNAL* Wednesday, December 6, 1933

As in all small villages, people tended to know each other. While in Goworowo, Sylvia Blum had been acquainted with Mates Rubin. She had been friends with the girl he had been seeing in Goworowo. To avoid being drafted into the Polish military in 1924, Mates at age 16 illegally left Poland. Because of his status, it was impossible for him to obtain an American visa. Immigration to Cuba was appealing due to the tropical weather, friends in Havana, limited anti-Semitism and, most importantly, the country's willingness to accept eastern European immigrants with limited questions; therefore, Mates immigrated to Cuba.

Cuba, at that time, was a heterogeneous mix of ethnic/racial groups – Caucasians, mulattos, and Afro-Cubans with its attendant mix of cultures, traditions, and religions. The government welcomed the influx of Jewish immigrants with their potential to reactivate the faltering Cuban economy.

Havana had the largest Polaco (Polish) community in Cuba. All immigrant Jews including Polish, German, French, Hungarian, and Turks were called Polacos by the local population as an identification of a person without an English speaking accent rather than as a derogatory term. About 75 percent of the country's 12,000 Jews were living in Havana. In the 1920s, the city was a thriving Jewish community with five synagogues, a Kosher restaurant, one Jewish high school and five Jewish elementary schools. The immigrants strove to emulate their accustomed village lifestyle in this new world.

Sylvia, as a minor upon arrival in the United States, had been auto-matically granted, by virtue of her father's, Shalom Joseph's, naturalized citizenship, derivative citizenship. In addition to being acquainted and the families knowing each other, perhaps her citizenship was a reason Mates' older brothers, Morris, Louis, and Sam arranged the match.

According to Section 6 A1 of the Johnson-Reed Act of 1924, *"Fifty per centum of the quotas of each nationality for such year shall be made available . . . to the following classes of immigrants… who are the husbands of citizens of the United States by marriages occurring on or after May 31, 1928."* After living in Cuba for ten years, the brothers had found a way for Mates to obtain a visa to join them in the United States.

Havana – Sylvia Blum and Mates Rubin (3ʳᵈ & 4ᵗʰ from left)

A wedding was planned. Sylvia traveled to Havana. The wedding took place on March 14, 1934 (and again in a formal wedding in the Bronx, New York on May 10, 1936). Sylvia spent three months in Cuba with Mates prior to returning to New York while he remained in Cuba.

Mates' brothers had established themselves in the United States since the early 1920s. Being financially stable they hired an immigration facilitator – Abe Linder to expedite Mates' immigration. He was instrumental in bringing Mates, legally, from Cuba into the United States.

Sylvia and Mates Rubin

Seated: Hilda Blum, Sylvia Rubin, Joseph Blum —
Standing: Dorothy Blum, Norma Blum, Abraham
Itzhok Blum, Mates Rubin, Nettie Blum

At age 27, Mates arrived in New York on March 2, 1936 aboard the S.S. *Pennsylvania* with $35. in his possession. Under the name of Murry Rubin, petition number 382932, he filed for naturalization in October 1940.

Despite the negative court ruling, Abe Linder continued his work as an immigration "fixer". As the 1930s progressed, with a changing political situation in Europe, there was an even greater urgency for the oppressed European Jewry to immigrate to the United States. Having been successful in bringing Mates to the United States, the family firmly believed that Linder had the skills and the proper contacts to facilitate bringing Elka to America.

Goworowo   *14 August 1938*
Dear Bubbe and Zayde

I am doing fine and hope that you are fine also. I like to inform you that we received a reply from the American consul. There are a lot of requests to fulfill. On the 16th, we will go to the county seat (Ostroleka) to certify my birth certificate which we will forward it and some other documents to the consul.

I'll close now with best wishes for Bubbe and Zayde, best regards to my Auntie Sylvia and her husband. Regards for Itzhok, Nettie, Norma, and Dorothy.

Your Granddaughter,
Elka Taus

The United States immigration regulations were in a state of constant modification. The State Department issued frequent updates to the policies which each foreign consul office interpreted differently. It is uncertain with whom Ruchel Leah was in communication at the American Consulate in Warsaw as no records are in existence.

The consuls, consular officers as well as their clerks, would have been tasked with processing and dealing with different aspects of the visa application process.

Obtaining a visa was not a simple procedure. It was both complicated and costly. The preliminary step was to provide birth/marriage records, a statement from the police attesting to the individual's character, a valid reservation for transportation, affidavit of support from a United States citizen, medical exam, and an interview at the consulate which required the receipt of a quota number to even make the interview appointment.

A significant change in policy was issued in September 1938 which allowed a potential immigrant to apply for a visa prior to presenting the financial affidavit.

In the villages of pre-war Poland, formal birth certificates did not exist. A child's birth was recorded in the registrar's office of the town hall and/or for Catholic children, church baptismal records. Anschel obtained a copy of Elka's birth registration from the town clerk to bring to Ostroleka, the county seat, for the verification stamp.

Both Elka and Surcha's births were registered seven years after their actual dates of birth, respectively. There was a fee involved in birth registration so it was not generally done unless it was necessary for a specific reason. The registration was likely a prerequisite for attending school since each girl was seven at the time of her birth registration.

Elka's Birth Registration

It happened in the town of Goworowo, on 24th of June 1931, came Anschel (or Azriel) TAUS, shoemaker, 33 years old, living in Goworowo, with 2 witnesses (…) and presented before us a baby girl born in Goworowo on the 26th of August 1924, to his wife Ruchla Leja (Ruchel Leah) *maiden name Blum, aged 31. The name of the girl was given as Elka.*

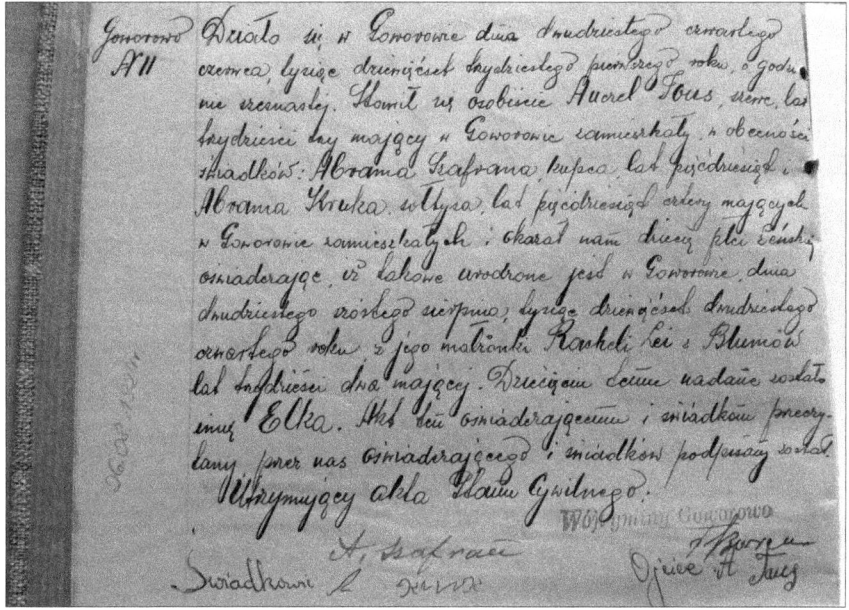

Elka Taus Birth Registration

Surcha's Birth Registration

Registry happened in Goworowo on 17th of August 1936 on1 PM (1300) , came Taus Azrielm (Anschel) *shoemaker, 34 Yo (….)*

And showed a baby girl born in Goworowo on 5th of March 1929 on 11 in the morning, from the woman Ruchla Leja (Ruchel Leah) *nee BLUM*

The administration of the Republic of Poland (Rzeczpospolita Polska) was based on a three-tiered system. On the lowest tier were the "gminy" – local towns and village governments like Goworowo. These were grouped together to form "powiaty", similar to counties. Ostroleka was the powiaty for Goworowo. The counties were merged to create "wojewodztwa" (voivodeships – provinces) which, in this

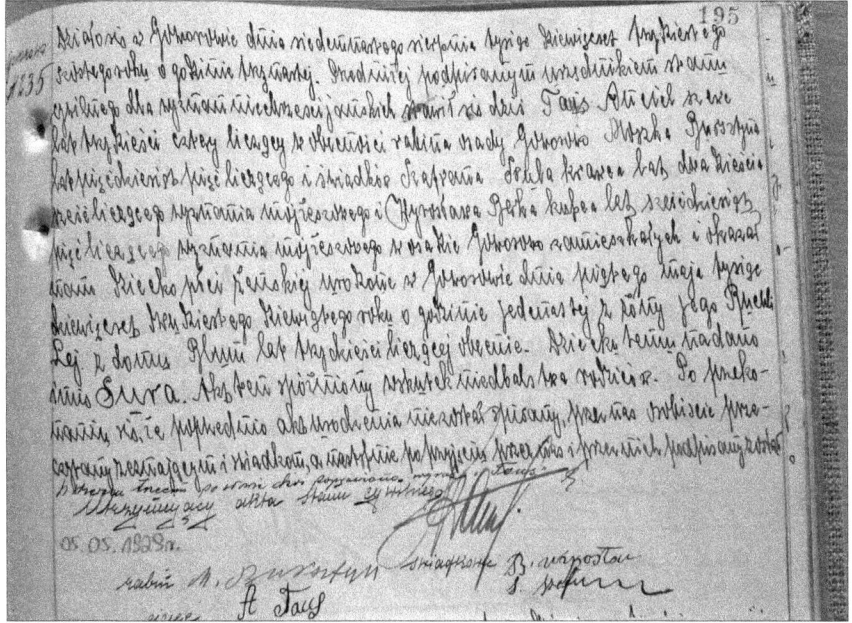

Surcha Taus Birth Registration

case, the province was centered in Bialystok. Because of the government structure, Anschel and Elka traveled to Ostroleka, the county seat, for certification of the birth registration.

Goworowo   *20 February 1939*
Dear Brother Abraham Itzhok:

I received your letter. It brought me much joy. Dear brother, had you sent me a large sum of money it would not have meant as much to me as your letter. I am very thankful to you for it. Every day I looked forward to the mail delivery hoping to receive a letter from you. Your letter awakened in me the tragic life that we live. I have no fantasies but, I am thankful for your letter. You write in reference to Elka that you received a letter from the consul and that you have forwarded to the consul the new financial papers. I beg you to do so as soon as possible and forward to the consul without delay, requesting (begging) to send Elka a (quota) *number. I have it from reliable sources that those papers are important; without them no number or visa is issued. The man I have contact with has connections whom I never gave any money. If and when she gets the visa then he will get paid. I was aware that you will receive such a letter from the American consul. My source informed me that much. Please forgive me for saying again, prepare the financial papers and send it off to the consul.*

Thank you for inquiring about Anschel's health. He is about the same. Medications keep him going. The weather is very nasty, wet and raining all the time. The damp weather certainly does not help him any. He has not been to the doctor in Warsaw this year. When he gets an attack, we do all we can. It is a hard life. If he could spend some time in the forest, it might give him some relief.

Anschel Taus 1921

When he feels better, he does some work. We badly need the meager income from his work. It is a very tragic life that we live that a sick man has to be the family provider. It is very difficult for me to watch him work under these conditions. Perhaps that is the way it has to be. You asked about me, well I can....(page 5 and any subsequent pages of the original letter are missing)

Life was difficult in the shtetl yet, everyone had dreams of a brighter future.

Was this "contact" a person whose services was utilized by one of Ruchel Leah's acquaintances or was he a fictitious person created to exert pressure on the family's facilitator, Abe Linder? Living in a small shtetl, it seems unlikely that Ruchel Leah would have come in contact with an individual who could give reliable, current advice pertaining to Elka's United States visa process, but it was not impossible.

While "we did not have enough financial backing to sign for her" (Abraham), the new financial papers requested did not pose a problem. It was suggested that a surety of $2000. was required. Abe Linder had arranged for an individual, with substantial financial resources, to sign a guarantee for Elka through her age of maturity – 21. This guarantee confirmed that, upon arrival in the United States, she would not become a public charge. If the amount guaranteed on the affidavit was deemed to be sufficient, no additional funds were required.

A quiet, intelligent man, Anschel was considered to be a "first class" professional shoemaker. He and Ruchel Leah were married on October 21, 1923 in a ceremony performed at 5 p.m. by Rabbi Alter Moshe Mordechai Burstein (who was murdered in August 1943 in the Treblinka death camp).

Rabbi Alter Moshe Mordechai Burstein

The young couple moved into the small back room in the home of Ruchel Leah's parents. The large front room served as the shoe shop during the day and a multi-functional living space. Prior to his marriage, Anschel worked as a shoemaker alongside his prospective father-in-law, Shalom Joseph. When Shalom Joseph immigrated to the United States, Anschel took over the operation of the shop in support of the entire family.

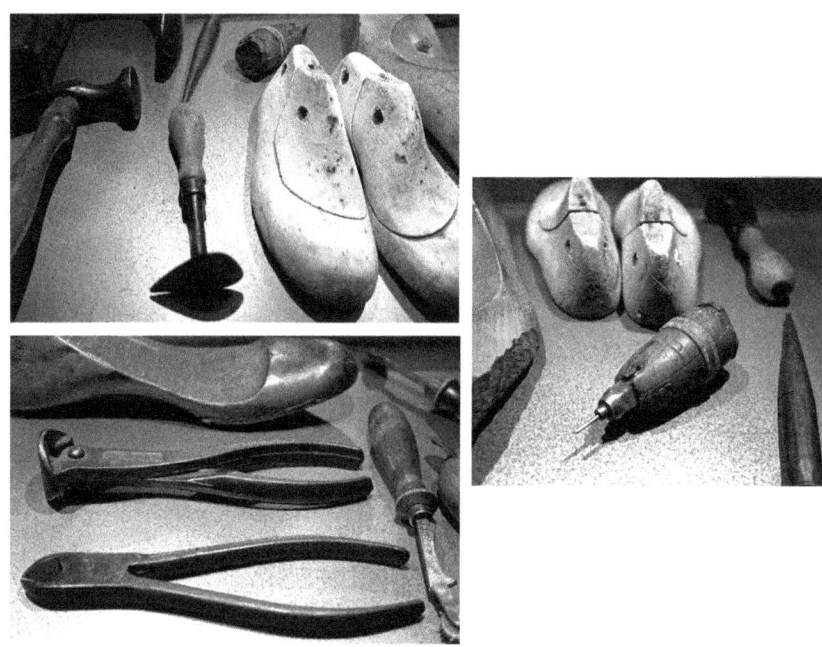

Shoemaker Tools

By the mid 1930s the situation in the local shoe market had deteriorated. There were many other shoemakers in the village which increased competition for a diminishing market. Peasants as well as other Jews were traveling to cities like Ostroleka and Bialystok to buy their footwear in stores instead of ordering them from the local shoemakers.

From all available information, Anschel most likely suffered from asthma. There are many different types of asthma – adult-onset asthma, allergic asthma, occupational asthma among others. Anschel exhibited definite respiratory issues such as shortness of breath, wheezing, and chest tightness. These attacks, often caused by indoor allergens such as feathers and mold, affected his ability to work. It is known that people with asthma have a high rate of anxiety, psychological stress and depression. Medications were available, at the time, to help alleviate the breathing difficulties.

Anschel was able to obtain the medications prescribed by the doctor in Warsaw from the local pharmacist, Goszczyński who lived in a two story brick home near the synagogue.

Epinephrine (adrenaline) was used as early as 1910 to rapidly open airway passages. At first, it was only available in an injection form administered at the hospitals. By the 1930s, epinephrine was available as an inhaled medication using a nebulizer. While electronic nebulizers existed, the most common nebulizers used were hand squeezed rubber bulbs. The epinephrine reduced the swelling which constricted the muscles around the lung passages thus offering short-term relief from the asthmatic symptoms.

Another medication, Ephedrine, the active ingredient of the herb, Ephedra was in common use for the treatment of asthma. By the 1920s it was available to offer temporary relief of shortness of breath, chest tightness, and wheezing due to bronchial asthma.

Fresh air, such as in a forest area, was known to help prevent the onset of an asthmatic attack. The trees filtered allergen particles out of the air. The naturally purified air decreased the risk of different respiratory illnesses including asthma.

Date Unknown

I wrote you many times that you have to send new papers to the American consul. Recently I received a reply from the consul that you have to furnish them with an affidavit that you will be responsible for the well-being of Elka until she reaches maturity. That is the law in the United States of America. Do not delay. Please furnish the consul the necessary documentation. There is no way she will get a number without it. Mr. Linder will verify that the document is a must to secure a number for Elka. There is no doubt in my mind that it has to be done. No two ways about it....

Dear parents, what is the problem that you do not write much to us? Is there anything wrong? Abraham Itzhok also did not write much about you except to send your regards. Please write about everyone; write about my sister and her husband (Sylvia and Mates). I am hurt that she does not write. How is my sister, Nettie? Also about Norma and Dorothy? I hope that this finds you in the best of health. Heartfelt regards to my dear parents. I beg you again to make sure you file the documents with the consul. Everyone sends their regards. Moshe sends his regards.

Your daughter,

Ruchel Leah

While the date of this letter is unknown, the contents dictate the placement at this point in the sequence of letters.

The immigration laws of the United States were not welcoming, particularly to Jewish immigrants. In the midst of the Great Depression, many feared the additional burden immigrants would place on the national economy. As early as 1930, President Herbert Hoover reinterpreted immigration legislation to bar individuals "likely to become a public charge" which even included individuals capable of working. The rationalization being that with the high existing unemployment rate, it would be impossible for an immigrant to find employment.

By 1929, the United States immigration quota for worldwide immigration was further limited to a total of 153,879 new immigrants with the quotas calculated based on the national origins of United States residents as reflected in the 1920 census. The total yearly quota granted to Poland was 6,524 immigrants.

While economic concerns played a major role in formulating immigration policy, so did fear and hatred. Racism and anti-Semitism as well as fear of communist infiltrators and Nazi spies had an influence on immigration policies. The prevailing tone of the general American population, at the time, was one of isolationism.

Anti-Semitism was a key factor in shaping public opinion against increased immigration which was fueled by influential public figures like Charles A. Lindbergh who was unashamedly pro-German and an anti-Semite.

While living in Europe, Lindbergh became enamored with the German national "revitalization" even allowing himself to be decorated by the Third Reich. By April 1939, Lindbergh worked towards keeping the United States out of a potential war in Europe. In an article for *Reader's Digest,* he stated *"that our civilization depends on a Western wall of race and arms which can hold back…the infiltration of inferior blood."*

Testifying before the House Foreign Affairs Committee on January 23, 1941, Lindbergh suggested that the United States negotiate a neutrality pact with Nazi Germany. He was in opposition to the Land-Lease policy which offered cash and military aid to any country "friendly" to the United States' war effort against the Axis powers (Germany, Italy, and Japan).

In a speech on September 11, 1941 in Des Moines, Iowa, Lindbergh identified the groups he believed were pushing the United States into a war against Germany, *"The three most important groups who have been pressing this country toward war are the British, the Jewish, and the Roosevelt Administration."* He went on to say, *"Instead of agitating for war, Jews in this country should be opposing it in every way, for they will be the first to feel its consequences. Their greatest danger to this country lies in their large ownership and influence in our motion pictures, our press, our radio, and our government."*

President Franklin D. Roosevelt did not personally respond, however the White House press secretary released a statement which noted the "striking similarity" between Lindbergh's statements and "the outpourings of Berlin in the last few days."

Anti-Semitic radio preacher, Father Charles Coughlin embraced and amplified Lindbergh's message. Father Coughlin, a Roman Catholic priest, had a listening audience of up to 15 million who heard his anti-Semitic rantings along with his religious messages. He accused the Jews of manipulating financial institutions and conspiring to control the world.

The anti-Semitic message was spread by other prominent Americans such as Henry Ford and Robert E. Wood, CEO of Sears, Roebuck, & Co., who was also the Chairman of the America First Committee (Lindbergh was the Spokesperson).

The America First Committee was an isolationist, anti-war pressure group which also served as a forum for many anti-Semitic and pro-fascist speakers. It is unknown whether members were attracted to join the America First Committee by anti-war feeling, isolationism or white supremacy. By Fall 1940, the Committee had 8000 members including politicians – Gerald Ford, Sargent Shriver, a young John F. Kennedy; authors – E.E. Cummings, Sinclair Lewis, Gore Vidal, and Walt Disney. After the United States entered the war on December 10, 1941, the committee was dissolved.

The public was heavily influenced to encourage Congress not to relax the immigration laws, but to make them even more restrictive. As the United States was working its way out of the Depression, government officials tended to embrace this isolationist policy.

Most officials, including President Roosevelt, were in denial regarding the severity of the existing situation of anti-Semitism in Poland. They repeated the rhetoric they had heard regarding the Polish Jewry from representatives of the Polish government – Count Jerzy Potocki, ambassador in Washington (1936-1940) and Jozef Beck, Polish Foreign Minister (1932-1939). The prevailing anti-Semitism in Poland was a response to the fact that *the Jewish grain dealer and the Jewish shoe dealer and the Jewish shopkeeper were controlling the Polish economy*. The Jewish population was *scapegoats to whom to point in order to satisfy the landless and unfed peasantry, and the Jew is the convenient and traditional and historical scapegoat*. *The Jews Should Keep Quiet: Franklin D. Roosevelt, Rabbi Stephen S. Wise and the Holocaust* by Rafael Medoff, 2019

It is unclear what criteria was used to actually determine who received a quota number and confirmation for the interview appointment. The individual seeking a visa had to first be placed on a waiting list for the interview. No interviews were granted until the yearly quota numbers became available. So, it became "a chicken and an egg" situation. Was it luck of the draw or was graft involved?

Along with other documents, the paperwork from an American financial sponsor committing to the assumption of financial responsibility for the arriving immigrant had to be submitted to the consul. The sponsoring individual needed to present to the consulate recommendation letters as to his standing in the community, bank letters affirming his solvency, and a copy of his United States tax return. Mr. Linder was hired to obtain the proper financial documentation and corresponding recommendation letters which was all that could be accomplished from the United States. Mr. Linder had the financial sponsor in place. The remainder of the visa requirements had to be secured and furnished by Ruchel Leah.

After a 1939 procedural change, the immigrant needed to prove that passage out of Poland had been booked. Tickets were costly to the average immigrant. The average steerage class ticket was $30. ($570. current value) Transit stamps had to be placed in the passport for each country that the immigrant needed to travel through to reach the ship's port of departure. The fee for the transit stamps varied depending upon the country. The required stamps needed to be collected in the specific order of travel. If departure was purchased from the port of Gdynia, Poland then no transit stamps were necessary as no borders were crossed to reach the port of departure. Any mistake would require repeated visits to the specific government offices which meant an incurrence of additional expenses. There is no documentation or verification in the letters that Ruchel Leah ever implemented this stage of the immigration process.

By the time the immigrant received the call for an interview, often many documents and/or transit stamps could have expired. The immigrant had to re-obtain the expired documents at an additional cost of time and money. The applicant had to present, at the interview, the appointment letter, five copies of the visa application, two copies of the birth certificate, the quota number, a police report attesting to good conduct, as well as the affidavit of support and a medical examination report. Most documents were typed and presented with carbon paper copies, each at an additional cost to the applicant. The State Department official at the Consulate scrutinized all the documents to insure the paperwork was in order and that the individual would pose no threat to the national security of the United States.

If everything was in order, the immigrant's passport was stamped with the entrance visa to the United States. Once issued, a visa was valid for only four months.

From the tone of her letters, Ruchel Leah's frustrations began to become apparent. She expresses feelings of alienation and isolation from the family. They do not write as often as she feels they should and when they do, she feels the letters are impersonal. Ruchel Leah, with everything going on in her life, made the effort to correspond on a regular basis. It appears that the family did not reciprocate to the same level.

Ruchel Leah was not being ignored. Everyone in New York had become absorbed in their own hopes, anxieties and experiences in this new world that, perhaps they did not recognize the positive benefits a simple letter would bring to the family from Goworowo. They simply did not write on a consistent basis as she would have liked.

Only her father, Shalom Joseph, Abraham, Sylvia, Mates, and Nettie were literate in Yiddish. Nettie's basic education was from Polish public school, however, she was tutored in both Hebrew and Yiddish in the afternoons. Hilda could neither read nor write Yiddish or Polish. Sylvia's education was limited to having attended kindergarten in

Russia during World War I. Upon returning to Poland, she did not attend school, but helped her mother care for Moshe and the younger children, yet somehow learned to read and write Yiddish. Norma could print a little in Yiddish but, according to her, "not well enough to write letters". Since Dorothy was seven when she left Europe, it is assumed that she never learned to read or write in Yiddish.

Life was not as idyllic in the "die goldene medina" (the golden land) of New York as Ruchel Leah might have imagined it to be. The family had their own struggles, yet they made every effort to properly process Elka's visa application and, in general, offer Ruchel Leah financial and moral support. Ruchel Leah, left behind in Poland with her family and Moshe, believed that they should have been doing more.

Goworowo   *24 February 1939*

Dear Parents, Sisters, Brother-in-law and Brother,

Hope my writing finds you well. I wrote you a letter this week but I am repeating the same thing in this postcard that you should send the papers that were requested to the consul, without delay. The consul bases his decision on those papers. Perhaps he will decide to send her a number. Even to get the visa appointment you do not need any papers. And the passport you do not bring it with you either. You send it in the mail to the Consul and there everything is received. They look at the papers and then interview the person.

Please my dear brother, forgive me for writing to you in this manner. Please expedite those papers since I have come to the conclusion that it is the most important document that the consul bases his decision to approve the entry application.

Here everything is about the same. This winter we had our share of rain and cold. It is not the best for your health, especially for Anschel. There has not been any work since Christmas. Please write about what is going on in the family. I cannot figure out why my dear sister Sylvia does not write. I wrote to Sylvia but did not receive a reply from her.

Heartfelt regards to all.
Your daughter and sister
Ruchel Leah Taus
The children send their love.

The cold, wet winter of 1939 had been extremely strenuous for the family on many levels. Anschel was not making enough money to support the family's basic needs – food and a dry, warm environment. Ruchel Leah had become more desperate in her pleas, yet she was apologetic for the demanding tone of her letter.

Goworowo   *7 March 1939*
Dear Parents, Sisters and Brother

It is already eight days since I received the money ($40.00). I did not respond immediately. I was expecting some mail from you. I do not understand the reason why I have been receiving so few letters from you this winter. I worry continuously about you. I have written to you numerous letters and postcards but received no reply. However, I did receive a letter from my brother Abraham Itzhok. He really saved my life. I was nervous and upset with the lack of news from you for such a long time. Did I insult my sister (Sylvia) when I wrote to her after Sukkot (October 9–16, 1938), asking her to write to me all that is going on with her. Is this the reason for her not writing to me?

I wrote a letter and postcard to my dear brother to send the required papers to the consul. Perhaps he will send the number. This week two people from town received the visas to immigrate to America. One is Esther's (Szafran) son, Mendel (Aron Mendel Szafran).

There is not much to say or write about ourselves. We live, hope for better times and pray to God that we live that long.

Dear Nettie, please write and inform me the reason that I did not hear from anybody. The last I heard from you is a note you wrote and a letter from Mr. Linder.

It seems to me that you like to irritate me. I had a terrible winter. I suffered a lot over Moshe. I shed many tears and suffered because of him. He does not show any appreciation no matter what I do for him. Perhaps that is the way it has to be.

I thank you all for the money you sent us. You sent it the correct way.

I close with heartfelt regards to all. My children send their regards. On March 3rd Surcha celebrated her 10th birthday. Stay well.

Your daughter,
Ruchel Leah

Hilda denied herself even the smallest of luxuries so that she could afford to help her daughter. When she bought new clothing, she wore it once, sending it directly to Ruchel Leah. In that way, she was sending "used clothing" which made it easier for Ruchel Leah to receive the parcel.

Every week, the family put any money that could be spared in a little pushke (container where money would be accumulated,

Postcard March 7, 1939

generally for charity) until they had accumulated the $40. sent to Ruchel Leah. Forty dollars in 1939 ($750. current value) was a considerable amount of money. The average annual household income in 1939 was $1,368. ($26.30 per week). Shalom Joseph worked as a shoe repairman at a shop at 74 East 113th St. in Manhattan. He earned "10 cents a sole". Since both Sylvia and Abraham were working, they were able to regularly contribute to the pushke. Sylvia worked in the needle industry while Abraham was an interior design clerk at A. Schonfeld Decorators in Brooklyn making $30. per week. According to Abraham's accounting ledger, on February 18th he contributed $10. to RLT (Ruchel Leah Taus).

Money could be transferred to Poland by means of an Electronic Fund Transfer (EFT) either by a Western Union wire transfer or a bank transfer. Once money was paid to a Western Union office, the operator would transmit a message and "wire" the money to another

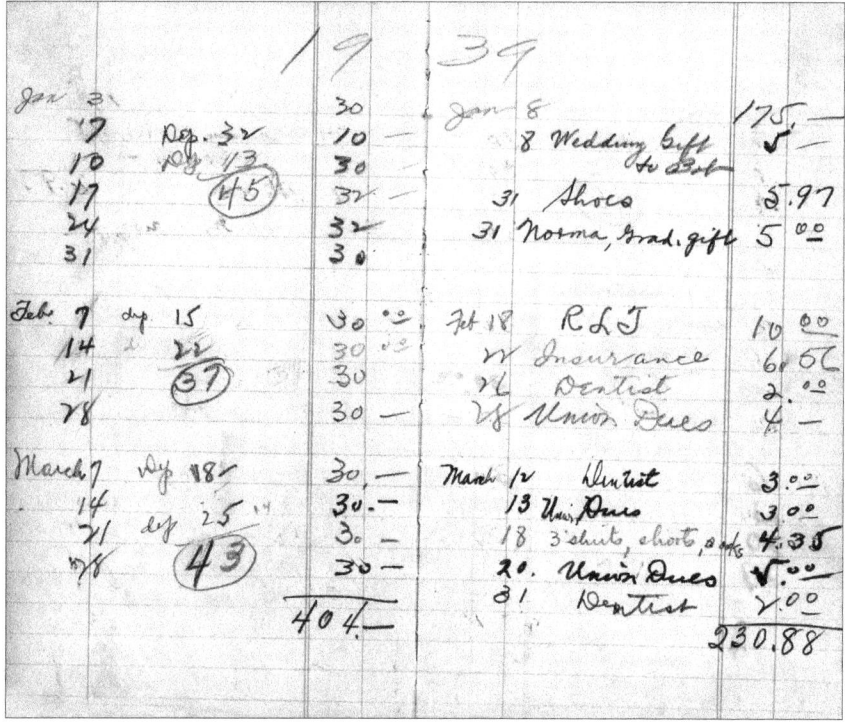

Abraham's Accounting Ledger Page

office worldwide, using passwords and code books to authorize the release of the funds to the recipient at that location. The sender paid a transfer fee when the funds were transferred which was a higher fee at Western Union than the fees charged by a bank.

Alternatively, if money was transferred via a bank transfer, in addition to the initial transfer fee, each transmitting bank deducted a fee for the services until the funds reached the final destination. The best method, for the recipient to receive the maximum amount of cash, was to transfer funds via banks with the fewest number of inter-bank connections.

All financial matters, personal or business, were transacted at one of four banks in Goworowo – The Merchants' Bank, Bank Zydowski

Kredytowy (Jewish Credit Bank) co-founded by Itzhok Kasavski, the Artisans and Retailers Bank on Ostrolenka Street founded by Sholom Pltake from Rozan, and the Hebrew Free Loan Society.

Two houses away from Ruchel Leah's home on Long Street was the home and colonial store (sold food and other consumer products) owned by Avrom and Esther Szfran. It was considered among the largest colonial stores in the village. Ruchel Leah, like her mother, Hilda, shopped at Szfran's on credit which was a customary way of life in the village. As long as the credit was repaid within a reasonable period of time, Esther Szfran, who operated the business, placed no limits to the amount of credit she extended to Ruchel Leah.

Esther Shafran

When someone needed a loan, they generally went to the Jewish Credit Bank which was run by six prominent families in the village. The bank would issue the person credit so that they could secure necessities. Some women, like Hilda, had husbands in America, so until they received money from America, they would "buy" what they needed on credit. Often there was a long wait to clear the accounts as the dollars had to arrive and then be converted to zloty (Polish currency). Once the account was cleared, the individual was issued an additional line of credit. Ruchel Leah was diligent in repaying any loans. She would pay her debts when Anschel was capable of working or when she received funds from the New York family.

On March 6, 1939, Esther Szfran's son, Aron Mendel, age 19, was issued Visa QIV 5791. It is unknown when the visa process actually began that resulted in the issuance of the document. Upon receipt of the visa, plans were immediately made for him to travel to the port of Gdynia via train from Bialystok for departure aboard the M.S. (Motor Ship) *Batory* with a scheduled arrival date in New York of May 2, 1939.

Gdynia was a major seaport constructed after Poland regained its independence in 1918 located on Gdansk Bay on the coast of the Baltic Sea between the Free City of Danzig (Gdansk) and German Pomerania. The port and shipyard were completely destroyed by the German invasion forces at the onset of World War II.

The M.S. *Batory*, named after the 16th century Polish king Stefan Batory, was built at the Cantieri Riuniti dell'Adriatico Monfalcone Shipyard in Trieste, Italy and launched on July 3. 1935. At the time of the launch, the

M.S. Batory

owner, Gdynia America Line, did not have sufficient funds to pay for the ship. A barter was agreed upon. Poland gave Italy five years' worth of coal in exchange for the value of the ship.

The ship became a symbol of Polish emigration. In May 1936 the M.S. *Batory* went into service on the Gdynia-New York route. By 1939 she had transported over 30,000 immigrants to the shores of America.

With the outbreak of war, the M.S. *Batory* was mobilized to serve as a troop transport and hospital ship by the Allied Navy. She played a crucial role in several special assignments – secretly shipping Polish national treasures to Canada for safekeeping, the evacuation of

Dunkirk, and transporting approximately £40 million of the United Kingdom's gold reserves from Scotland to Montreal for safety.

In 1946, after being refitted, the M.S. *Batory* returned to civilian service until she was decommissioned in 1971.

It appears that Moshe's condition might have deteriorated or Ruchel Leah was simply finding it more difficult to deal with his erratic behavior. The cause of his affliction was never identified, therefore, measures were never implemented to assist in coping with what appears to have been autism. If he was autistic, it is known that the individual seems to function best following a consistent routine and familiar surroundings. Perhaps Moshe was beginning to notice the changes taking place in town and within the household. It is conceivable that his behavior became worse as he tried to adjust to the changes in his environment.

Goworowo   *10 March 1939*

Dear Bubbe and Zayde,

I am well and hope to hear from you that you are both well. How is my Aunt Sylvia and her husband? I am glad to inform you that Daddy is feeling better, thanks God.

Dear Grandparents, what you wrote in your last letter that the American consul wrote you that the immigration was postponed for six months is not correct. Two people from town recently received their visas. Another person has to appear before the consul the first day of Passover (April 4, 1939) *for his visa. All these people furnished the consul with financial papers on behalf of the emigrants. It seems that there is no other way. You must try to secure such an affidavit on my behalf. Perhaps, I too, will receive a number which will lead to my being called to appear before the consul to get a visa. Forgive me please for calling to your attention to the fact but, there is no other way.*

Dear Aunt Nettie (age 23), I am curious to know how you spend your time. Do you have steady employment? And did Norma (age 17) find employment? Does Dorothy (age 16) still attend school and in what grade? I would love to know about all of you. I finished school last year. Since there is no higher education available here, no one has the opportunity for a higher education.

Surcha is in fourth grade. She is a very good student. Please forgive me for not writing often. I get depressed when I hear other people in town are leaving for the United States and I cannot. However, one must have faith and hope that someday I'll go to America.

Norma, thanks a lot for your English letter. You received very good compliments on your handwriting and style of writing. I sympathize with you to the fact that while you graduated high school, you cannot continue with your education as I am in the very same position. The opportunities here are limited. I can become a seamstress. I would not mind entering into photography but to study it would cost a few thousand zloty.

Many thanks for your photograph. You are a very pretty young lady. Whoever looked at the photo was amazed how good looking you turned out to be.

I close with love and best wishes to Bubbe, Zadye, Sylvia, Itzhok, Nettie, Norma, and Dorothy. Surcha sends her best regards to all of you. May my letter reach you and find you in best health.

Your grandchild,
Elka Taus

There is a remarkable similarity in the tone and content of Elka's letter to those written by Ruchel Leah. Was the purpose to elicit additional sympathy for the situation with the pleas coming from a child so that efforts on her behalf would be intensified or was it mere coincidence?

It is apparent that Ruchel Leah did not understand the import of the consul's statement that *immigration was postponed for six months* which actually meant that Elka would not be considered until the new annual quota was instituted which was scheduled for June 1939.

Both Elka and Surcha attended the Beit Yaakov (House of Jacob) School in Goworowo which opened in 1928 co-founded by Hershl Rubin and Levi Varshaviak (whose active role was later replaced by Yisroel Burshtin) with Miryem Ruchel Hertsberg as president of Bnos Agudat Israel (a youth club) and as one of the principals of the school. The school system had originally been founded in Krakow, Poland in 1917 by Sarah Schenirer as an Orthodox Jewish educational movement for girls. Up until that time, there had been no tradition of formal education for girls within the Jewish community. Girls were taught at home usually by their mothers or other female relatives primarily on how to fulfill the domestic roles they would assume as adult Jewish women.

Early in the 20th century, it began to be recognized that it was an economic necessity for girls to attend school to acquire the linguistic and vocational skills necessary to support a family. There was also pressure by the Polish government to educate Jewish children in non-religious venues. To avoid sending girls to secular or even Catholic schools where they would be influenced by current cultural and social trends, many rabbinical leaders endorsed the establishment of the Beit Yaakov Schools.

Elka at Beit Yaakov

Surcha at Beit Yaakov

By 1921 the Beit Yaakov Schools were adopted by Poland's Agudat Israel as its educational arm for girls and women. Agudat Israel began as a political party representing ultra-Orthodox Jews in Poland so this endorsement was paramount to the expansion of the schools. On the eve of the German invasion of Poland in September 1939, there were about 250 Beit Yaakov schools with over 40,000 students throughout the world.

The movement grew to include many types of programs: supplemental (afternoon and weekend) religious schools for girls who attended Polish school during the day; all-day schools where the pupils were taught both Jewish and secular subjects; teacher training seminars; a textbook publishing house, and a monthly Yiddish journal; summer camps, youth clubs – Batya (Daughter of God) for girls and Bnos Agudat Israel for teenagers – and international conferences for Jewish women. In some of the larger cities the grade levels extended through high school, offering business and vocational training, but in smaller villages like Goworowo, the education ended with the completion of middle school.

At the Polish Beit Yaakov Schools, Yiddish was the language of instruction, with limited exposure to Polish and German language and literature. The curriculum in Jewish studies included the Torah (Old Testament) and traditional commentaries, Jewish philosophy, and those religious laws incumbent on women.

Students were taught not only the specific prayers and duties which Jewish women were expected to know but were presented secular subjects through the prism of religious faith. Literature was a venue for teaching the values of Jewish living; the wonder of God's creation as the underlying theme was taught in science classes while the study of German was deemed necessary to understand Rabbi Samson Raphael Hirsch's (1808 –1888 – German Orthodox Rabbi) biblical commentary in its original language.

Elka graduated from the seventh grade at the Beit Yaakov School with no viable option to continue her education in the small shtetl. To further her education she would have had to travel to a larger city such as Bialystok or even Warsaw. There she would have had to have a place to live and a means to support herself. Without money, it was an impossible dream. If she were to stay in Poland, she would have had to learn a trade or get married. Being apprenticed to a seamstress appeared to be her only viable alternative, yet one in which she was not interested.

Norma, too, began her education in Goworowo, at the Beit Yaakov School, continuing her schooling in New York.

Norma at Beit Yaakov

Upon graduation from James Monroe High School in the Bronx, New York in December 1938 she entered the work force as a low salaried stenographer in an attorney's office working for a female attorney alongside her sister, Nettie. While Norma had the aptitude for a higher education, economics dictated another direction in life.

Norma's High School Graduation

10 March 1939

Dear Sister Norma,

We received your letter with your photo for which we are very thankful to you. I can fully sympathize with you to the fact that you cannot continue with your education in spite of your having a great desire for knowledge. Nevertheless, be grateful that you managed to graduate from high school. I wish you good luck and happiness in your future undertakings. Anybody that looks at your photograph makes highly favorable remarks as to how beautiful you look.

Dear sister, please write more often as I always like hearing from you. Stay well. Everyone sends you warmest regards. Anschel's health is up and down. That is how we live. It is not the best in the world. Moshe sends his regards. Give our regards to my sister Nettie and brother Itzhok.

Your sister,

Ruchel Leah

Goworowo   *12 March 1939*

Dear Parents, Sisters, Brother-in-law and dear Brother,

I was very happy to read that you are all, thank God, in good health. All winter long I was very anxious to hear from you. I was out of my mind. But why talk about the past. Let's hope and look for a better future. Your letter, in fact, caused me some pain. Somehow I felt that it would turn out that way. I suppose one cannot control events.

I received the $40.00 you sent for which we thank you all very much. I gave my mother-in-law her share (a portion was sent specifically for Schwartza Dvora Taus) *for which she* *thanks all of you and wished you good health. The same day I received your letter, I received the photograph of my dear sister Norma. It is hard to describe our joy as we admired how pretty a young lady Norma turned out to be. Anybody who got to see the photograph expressed great admiration. I wish you, my dear parents, much nachas* (proud enjoyment) *from your children there. You certainly do not have much nachas from the children here. May God include us with those who need help.*

I have been sending you postcards as I thought that they would get to you faster. I assume you received them. I have written numerous times about the affidavit the consul requests. I took it upon myself and wrote a letter to the consul questioning him why he has not sent Elka a number. He replied that he wrote to you but has not received any of the documents which he requested. It seems that by not filing the correct papers you are causing the delay. I beg you, dear parents, please send the consul the required papers without delay. You wrote in your last letter that immigration was stopped for a while yet, some people in town have been getting their visas. Baruch's (Kuperman) *son-in-law* (Baruch Meyer Goldberg) *had some difficulty yet, he was called for the second time to appear before the consul on the second day of Passover (April 5, 1939). He is confident that he will get the visa this time. Their relatives in the United States furnished affidavits that they have money assigned to support the immigrant.*

You asked what Elka did during the entire winter. She kept herself busy reading Yiddish and Polish books and practiced her violin daily. As you know, there is no education facility in Goworowo higher than the seventh grade. We did not try to teach her a trade as I figured she would soon get her visa. There is no point doing that and learning to be a seamstress did not seem to excite her either. The situation keeps me confused.

Right now, I do not have much more to write. Everything is about the same. No improvement in the situation.

Your son-in-law, Anschel sends his heartfelt regards and wishes you a healthy and happy Passover. Regards for my parents. Regards for my dear sister and her husband. What is the reason you do not write? I keep writing to you but receive no reply. Your father-in-law (Mendel Chaim Rubin) *had a party this week honoring his grandchild's upcoming wedding. The party was held in his daughter's house. However, we were not invited. That is the kind of people they are. We felt shamed in front of others for not being invited.*

Heartfelt regards from your daughter, sister who wishes you the best. My girls send you the best regards.
Ruchel Leah Taus
My in-laws send the best wishes.

Residing next door, with both properties adjacent to the Rotenski apple orchard, were Rachel Leah's in-laws, Itche Yosel Taus, the village grave digger and Schwartza Dvora Kruk Taus, a midwife.

The term "schwartza" while meaning black in Yiddish was not considered to be a derogatory term even when used in reference to an individual. In reality, it was used as a term of familiarity and endearment. Since she was a young girl, everyone called Dvora, "Schwartza" Dvora. She had a dark, swarthy complexion, deep brown eyes, and coal black hair thus earning her the appellative of "Schwartza".

Having known Moshe since he was an infant, Schwartza Dvora, in all probability, assisted Ruchel Leah in his care. He was familiar and comfortable with her so she was able to be offer succor without disrupting his normal routine. The family probably sent the small monetary gift to her in appreciation for her supplemental care of Moshe.

Lazar Frydman

Anschel's youngest sister, Feige, her husband Lazar Frydman, and their children – Chaim age 6 and one year old Razale – lived with Schwartza Dvora and Itche Yosel. In addition to being a baker, Lazar worked for many years with the burial society alongside his father-in-law. Lazar was also an active participant in the Goworowo branch of the BUND (abbreviation of Alge-meyner Yidisher Arbeter Bund in Lite, Poyln un Rusland – General Jewish Workers' Union in Lithuania, Poland and Russia).

Founded at a secret convention in Vilna, Lithuania, then under Russian dominion, on October 7-9, 1897, the Bund concentrated its activities on the political sphere with the party becoming an important factor in Jewish public life. It was initially an underground, clandestine movement. Their ideology of secular Jewish nationalism was sharply opposed to both Zionism and religious orthodoxy.

When the threat of a German invasion of Poland's Russian terri-tory became apparent in November 1914, the central committee of the Polish Bund declared a complete dissociation from the Russian movement. Though still a clandestine organization, the new German occupation authorities enabled the Bund in Poland to emphasize

Jewish demands, set up trade unions, workers' kitchens, cooperative shops, and a network of cultural institutions. With the creation of the Republic of Poland in 1918, the Bund was able to function as a legal, independent political party. During the early years of the Republic, the Polish Bund was persecuted because of its opposition to the Polish-Soviet War (1918-1921) but continued to exert political influence on behalf of the Jewish population.

Some Bund activists were imprisoned at the Bereza Karuska (Belarus) concentration camp from June 17, 1934 until the guards, fearing the German advance, fled in September 1939. All the prisoners were released. The camp was designed to detain people who were viewed by the Polish state as a "threat to security, peace and social order" without any formal charges. More than 3000 people had been detained at the camp.

Bund Meeting Lazar Frydman top row at right Zisket Taus middle row at right

The Goworowo branch of the Bund was founded and lead by Leybn Kersh who later became a prominent leader in the national organization where he lead the youth movement. He was among those murdered in the Warsaw Ghetto Uprising between April 19 and May 16, 1943.

Jewish life in Poland in the 1930s had become increasing difficult caused by the inherent anti-Semitism prevalent in the country. Polish anti-Semitic activity was further amplified by the worldwide economic depression with the Jewish population being blamed as a scapegoat for the country's financial difficulties. *"Although in the wake of World War I Poland had signed 'minorities treaties' that were supposed to protect Jews as well as other ethnic minorities, anti-Semitic discrimination and occasional outbursts of anti-Jewish violence became the norm in the years leading up to World War II. Local anti-Jewish boycotts also were common. Gangs of anti-Semitic thugs pressured Christian landlords, artisans, and shopkeepers to refrain from doing business with Jews. Those who cooperated with the boycott were given signs to place in their windows announcing that they dealt only with 'Aryans'. Those who refused had their names published in extreme nationalist Polish newspapers. The boycott enforcers also frequently carried out physical assaults on Jewish businesses, demanding that they close down, and the attacks sometimes escalated into all-out pogroms.... The Polish government, for its part, endorsed anti-Jewish boycotts as necessary to realize the 'Polonization' of the nation's economy, which Polish authorities claimed was under Jewish domination."* The Jews Should Keep Quiet: Franklin D. Roosevelt, Rabbi Stephen S. Wise, and the Holocaust by Rafael Medoff, 2019

The Bund's greatest political influence was achieved on the eve of the Holocaust between 1936 and 1939. After Adolf Hitler

(1889-1945) began his rise to power in Germany in 1933, the Bund was instrumental in the campaign against the increased anti-Semitism within the Polish government and general population. Tremendous success was achieved in the municipal elections. The Bund organized self-defense groups, a protest strike after the pogrom of Przytyk in 1936, and a Workers' Congress against anti-Semitism (banned by the Polish authorities as was a proposed Congress for the Struggle of the Jewish Population in Poland in 1938).

A boycott of Jewish trade called by the National Democrat movement resulted in a riot at Przytyk on March 9, 1936. During the boycott demonstration, two Jews and one non-Jewish Polish citizen were killed, several dozen Jewish dwellings and shops were destroyed and more than 20 people were severely beaten. In 1936, 90% of Przytyk's population of 3,000 were Jewish and the market had been a hub for neighboring villages.

The trial of the 14 Jews who fought back in the riot and 42 non-Jews who were arrested took place in June 1936. There was a disparity in the severity of the sentences received by the Jewish and non-Jewish defendants. While three of the Jews received prison terms for using firearms and killing one of the Poles, the four non-Jews who were accused of killing a family were acquitted for lack of evidence. In addition three Jews and 16 non-Jews were acquitted for lack of evidence while eight Jews and 22 of the accused Poles received sentences of up to one year.

After the trial, the wave of anti-Semitic violence subsided, to a degree. The authorities began to take action against such violence as it was viewed as being not only an attack against the Jewish population but also against the government authorities. The action of the Jewish self-defense group in Przytyk illustrated that the Jewish population would not allow themselves to be attacked and victimized without responding in kind.

There was a profusion of active political/social organizations in Poland during the interwar years. Differing goals and ideologies led to conflict and arguments, often within the same household. As a small shtetl, Goworowo was not immune to the ideological rifts prevalent in the country.

In contrast to the Bund, Zionism, also founded in 1897, by Theodor Herzl in Austria was a prominent political movement in Goworowo. The Zionists sought the re-establishment and ultimately the development/protection of a Jewish national homeland in what was then known as Palestine (Israel). By 1920, Chaim Weizmann, as president of the World Zionist Organization, was the guiding force of the Zionist movement. In 1949, he was elected as the first president of Israel.

Prior to immigrating to the United States, Abraham had been an ardent supporter and member of the Ha Shomer ha-Tsair, The Young Guard, a Zionist-socialist pioneering youth movement.

Ha Shomer ha Tsair Abraham bottom row right

In late August 1929, the Ha Shomer ha-Tsair, in Gowowro, organized a protest demonstration spurred on by the Hebron Massacre in Palestine. For generations, the community of 800 Jews in the ancient city of Hebron had lived peacefully surrounded by their Arab neighbors. On the eve of August 23rd, the Arabs were incited to violence by rumors that the Jewish population in Palestine planned to seize and control the Temple Mount (venerated as a holy site by Judaism, Christianity, and Islam) in Jerusalem. For three days, Hebron became a city of terror as the Arab residents led a massacre against the Jewish community. In the end, 67 Jews had been killed, many others seriously wounded, homes and synagogues were destroyed. The survivors were relocated by the British authorities to Jerusalem. After hundreds of years of peaceful coexistence, no Jews were left in Hebron.

The Ha Shomer ha-Tsair group in Goworowo, in support of Zionism, asked everyone in town to close their doors and window shutters during the protest demonstration and speeches as a symbol of solidarity. Anschel, a Bundist, did not agree with the Zionist philosophy, so refused to close the shutters.

At 15, considering himself to be the man of the house, Abraham was particularly perturbed with Anschel's lack of support and Ruchel Leah's stance with her husband. "Some of the boys in my group wanted to use force to close the doors, but I called it off" (Abraham). As a result of this refusal, Abraham ceased speaking to both Anschel and Ruchel Leah for a year. The day prior to the family's departure for the United States, June 12, 1930, Abraham went to the small back room occupied by Anschel and Ruchel Leah to say good-bye.

It is theorized that at some point in this conversation, Ruchel Leah gave Abraham her "waxing crescent moon" locket which conceivably her father had brought to her as a gift upon his return from the United States in 1913. The gold shell locket, set with spinel stones, had been manufactured by Wightman & Hough Co. (1856-1922) in Providence, Rhode Island.

Anschel and Ruchel Leah 1923

Ruchel Leah gave Abraham the locket, her most valuable possession, to sell on the journey to the United States should the family find the need for extra money. If it was not necessary to sell the locket, she instructed him to hold it for her eventual arrival in New York, the arrival of one or both of her daughters, or barring either, to give it to his future wife with her blessing. The locket, with its promise of a brighter future, eventually belonged to Abraham's wife, Rebecca Offenberg Blum.

In those trying times, the shtetl was rampant with gossip particularly when someone received a visa to emigrate to the United States. News that Baruch Kuperman's son-in-law had a second interview

*Abraham and Rebecca
Offenberg 1938*

with the American consul traveled faster than lightening through the gossip channel.

Having arrived in the United States on February 19, 1930 aboard the SS *Paris* from Havre, France under Visa #5097 issued on November 21. 1929, Baruch Kuperman, a shoemaker and Goworowo synagogue council member, began planning to bring his entire family to the United States. He left his wife, Chana Ruchel Glotzer Kuperman and five children – Taube (Goldberg who lived in Ostroleka), Fannie, Malka, Naftal, and Freda – in Poland. His oldest son, Isidore was already living in Brooklyn, New York.

Within a couple of years, on November 13, 1934, Naftal, Visa #QIV 3852, arrived in New York aboard the SS *Pulaski* from the port at Gdynia. Now, Baruch Kuperman's son-in-law and family had an appointment with the American consul for their visas. Ruchel Leah could not comprehend how Baruch Kuperman, whose financial situation was similar to her family's, could arrange the proper documen-

Baruch Kuperman

tation for immigration, yet her family did not seem able or willing to do so for Elka.

67

Sailing aboard the MS *Batory* on April 22, 1939, Baruch Meyer Goldberg, his wife Taube Kuperman Goldberg and children Jankiel age 5 and Szejna (Shayna) age 10 had visas issued by the American consulate in Warsaw on April 4, 1939. Ruchel Leah was exasperated at what she perceived to be inactivity on the part of her New York family in obtaining the necessary documentation for Elka's visa.

Private libraries were prolific throughout Poland during the interwar years. Shelves were filled with a wide variety of books unlike those traditionally found in the collections of yeshivas or synagogues which only held religious volumes. While most Orthodox Jews opposed this spread of secular literature, the libraries quickly became an essential part of life in the shtetls.

Elka availed herself of literature by Shomer (Nahum Meir Schaikewitz 1849-1905), Sholem Aleichem (Solomon Naumovich Rabinovich 1859-1916), and other popular authors at the various libraries in Goworowo. Named after Yosef Haim Brenner (Hebrew author 1881-1921), the Brenner Library was operated by the right wing of the Zionist movement. The Bund maintained a library along with the Peretz Library (named in honor of Yiddish author, I.L. Peretz) on half of the top floor of a house on Long Street. Chana Frydman, the widowed mother of Lazar Frydman was the founder and supporter of the Peretz library.

With an affinity for music, Elka began to study the violin in about 1933/1934 with Rafoyl Levkovitch who had come to Goworowo from Przasnysz to teach Hebrew in both private and group sessions. Levkovitch was a scholar, an advocate of the Haskalah (Jewish Enlightenment which was an intellectual movement), an expert in Hebrew and Hebrew literature, and was musically trained having played with the Warsaw Symphony Orchestra. In addition

to his Hebrew courses, Levkovitch taught violin with Elka as
one of his students. Somehow,
Ruchel Leah managed to
manipulate family finances to
purchase a violin and pay for
lessons so Elka could continue
to pursue her music studies.

Mendel Chaim Rubin was
Sylvia's father-in-law. He was
of a similar economic level as
Ruchel Leah and Anschel being
a shoemaker who raised a dairy

Elka Playing Her Violin

cow and sold milk and dairy products to earn additional income. An
upcoming wedding was a cause for celebration for the entire shtetl.
Not being invited by Mendel Chaim to his granddaughter's betrothal
was an embarrassment that Ruchel Leah found difficult to bear.

The betrothal was as important a festive occasion as the actual
wedding. During the affair, the parents of the couple recorded the
terms of the engagement, the names of the bride and groom, their
parents, the dowry, and the gifts. The future bride and groom signed
the document which was then read to the attendees. A dish was
broken – Mazel Tov was shouted – the engagement was official.

The lack of an invitation was a personal insult and a shonda
(scandalously shameful). Everyone in the village knew Ruchel Leah
had been slighted. She was no stranger to the Rubin family. She
considered herself to be mishpachah (an entire network of relatives by
blood or marriage) by virtue of her sister Sylvia's marriage to Mendel
Chaim's son, Mates. They **were** mishpachah.

Mendel Chaim hosted the party at the home of his daughter, Bejla Leja Rubin Cymerman in honor of her 15 year old daughter, Sura. There are no records that Sura ever married the man to whom she was engaged.

Goworowo   *7 April 1939*

Anschel looks real bad. That is how my life is. With God's help, when he feels better, he looks good and can even do some work. The condition is bad when he gets sick and cannot work. With no income of any kind, the situation can get unbearable with no money for medicine. What's the use of talking? I cannot convince the Almighty to restore his health.

As far as his not writing you, you know the reason. He feels that his writing is not up to standard. However, he is very much concerned about each one of you. He was very happy to see Norma's photo as if it would have been his own child. He is more concerned about you than his own brothers (Zisket and Fishel).

You asked about the exchange of dollars – We got 7.65 zlotys for a dollar. You did the right thing. Otherwise I would have received only 5.20 zlotys for a dollar. I would have been heartbroken for the loss of the difference.

That is about all I have to write.

It is the week of Passover and Anschel went to the shul (synagogue). *Your son-in-law sends his best regards to all of you.*

Your daughter,
Ruchel Leah

In addition to his younger sister, Feige, Anschel had three other siblings who were all living abroad. His older sister, Elka Taus Ter had immigrated along with her husband Leibel Ter and daughter

Rachel to Paris prior to World War I becoming naturalized French citizens on January 26, 1926. Residing at 88 rue Philippe de Girard 18th arrondissement they had three additional daughters – Madeleine who died in 1923 at age 5, Lucienne, and Helene.

His brother, Fishel Taus, Richla Frydman Taus, his wife, along with their daughter, Resla moved to Paris around 1923 and established himself as a tailor. Initially he lived with his sister and brother-in-law. After June 1930, Fishel, Richla and their daughters, Resla and Claudine moved into an apartment at 60 rue de la Chapelle.

Immigration to the United States was in the cards for Anschel's brother, Zisket Taus and his wife, Sura Schmeltz. Sura had two brothers, Aaron (Harry) and Hymie who had previously immigrated to the United States.

Aaron arrived in New York on September 18, 1920 aboard the SS *Susquahanna* which sailed out of Bremen, Germany. Aaron's wife Liba and daughter, Shirley (Shana) Schmeltz Freedman joined him on December 27, 1927. Hymie immigrated on November 13, 1921 via Rio de Janeiro on the SS *Southern Cross* which was operated by the Munson Steamship Line. Sura's brothers, Abe and Reuben immigrated to the United States in 1932.

Abraham, Reuben Schmeltz, Abe Schmeltz, Shirley Schmeltz, Coney Island, New York 1934

It was perceived that it would be easier for Zisket and Sura to obtain an American visa since her brothers were already in the United States. Therefore, Zisket changed his surname from Taus to Schmeltz. Preparations were underway in the early 1930s to immigrate to America.

Convinced by some acquaintances that their opportunities would be better in Brazil, Mexico, or Cuba, they chose to immigrate to Brazil instead of the United States. Zisket along with Isaac Waizbort, the husband of Sura's sister, Rivka (Regina), left for Brazil to make arrangements for their new lives. Sura and Rivka subsequently traveled together to join them in Brazil.

Rivka Waizbort and Sura Schmeltz

At the time, Brazilian naturalization was mandatory. It was common practice to change a difficult sounding name to be more acceptable to the Portuguese speaking Brazilians. Zisket Schmeltz now became Jose Schmelcz and Sura became Sara Schmelcz.

Passover commemorates the story from the Book of Exodus in which the enslaved Jews in Egypt gained their freedom. There are strict religious guidelines for the celebration of the holiday as there is an injunction that every generation must act as if they were part of this exodus. Preparations often began weeks prior to the first Seder (festive meal signifying the beginning of the holiday). The house, particularly the kitchen, was scrubbed from top to bottom. Food with leavening agents, the five grains – wheat, barley, rye, oats and spelt which sits in water for more than 18 minutes – is called

chametz which is forbidden to be consumed on Passover. According to Jewish law, pots, pans, dishes and utensils used throughout the year absorb the chametz and, therefore, are not allowed to be used during the eight days of Passover. They are either changed for specific Passover sets or there exists a series of stringent rabbinical procedures to make them "Kosher (to be pure, proper, and suitable under Jewish law) for Passover".

Sara and Jose Schmelcz daughters Eva and Rela –Marriage Contract in Background

Even with the lack of funds to "properly" observe the holiday, the family endeavored to celebrate the Exodus from Egypt as best they could. They had hope in the midst of despair.

On the night before Passover began, it was customary to search the house, with a candle, to seek any chametz crumbs. If any crumbs were found they were symbolically swept up with a feather and then burned. Traditional Passover fare – chopped chicken liver, gefilte fish, matzo ball soup, charoset (fruit/nut mixture), boiled potatoes, carrot tzimmes (sweet vegetable side dish), homemade raisin wine – was prepared within the family's financial limitations. Life and tradition continued.

Every zloty counted towards the family's well-being and basic survival. It was important to maximize the exchange rates of the received United States dollars. This resulted in the emergence of a "grey market" exchange. The official national bank exchange rate in pre-war 1939 was $1 yielded 5.20 zlotys. By exchanging the money at the grey market budżetowy (financial exchange), Ruchel Leah was able to gain 2.45 zloty for every dollar exchanged.

5 Zloty Banknote 1930

Goworowo   *7 April 1939*

Dear Bubbe, Zadye, and Aunts,

We received your two letters. We read them with pleasure hearing that you are all well, thanks God. We received Norma's photograph. We all admired how pretty she looks. My desire is to see her personally, the same for all of you.

Why are you mad at me? I do not know the reason. I am not mad at you. I was talking to you but you did not answer.

Your grandchild,

Surcha Taus

In one of the few letters existing from Surcha, she expresses her longing to see the family and chides them for not writing to her. Did Surcha, a 10 year old child, formulate this letter or did Ruchel Leah direct her to write it?

Goworowo   Date Unknown (stationary is similar to the letter written on 7 April 1939)

My dear brother Abraham Itzhok,

Please send me your address where you work as I want to write to you directly without anyone else knowing the topic or the content of the letter.

Now, what have you been doing in regards to Elka's situation? I hope that you are trying to arrange an assignment of some money on Elka's behalf. There is no hope for Elka without that certificate. I have written numerous times but never receive a reply.

Again, please send me your employment address which will enable me to communicate with you on an important matter.

Best regards from the depth of my heart. Everyone sends regards.

Elka is well and she looks real good but, she worries a lot.

Your sister,

Ruchel Leah

Increasingly frustrated and seemingly desperate to obtain an immigration visa for Elka, Ruchel Leah conceived a plan she wanted to propose privately to Abraham. She rationalized that if Elka was married to an American citizen, the husband would have a better chance of bringing his wife to the United States under immigration spousal stipulations as defined by section 9 of the Johnson-Reed Act of 1924. This section allowed for "the wife, of a citizen of the United States who resides therein at the time of the filing of a petition" to enter the United States quota exempt. What Ruchel Leah did not know is that the Act further defined the terms "wife" and "husband" to exclude a proxy or picture marriage.

She proposed that Abraham marry his niece. While there are strict Judaic laws regarding incest dating back to Biblical times, the marriage of a man and his niece is not specifically forbidden by the Torah (Old Testament).

Abraham rejected the concept. Even if he had not, it would have been impossible to implement. While permitted by Talmudic law, in addition to the restrictions imposed by the Johnson-Reed Act, in 1939, every state prohibited marriage between uncles and nieces, aunts and nephews along with other additional ancestor/descendant marriage prohibitions.

Goworowo   *9 April 1939*

Dear brother Abraham Itzhok,

We received your dear letter and read it with pleasure. I gathered that you are displeased with the fact that I engaged a man to help me with the problem of Elka's immigration. I can assure you that not much is involved. I doubt very much if the consul will issue Elka a visa based on the papers you furnished him. There is no reason he would honor them now since he previously rejected the same kind of papers. It seems to me that the documents the American consul will accept are the ones that assign a certain amount of money as a guarantee for Elka's support. Try your best to secure such a document and forward it to the authorities as soon as possible.

And now a few words about what is new in our shtetl. A large sum of money was sent by the American committee for distribution to the poor in the shtetl. Shai (Isaiah) *Kapikes was put in charge of the funds. He hesitated in making a distribution of the money and instead exchanged the dollars on the budżetowy* (financial exchange). *Then he distributed $520.00. Consequently, he made a few hundred dollars in this transaction. Now he does not want to share the gain with the people. It is quite a scandal. Now, Shai, the shoemaker, is a rich man.*

In the next letter, I will give you more details of the scandal. Be well.

Your sister,

Ruchel Leah

By the late 1800s, Jewish immigrants to the United States from the same geographical locations in Central and Eastern Europe began banding together to form Landsmanshaftn (people from the same region) societies as a familiar form of social organization. The Landsmanshaftn provided the immigrants with both a formal and informal social network; it was a means to stay in contact with friends and relatives still in Europe and provided a framework for financial and medical assistance. The Landsmanshaftn also purchased sections in various cemeteries so the immigrants would not have to be concerned about burial plots and be buried "among their own".

Early on, immigrants from Goworowo founded the Cheyras Bnai Aharon Shlomo Tehillim Anshei Govorovo Society commonly known as the Goworowo Landsman Society. A second society, Goworowo Young Men's Benevolent Association was established in 1909. Soon afterwards, a Ladies Auxiliary was created. The three organizations joined together to form a Relief Committee with the purpose of helping the new arrivals in America and sending financial assistance back to Goworowo for distribution to those in need.

When the money arrived in Goworowo, Shai Kapikes, a shoe-maker, was responsible for the distribution of the funds. Apparently, he converted the dollars to zloty on the grey market, keeping the profit from the difference in the currency exchange rates for himself.

Goworowo   *9 April 1939*

Dear Parents, Sisters, Brother and Brother-in-law,

I am glad to inform you that I received your letter and I enjoyed reading about your health. You asked whether or not I received Norma's photograph. I did receive it and immediately I responded in a letter that it was received. My dear sister looks stunning. I simply adore looking at your photos. On a holiday I display all your photographs and enjoy looking at them. The family photo hangs over my bed. I suppose we have to be grateful for that but longing for you is great. We figured if we are successful with Elka immigrating to the United States then we hoped we would eventually follow but, unfortunately, it is a losing proposition. It has been a year since we started Elka's immigration process without any results. I mentioned numerous times that you must assign a few thousand dollars on Elka's behalf otherwise the consul will not issue a visa. I understand that perhaps you do not have that kind of money. Without it the consul will not budge. The consul wrote to us that he needs another statement from you about being in position to support her. Without such an affidavit, he will not issue any number. I believe that you should be acquainted with the immigration laws and requirements.

Quite a few people from Goworowo have left for the United States namely Shalom, the butcher. His family assigned a certain sum of money. Therefore, he got his visa. I have nothing against you if you give up on the whole deal.....

But Elka just finished school and was considering her future. There is not much for her in Goworowo except for her to become a seamstress. After hearing from you I will be compelled, to my disappointment, to have her learn a trade and forget about emigrating. When a child is out of school, her mind and time is spent on other things and gets out of the habit of studying. Therefore, I was anxious for her to emigrate.

You question why I hired a man to help us with the emigration problem. You do not have to worry about it. First, I never gave him any money. Second, he can do us no harm. The only time he would be compensated is if he would succeed in getting a visa. It seems to me that your consultant (Mr. Linder) *is misleading you. The Kuperman family did not have an attorney* (consultant) *but submitted an affidavit for $3,000. for a family of four. They already received their visas and after Passover, they are leaving for the United States. The only hope for Elka to get a number and a visa is for you to file the affidavit. Without it, there is no chance whatsoever to get one. I am anxiously awaiting a reply from you on my request.*

And now, my dear parents, I was delighted to hear the good news that my dear sister Sylvia is expecting. Make sure that she does not work too much. Help her as much as you can. Anschel and I are very happy about the good news.

You asked about Anschel's health. Well, he is about the same. Sometimes, when he feels a little better he is capable of working a little and earning some money. Without the meager earnings it would have been entirely impossible to make it. On top of all that, the yearly tax is quite high. I asked the authorities for an exemption based on Anschel being sick but they rejected the request. However, if we got rid of the workbench and all showing that he is not working, it would help. Yet, we cannot make it without the little he makes when he is working. I submitted affidavits that he is a very sick person.

(Letter is not complete)

The pressures of daily existence were a constant challenge for Ruchel Leah. Between worrying about Elka's future, Moshe's behavior, Anschel's health, and financial struggles, Ruchel Leah was finding it increasingly difficult to cope with everyday life. Yet, with all of her difficulties, she still expresses delight in Sylvia's pregnancy and concern for her well-being.

We cannot fathom the struggle she had to be able even to provide food for the family or if the constant hunger of her family would ever dissipate. Everyday meals were based, for the most part, on coarse rye bread, herring, soup and, of course, potatoes. Meat, chicken, and fish were luxuries, therefore served only on the Sabbath and special occasions, if even then. Cheaper cuts of meat, chicken legs, and river fish were creatively prepared. Fish cakes were consumed which probably contained an abundance of potatoes and onions and very little fish. A favorite was matjes herring (salted young herring caught prior to spawning) which was more expensive than regular pickled herring so was only occasionally purchased. Soup was an evening staple – potato soup, borscht (beet soup) made with meat or meatless served with a dollop of sour cream, schav (sorrel soup) often with potatoes, and chicken soup.

Ruchel Leah stored, in the vestibule area between the main room and the back room, vegetables to be used during the winter months. Potatoes along with other root vegetables such as turnips, beets, radishes, parsnips, rutabaga, and carrots were put aside with an ample supply of pickled cabbage, cucumbers (pickles), onions and garlic.

Potatoes were the mainstay of the diet – cooked, stewed, baked. Potatoes were often eaten three times a day: boiled potato with herring, baked potato, potatoes with fried onions, knishes (a dough) stuffed with potatoes, potato kreplach (dumplings) and latkes (pancakes), potato kugel (pudding), boiled potato with fresh or sour milk, and potato soup.

It was estimated that a family of five would need to store approximately 2,250 pounds of potatoes to sustain them over the winter. Fortunately, an old Christian family friend had a farm on the outskirts of Goworowo and for years had allowed the use of a small parcel of land in exchange for collecting the waste from the Taus' outhouse which was used as fertilizer. The family planted a few beets and, of course, potatoes.

BULBES (Potatoes) – Yiddish folk song – 3rd stanza

Here – potatoes
There – potatoes
Here and there – potatoes
There and here – potatoes
But on Shabbos, after cholent
A potato kugel!
And Sunday, here we go again, potatoes

Since Jewish law prohibits lighting a fire on the Sabbath, a special dish, cholent was prepared on Friday to be served for dinner on Saturday evening. A mixture of a multiple variety of beans, onions, spices, buckwheat (kasha), potatoes, and a small bit of meat was placed in a special cholent pot. In all probability, on Friday afternoons, Ruchel Leah brought the cholent pot to the bakery where her brother-in-law, Lazar Frydman, worked. At the bakery, water was added to the mixture and her pot, along with those from other families, was placed in the oven. The oven had been turned off for the Sabbath but the residual heat of the cooling oven cooked the cholent for 24 hours. This was, perhaps, the original concept of a "slow cooker."

To help alleviate the financial burden, Ruchel Leah appealed to the tax office for an exemption of the PIT (personal income tax). Anschel's limited ability to earn a viable income due to his illness was the justification for the appeal. The request was denied.

In 1924, Poland introduced a unified progressive income tax based on earned and unearned income. The general population was suffering financially from the impact of the worldwide depression of the 1930s. Yet, the new tax law of 1936 increased the already burdensome tax rates.

Under the guidelines of this law, Anschel probably fell within the first range of income 1,500 – 1,550 zloty a year ($288. – $300.) which meant that his taxes were fixed at 440 zloty a year ($84.60) half payable on May 1st and the balance by November 1st of each year.

Income was calculated based on all earnings less the cost of doing business. If family members worked in the enterprise, the cost of feeding those members would be considered a tax deduction. No special fees or state tax appeared to have been levied in 1939. Without the exemption, Anschel was responsible for the minimal tax assessment of 440 zloty.

With Anschel's inability to work regularly and fewer clients, the family was in a dire financial situation, yet, Ruchel Leah continued to grasp for glimmers of hope. She courageously refused to concede defeat.

Goworowo   *13 April 1939*
Dear Parents, Sisters, Brother-in-law and dear Brother,
    I wrote you a letter about this same subject that I am writing about now. I am repeating what I have written many times before that it is important to furnish the financial affidavit and

send it to the American consul. Without it, nothing will happen. Dear brother, you wrote me recently that the consul wrote you that Elka will receive a number within six months after he receives additional papers (financial) *from you. I beg you not to delay. Do it as soon as you can. I feel that the man who is helping me with the case was instrumental in having the consul write to you. Had you furnished the consul with the required papers Elka would have had a number by now. I cannot understand the delay. Is it the cost involved in securing the papers? Spend another few dollars to secure the financial papers. In case your man* (Mr. Linder) *does not do it, have it done yourself. Do not let him talk you out of it. Do me a favor and do it. According to the information I have, it seems the consul, until recently required that a certain amount of money to be assigned for the immigrant. Then he would issue a number but, this has been changed. He now requires a financial statement instead. My contact assures me that the document carries more weight than any other in influencing his decision. In case you doubt the man I am dealing with, I can send you his address. He lives in New York. He has been successful with many of his clients. Not everybody knows about him. He will not do it for anybody. I cannot give you more details now but, eventually I might do so.*

I am sure if I were to ask you for a few dollars you would not have refused me even though you just sent me some money for Passover. I can assure you that everything will be in order.

I am very concerned about any delays as things get worse here from day to day. Also the immigration chances change for the worse. A few people from town left for the United States recently who I thought would qualify to leave after Elka but, it turned

out differently. They already left for the United States. Please do
not disappoint me.

Be well. A heartfelt regards from your brother-in-law, Elka
and Surcha. Special regards to my dear parents, sister, and
brother-in-law, sisters Nettie, Norma, and Dorothy. I beg of you
to take care of the matter. I expect an answer in about 4 weeks.

Your daughter, son-in-law and grandchildren send their
regards,
Ruchel Leah

Yiddish Letter April 13, 1939

With this letter one begins to wonder who was this mysterious
man with whom Ruchel Leah was in communication? Perhaps this
man had previously been successful in obtaining a visa for someone

from Goworowo, who is also unnamed. If she felt so secure that this man would be able to accomplish obtaining the visa for Elka and was so adamant regarding Mr. Linder's methods or lack of competency in handling the case, why is she being cryptic regarding his identity and contact information in New York?

Goworowo   *27 April 1939*

Dear Parents, Sisters, Brother and Brother-in-law,

I wrote to you a few times about Elka's possible trip to the United States. In order for Elka to receive a number from the American consul, you must furnish him with financial papers. However, it seems that the requirement has changed. It seems that now he requires that you need to assign a certain amount of money to or for the emigrant. The political situation here is very frightening. The talk is of war. We hope to God that it might not happen. That peace will prevail. Meanwhile, we live in fear.

How are you feeling? Are you employed? If we succeed and Elka leaves for the United States, I would sell the house and move somewhere else. I would have no regrets as the house is full of mold and mildew. No doubt Anschel would do a lot better in a drier climate and a healthier environment.

The fact that the consul did not write to us proves that he has no intention of sending her a number since no money has been assigned on her behalf. So far no one from here has left for the United States unless money has been assigned. If you do not have any money, perhaps you can borrow it. If you can accomplish that and send us the documents, we will forward them to the American consul.

The man you are dealing with (Mr. Linder) *will not do any good unless money is assigned. In the last few weeks quite a few people from town left for the United States. Szafran's son, Mendel, Baruch Kuperman's, daughter, her husband and children and Shalom Proske. Their relatives in the United States made the proper money arrangements. The ones who did not do it did not get called. I do not know why you engaged an advocate* (Mr. Linder). *He is not doing anything for you. You would have been better off if you were to work with H.I.A.S. like the Kuperman's did. Another person who received acknowledgement and approval that they will be the first on the list for the next quota is Yosef Krulewitz who was a friend of Abraham Itzhok. Of course, they made the required financial arrangement. The ones who made the financial arrangements in 1938 got their visas in 1939.*

I must be made of iron to survive all the tsuris (troubles and suffering). *Yet, this is not all. The problems our brother Moshe creates are indescribable. The grief he causes is unbelievable. He is well physically but, he does not listen. He does what he wants, no matter how detestable it is to correct it... I have been suffering with him for nine years. One would say, it is enough. I get upset with him which causes my blood pressure to go up. What can I do but suffer. I was considering to send him away somewhere. But, who would give up their health for Moshe? I remember the words you said about him....I do not feel comfortable writing about him but, you asked about him. I apologize if I disturb you. My heart ached. I felt like letting off some steam.*

The children are fine. Elka would have written a note but, she has a toothache. She will write to you next time.

Your brother-in-law sends his heartfelt regards. My children send their regards.

Your sister,

Ruchel Leah

Best regards to my dear parents. Why do you not have the children write to me?

Your son-in-law, Anschel sends his regards and wishes you good health. My children and Moshe send their regards. Best regards to my sister, Sylvia and her husband. Best regards to Nettie, Norma, and Dorothy. You all be well and please write.

Your daughter,

Ruchel Leah

On September 29, 1938, Great Britain and France agreed to cede to Germany the Sudetenland region of Czechoslovakia, with a majority ethnic German population, as an appeasement and deterrent to war. This was known as the Munich Agreement. However, the dark clouds of war began to drift across the European continent. After Germany, in violation of the Munich Agreement, occupied Bohemia and Moravia on March 15, 1939, Great Britain issued an assurance to Poland that in the event of any action by Germany which would clearly threaten Polish independence, to which the Polish government would have to resist by force, Great Britain would support Poland by all available means. In solidarity with Great Britain, the French government issued a similar statement.

Hitler signed a directive issued to the German armed forces on April 11, 1939 which stated, *"Quarrels with Poland should be avoided. Should Poland however adopt a threatening attitude towards Germany, 'a final settlement' will be necessary, notwithstanding the pact with Poland.*

The aim is then to destroy Polish military strength, and to create in the East a situation which satisfies the requirements of defense. The Free State of Danzig will be incorporated into Germany at the outbreak of the conflict at the latest. Policy aims at limiting the war to Poland, and this is considered possible in view of the internal crisis in France, and British restraint as a result of this."

In a speech to the Reichstag (German Parliament) on April 28, 1939 (one day after Ruchel Leah's letter), Hitler announced that Germany would no longer honor the German-Polish Non-Aggression Pact and the Anglo-German Naval Agreement signed in 1934, after the Polish government allegedly rejected an offer made regarding the annexation of the Free State of Danzig and the Polish Corridor. Hitler did offer to negotiate new non-aggression pacts with any other nation that requested them. This speech prompted the Polish government to negotiate a further alliance with Great Britain.

"I have regretted greatly this incomprehensible attitude of the Polish Government, but that alone is not the decisive fact. The worst is that now Poland like Czechoslovakia a year ago believes, under the pressure of a lying international campaign, that it must call up its troops, although Germany on her part has not called up a single man, and had not thought of proceeding in any way against Poland.... The intention to attack on the part of Germany which was merely invented by the international press..." Hitler

Peace was not to prevail.

The house facing Long Street belonged to the family. On the small lot, another home stood behind the main house. Near the back property fence there was a woodshed and a shared outhouse along with a garbage dumpster which was painted white with a tar coated inside. The house in back was owned by Hilda's half-sister, Elka Solka Liebowitz. When she moved, she rented it to a seamstress.

The main house consisted of two rooms – a front and back room separated by a small vestibule leading to a side entrance. Ruchel Leah and Anschel continued to occupy the back room while Elka, Surcha, and Moshe slept in the large front room which was multifunctional – shoemaker's workshop, living, cooking area as well as the bedroom. The structure of the house was consistent with that of most homes belonging to tradesmen in the village.

Blum/Taus Home Rebuilt around 1947

Light came from windows in both the front and rear of the house with further illumination provided by the naphtha (flammable liquid hydrocarbon mixture) fueled lamps. The house had no indoor plumbing, running water or electricity. A wood burning stove was used for cooking as well as heat. Water was drawn from a neighbor's well who lived two houses away, however, it was not potable, so drinking water was drawn from the Hirsh River, a tributary of the Narew River which was about three blocks away.

The house was constructed with unfinished wooden planks as walls and a wood floor. The planks were filled in with clay to make the home air and water tight. Yet, the clay seemed to foster the growth of mold and mildew. The walls were whitewashed for hygienic and sanitary purposes. Apparently the lime in the whitewash was ineffective in controlling the mold and mildew.

The allergens created by the mold, mildew, and soot from the wood burning stove had an adverse effect on Anschel's asthma.

To prepare for the Sabbath, the workbench, covered with a white sheet as a tablecloth, was moved to the center of the room. The entire house was cleaned – floors scrubbed until the raw wood planks were shining. The brass Shabbos candlesticks, which were polished to a high luster, were placed in the center of the table. Everyone dressed in their finest apparel even if some of the garments had patches. A feeling of peace and tranquility permeated the air on the Sabbath – a supernatural feeling, even in the midst of despair.

Seeing others obtain appointments with the American consul, receive their visas, and not receive confirmation from the family that the proper financial documents had been prepared added to Ruchel Leah's increasing anxiety and frustration. With war being imminent, she felt completely helpless. She was still hopeful that at least her children would have a better life; not one torn apart by poverty and war.

HIAS (Hebrew Immigrant Aid Society) and the European branch, HICEM were an international immigrant and refugee service founded in New York City in 1881 designed to help Jews who were immigrating from Imperial Russia. The organization provided meals, transportation, and employment counseling to the new arrivals. In subsequent years, HIAS merged with different shelters and Jewish housing associations while continuing to aid and assist Jewish immigrants. With the large influx of immigrants during the 1920s and 1930s from Eastern Europe, the organization grew to be national in scope. HIAS was instrumental in assisting many new immigrants make arrangements for the legal entry of other family members to the United States. The society provided basic subsistence, employment, citizenship instruction and location of relatives for nearly half a million immigrants.

In the pre-war years and during the war, the major efforts of HIAS were concentrated on financing and assisting emigration from Nazi Germany, Eastern and Central Europe to countries in both Western Europe and South America while imploring Western governments to adjust their immigration policies to increase their quotas for Jewish war refugees.

In 1940, with the focus on national security, the United States Intelligence Service insinuated that HICEM was an espionage agency created to ease 5th columnists entry into the United States.

After nine stressful years of caring for Moshe, which placed an additional physical and mental burden upon both her and the entire household, Ruchel Leah expressed stress and resentment that his care had fallen upon her. It was not a responsibility she wanted, just something she inherited when the rest of the family left for the United States. She was forced to accept it as her inevitable fate. She wished it could be otherwise, a different arrangement for Moshe's care but, in spite of all the difficulties he manifested, she continued to shoulder the burden for his well-being. While she expressed her emotional concerns, she apologized for her apparent frustration and anger. Ruchel Leah recognized Moshe as part of her destiny.

A rich tradition of folk remedies existed in rural Poland for common ailments. With no doctor or dentist in the shtetl, the villagers relied on babske refues (old wives' medicine) for the cure. Not all "cures" had any logic such as inserting a clove of garlic in your ear to cure a toothache. Toothaches were a serious ailment as they could lead to infection, gum disease, loss of teeth, and ultimately, even death from the infection.

A babske refues remedy of nettle root (which was readily available as it grew wild) tea which was believed to relieve toothaches and infections along with gargling with warm salt water would have been the suggested cure for Elka's toothache. The tea was made by boiling a cup of powdered nettle root in a pint of fresh milk or water. If Elka's toothache was not cured, then, prior to the condition worsening, she would have to see a dentist in Bialystok.

For any dental needs that required a dental appointment, the family traveled to Bialystok to see a female dentist, Dr. Pines. It is conceivable that she practiced at the Jaroszowka (a district of Bialystok) dental clinic, part of the Towarzystwo Ochrony Zdrowia Ludności Żydowskiej w Polsce (Society for Safeguarding the Health of the Jewish Population in Poland; TOZ) which had been founded in Warsaw in 1921 under the direction of Dr. Sura Sofia Syrkin-Binsztejnowa. The objective of TOZ, which was funded primarily by donations and foreign philanthropies, was to insure the health and welfare of the Jewish citizens of Poland.

To that end, TOZ promoted hygiene and provided adequate nutrition for infants and children. Vaccination against infectious diseases such as smallpox was administered at Jewish schools; food was distributed to 36,000 children in 69 towns. Hospitals, health and dental clinics were established for indigent Jews.

By 1939, TOZ operated 368 health and dental clinics and hospitals in 72 towns employing 1,000 doctors, nurses, and staff. When Germany invaded Poland, TOZ continued to operate with financial support from the American Jewish Joint Distribution Committee (AJDC). With the German creation of overcrowded ghettos, TOZ operatives attempted to supervise the sanitary conditions of the population. The German authorities did not prevent or interfere with their activities allowing TOZ to continue operating in some locations until 1942.

Hudson County Jewish Regular Republican Org. Inc.
Hoboken, New Jersey   May 5, 1939

My dear friend Mates,
  I am very, very sorry that I did not get to see you on Sunday. The reason is that I am very busy with the upcoming election. It keeps me very occupied.
  I am happy to inform you that I received a correspondence from Washington, which I am enclosing in this letter. It seems that the girl will be in America in a short while.
  With kindest regards to you and your family,
  Your friend,
A Linder

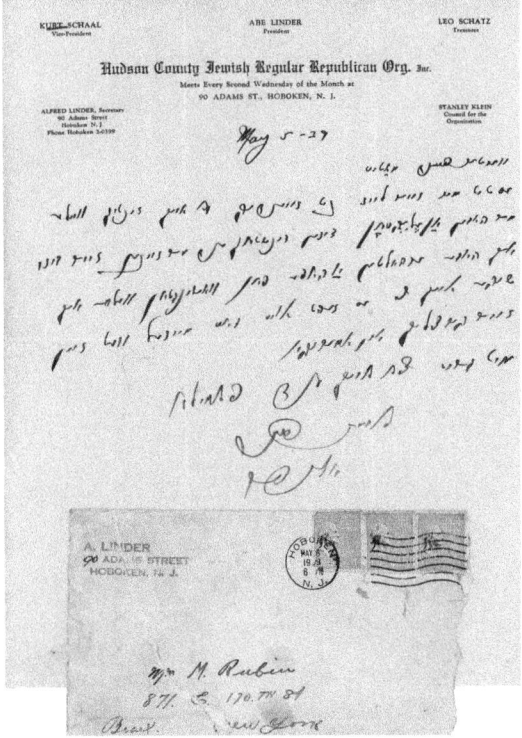

Letter from Abe Linder to Mates May 5, 1939

Communicating in Yiddish, Mates continued to be the family's liaison with Abe Linder regarding Elka's potential visa.

Washington, D.C.   *May 4, 1939*

Mr. Abe Linder
#90 Adams Street
Hoboken, New Jersey

Dear Abe:
    I have yours of April 28th 1939 requesting of me a letter sent to me by the Hon. Marcel E. Malige American Consul at Warsaw Poland.

Upon receipt of your last letter I immediately Cabled the American Consul at Warsaw Poland and requested of him to issue a VISA immediately to your friend Elka Taus and I am quite sure she will receive her VISA during the month of July as then the Polish Quota will be open and as soon as I receive word will notify you immediately.

With regards I remain yours as ever

Fred

P.S. Enclosed find a copy of letter sent to me by American Consul.

Fred Allan Hartley, Jr. (1902-1969) was a Republican New Jersey Representative to the House of Representatives having served ten terms beginning with the election of 1928. He represented, at various times, both New Jersey's 8th and 10th Congressional districts. Congressman Hartley's career was highlighted by being the co-sponsor of the Taft-Hartley Act in 1947 which was designed to curb labor unrest in the post war years.

Abe Linder, because of his connection with New Jersey Republican Congressional leaders, contacted Congressman Hartley to advocate on Elka's behalf.

The reference to the July date for Elka to receive her visa is based on the letter written on January 19, 1939 by Marcel Malige, American Consul – Warsaw. However, the July date was not feasible as the United States government had shut down the interview process during the months between the date the original letter had been written and Congressman Hartley's communication.

Warsaw Poland   *January 19/1939*

The Honorable
Fred A. Hartley
House of Representatives,
My dear Mr. Hartley:

I have the Honor to Acknowledge the receipt of your letter of Dec. 22nd 1938, regarding the Immigration VISA case of Elka Taus and, in reply, to inform you that Her name has been placed up on the list of persons who will receive appointments to appear at this office to execute formal visa applications and to undergo examinations when the status of the Polish quota permits. It is anticipated that an appointment for this purpose will be made in about 6 months.

The alien will be given ample advance notice of the date set for examination and will also be advised of the data required to make the evidence of support reasonably current. Such data as may be required should be presented by the alien at the time of examination and should not be sent direct to the Consulate General.

Sincerely yours,
Marcel E. Malige
American Consul

In 1938, Marcel E. Malige (1900-1991) from Lapwai, Idaho, became the 2nd Secretary in the Warsaw Embassy. In August 1939 he was re-assigned to become the American Consul and 2nd Secretary in Rio de Janeiro, Brazil.

Having been appointed Consul General in Warsaw in December 1938, John K. Davis was the senior diplomat when Germany began

96

bombing Warsaw in September 1939. After the embassy and staff were evacuated, Davis wrote a report, *Conduct of the Warsaw Consulate General During the Siege of that City*, while in temporary residence in Oslo, Norway. The dispatch offered a detailed description of the events regarding the siege of Warsaw, the embassy's role, and the ultimate evacuation. He noted "for all practical purposes we found ourselves living in the midst of a battlefield."

President Franklin D. Roosevelt was aware of the dangers under which the Consul General and his staff had operated. Prior to the State Department's receipt of the dispatch, President Roosevelt sent the following:

> *"The courage and devotion to duty of yourself and of the Foreign Service Officers and clerks of your staff are deserving of the highest praise and special commendation. I am happy to learn that you are now out of the danger zone and I wish to convey to each and all of you my sincerest thanks and appreciation."*

There are no existing embassy records which contain any correspondence from Ruchel Leah or the family in New York or any applications/documents pertaining to Elka's visa as apparently the records were all destroyed or lost in September 1939. Davis advises in his dispatch *"Consul Cramp, Vice Consul Birkeland, Mrs. Talmont and another clerk went to the Consulate General (office which had been vacated) to get some necessary records and had just left the visa section for the front of the office, when a shell entered the visa room in which they had been and exploded. A difference of perhaps two minutes was all that saved their lives."*

Marcel Malige's letter indicated that Elka's not receiving a visa was not an issue of correct documentation or financial affidavits but

Bombed United States Embassy in Warsaw

rather one of timing in relationship to the Polish yearly quotas. Mr. Malige only mentions the necessity of **current** financial documentation when she appears for her appointment with the embassy in about six months, meaning July 1939.

Goworowo   *10 May 1939*

Dear Parents, Sisters and Brother and dear Brother-in-law,

I did not receive any mail from you in spite of the fact that I wrote you a few letters. It seems to me that you are not very interested in us even though the terrible storm is awaiting us here. Every American knows of it. I am sure you are aware of it also. I know that we are not the only ones yet our heart aches to know that we have such bad luck to be caught up in this coming war. I always had hoped that somehow, sometime I would get to be with you but what is the use of idle talk when it seems to me, my dear parents, that you are not interested in us. Had you tried harder, we would have been in the United States by now.

I know that Anschel is a sick man, but we would have taken him to the forest for a while to recuperate before taking him before the consul. He could have passed the exam. Had Anschel felt that he would be rescued from the present situation, no doubt his health would have improved.

I know my unfortunate predicament. You left Moshe for me to take care of him; to cater to his needs and if you bring us over to the United States, who will take care of him? I may die before him. Where will he stay? Because of him, I have wasted my life. It is very difficult for me to handle the situation.

Observing the fact that Baruch Kuperman succeeded in bringing the entire family over to the United States during the same time that you started the process with Elka. They are starting with their other daughter. And you doubt if my daughter is human. You can hardly find another child like Elka. It seems that she has no luck. Perhaps you will have a chance to meet Esther's (Szafran) son, Mendel who may advise you how to go

*about to deal with the immigration (or how they succeeded).
You depend too much on Mr. Linder who mislead you all along.
Thanks to him that my child....*

*From the very beginning I have been telling you that unless
you assign some money on her behalf, she will not get a visa.
Your consultant advises you the opposite. Check with Avromel
Schmeltz* (Avrom Meyer Schmeltz, a tailor) *who tried to bring
over his bride. He did not succeed until he assigned some money
on her behalf. The same is repeated many times with other people
from town that as soon as they arranged the financial papers
they got called for a visa. In 1938 the time was right for all of
us to immigrate to the United States. We missed the opportunity.
All the trials and tribulations and suffering was for nothing. I
rationalized and figured that you are not rich therefore you are
trying only for Elka, but you ignored my advice. I asked you
many times to inquire from those who succeeded in bringing their
relatives to the United States how they did it. You claimed that
for Elka you do not have to assign some money. It is an exception
while I keep telling you that it is not so. Only those whose relatives
assigned money got their visas.*

*It is very hard to describe how bad the situation is here
now. We find ourselves in a deep cave surrounded by snakes.
All because we are Jews. It has been two weeks since Baruch's*
(Kuperman) *son-in-law left for the United States. Conditions
since then have changed for the worse. I tremble in fear in trying
to describe the situation.*

*After so many years in America one would expect that just
like other people you would have your children with you. You
would have tried harder to get us there and we could have looked*

forward to a better life. I am not saying that you live in luxury but, if you would have any conception what our life is, you would have found a way to get us out of here. I was surprised that Baruch's son-in-law is on his way to the United States. Kuperman is not a rich man but he managed to get, borrow, or whatever, money to satisfy the immigration authorities in order to rescue his family to the United States.

When you, my dear father, wanted to leave for the United States, you wrote to your friends asking for help. The situation here is now much worse. It is like comparing a person who is sick with one disease to a person who has multiple diseases. Such is the situation now.

I have written enough about the subject. I hope it does not disturb you too much; however, you should not be surprised since it hurts so much. The thought of war is on one's mind. What will become of us?

I would have settled if at least one child could be saved. Yet, it seems that did not materialize.

About Anschel's health. The situation is about the same. Sometimes better, sometimes worse. If the situation would have been peaceful, it would have been the best medicine to leave Goworowo, move to another town where the air is cleaner. Here the climate and the condition of the house – mold is very bad for his health. He hardly has any work due to the unsettled condition. We are always in need of money for special taxes and fees.

Now my dear parents, write to me. How is your health and how is my sister, Sylvia?

I seem to hear some news in Goworowo which disturbs me greatly and the news comes from people close to us…

*Please write about your life in the United States and how is your
health. I do not want to repeat the same thing that you write one
letter for every three I write you. Are you so busy that you cannot
find the time to write? And what have you done lately for Elka's
situation to make progress? You have to assign money on her behalf.*

*Josef Krulewitz received a number for his visa. For years he
tried to obtain it. He succeeded only after his relatives assigned some
money. I have not much more to write. I know one thing that if I
had wings I would have liked to fly to see you as my longing for you
tears me apart.*

*Your son-in-law sends his best regards to you and his sister-
in-law, Sylvia and her husband and wishes them a happy life.
Heartfelt regards to Nettie. She writes very little. I would like to
hear from her. And heartfelt regards for Norma. Did she get a job?
Regards to Dorothy. We wish her happiness. I would like to hear
from her. I would be glad to reply and to write to her. I would find
time to do it. Elka and Surcha send their sincere regards.*

*Please write whether you get to see some of the new arrivals
who came from Goworowo.*

Your daughter,

Ruchel Leah

There is no doubt that an appointment with the consul would
have psychologically improved Anschel's health. However, given his
medical issues, it is doubtful that his health would have been classified
as Class A which would have cleared him for immigration. In reality
he would have probably been classified as Class B meaning that he
had a chronic condition which conceivably could render him as a
public charge in the future.

News of the approaching storm was electrifying the entire country. There appeared to be no doubt in anyone's mind that war was imminent after Foreign Minister Jozef Beck's speech to the Sejm, the Polish lower House of Parliament, on May 5, 1939.

Beck (1894–1944) was largely responsible for setting Polish foreign policies during the 1930s. During this speech, Beck staunchly refused Hitler's demand to subordinate Poland by turning it into a German puppet state.

Hitler had demanded that Poland turn over to Germany the area of Pomerania and to join the Anti-Comintern Pact, which was directed against the Soviet Union. Had Poland agreed to the German annexation of Pomerania, Poland would have essentially relinquished any access to the Baltic Sea. This would cut off its main trade routes making the Polish economy totally dependent upon Germany.

The demands for an extraterritorial rail and highway corridor running from East Prussia to the Free City of Danzig in exchange for vague territorial promises of Soviet territory inhabited by Ukrainians and Belarusians in a hypothetical future war was also rejected.

"Peace is a precious and a desirable thing. Our generation, bloodied in wars, certainly deserves peace. But peace, like almost all things of this world, has its price, a high but a measurable one. We in Poland do not know the concept of peace at any price. There is only one thing in the lives of men, nations and countries that is without price. That thing is honor." Josef Beck May 5, 1939

Conditions throughout Poland were getting worse, economically and politically. The hate filled German propaganda machine began sending agents into Poland to create strife and agitate the Polish people against the Jewish population. Anti-Semitism was becoming more rampant as war with Germany was impending. Fear became a constant factor of everyday life.

The letters are permeated with emotion – frightened that her family had been forsaken by those in the United States. It is almost as if Ruchel Leah had a premonition of what would transpire during the inevitable war with Germany. While she resented being left to care for Moshe and thus having, in her words, "I have wasted my life", she still expressed concern for his well-being should the family succeed with their immigration to America knowing he would not be medically approved for a visa.

"We had not abandoned them, we had no choice." (Abraham) Life in New York was not in reality the "goldene medina" of European folk tales. The family struggled to live, adapt to their new world, continue living their own lives and, yet still had the plight of Ruchel Leah and the family in the forefront of their thoughts.

Faced with continuous trials and tribulations, Ruchel Leah was not ready to resign herself to accept her fate. Communication with the family in the United States appears to have been a "life line" of hope. It was inconceivable to her that no one seemed to find the time to return her correspondence in the same abundance as she was communicating. She remained confident that, if she pushed the family in New York hard enough, she would, at the very least, succeed in "visa salvation" for one of her daughters, Elka, and the family left in Poland would not have been forsaken.

Psalm 22

> *Eli, Eli, lema sabachthani – My, God, my God, why have you forsaken me? Why are you so far from helping me, from the words of my groaning? O my God, I cry by day, but you do not*

answer; and by night, but find no rest … My mouth is dried up like a potsherd, and my tongue sticks to my jaws; you lay me in the dust of death. For dogs are all around me; a company of evildoers encircles me. My hands and feet have shriveled; I can count all my bones. They stare and gloat over me… Deliver my soul from the sword, my life from the power of the dog! Save me from the mouth of the lion!

Her situation, in retrospect, recalls Esther of the Purim story fighting for the survival of her people. On the holiday of Purim (Feast of Esther), Psalm 22 is traditionally recited. The psalm is a plea to God to be saved. In the story of Purim, which took place around the year 357 BCE, Esther, a Jewish Queen of Persia learned of a plot by the Prime Minister, Haman, to annihilate all the Jews in the Persian Empire. With the encouragement of her cousin, Mordecai, Esther approached her husband, King Ahasuerus (assumed to be the historical King Xerxes I), who was unaware of her religious background, to plea for the survival of the Jews in an attempt to save them from annihilation. Esther succeeded in her mission while Ruchel Leah continued to plea.

Goworowo   *1 June 1939*
Dear Parents, Sisters, Brother, and Brother-in-law,

It has been a long time since I have heard from you. I keep wondering why the delay. Hope everything is well with you. I still did not receive a reply to the letter I sent to you at Passover time (April 3 -11, 1939). When I do not hear from you, it seems to affect my health, so please write more often.

Now I want to let you know that I received a reply from the American consul on my request for information on the application which I sent to him a few weeks ago. His reply was that he sent to you the papers listing the requirements but did not receive any reply from you. I gather that is the reason Elka did not receive a number. What is the reason for not sending a reply? Did you change your mind about Elka coming to the United States? I am ashamed to continue writing to you about sending the proper papers to the consul. Without the required papers he will never send a number for a visa. It seems that you listen to your immigration consultant.

Nothing new around here. Anschel does not feel good. He has not been feeling well since Passover and now Shavuot just passed (May 23, 1939). Please write telling me the reason for changing your mind about Elka's immigrating to the United States.

Your daughter,

Ruchel Leah

No one ever changed their mind regarding Elka's immigration to the United States. This was Ruchel Leah's assumption based on the lack of results. In reality, the family was even more determined to obtain a visa for Elka and the remainder of the family because of the news reports coming from Europe but was stymied by red tape and immigration quotas. All possible efforts were being made while working within the system.

Goworowo   *7 June 1939*

Dear brother, Abraham Itzhok,

Your dear letter was received with happiness and content- ment. It eased my anxiety. It has been a long time since I have heard from the family. Many thanks for the $20. you sent us. I can hardly believe what you wrote that Elka will soon *receive a number for her visa. Perhaps the American consul had a change of heart or perhaps he deals differently with an American citizen than with a Polish citizen. I feel disappointed that you wrote that I keep writing that others, in the same position as Elka have received their visa and that you should look into how they did it. How can you judge a mother who is willing to part with her daughter, perhaps never to see her again? But since the fear of war is imminent and we are not sure of our future, we are hoping to save at least one child. I know, for sure, that I will suffer that Elka will not be with us. But, I do not think of us. I think only of her welfare. I am sure she will get the right upbringing and education. Here she has limited opportunities. Daily, she practices the violin and reads Polish literature. For a while she was studying English but quit as the cost was quite high. But I intend to start her English studies again, real soon. Her English teacher is Leyke Rothstein. You may remember.*

Elka occasionally tutors others in music thereby earning a little. I hope when she gets to America she will continue with her music education. I can depend on you that you will arrange everything and take care of her general education.

She is kept busy. She, like others in her age group, belongs to youth groups. She belongs to Betar. I, personally, can do without it but, you have to follow what others do.

There is not any new news to write about. Anschel has to get out of town for his health. When he leaves, I will let you know. What is the reason that I seldom hear from the family? Nobody seems to write much. I am very anxious to hear from each one about their health and general well-being. How is my sister,

107

Sylvia? Are you still working in the same place? Are you still dating the young lady that is on the picture you sent us?

Best regards to you and your loved ones. Your brother-in-law sends his heartfelt regards and he hopes to someday see you. Elkale and Surchale send their regards. Stay well. I apologize for writing so much.

Your sister,

Ruchel Leah Taus

After multiple diplomatic meetings held during May 1939, it would appear that Poland was preparing for a predestined war with Germany. Great Britain had previously announced, at the end of March 1939, that it would defend Poland from any German attack. In April, Josef Beck was in London negotiating the terms of the British-Polish aid treaty. A mutual help agreement between France and Poland was signed in Paris by the Polish ambassador, Juliusz Lukasiewicz and the French Minister of Foreign Affairs, Georges Bonnet on May 12th. By May 16th, General Waclaw Stachiewicz, Chief of the General Staff of the Polish Army, ordered the creation of a plan to fortify the Polish-German border. Polish-French and Polish-British military negotiations were concluded by the end of May.

The entire country was bracing itself for the inevitable storm of war.

Betar, an acronym for Berit Yosef Trumpeldor (Joseph Trumpeldor Alliance), was a youth movement founded in 1923 in Riga, Latvia. Conceived as a small scale local organization, Betar's platform was vague. After several years, Betar became the official youth movement of the Union of Zionist Revisionists founded by Ze'ev Jabotinsky.

The Zionist Revisionists' ideology was to revise the policies of the official Zionist movement: to create a country with a Jewish majority in the ancient Land of Israel (Palestine) on both sides of the Jordan River; to encourage a massive Jewish settlement in Palestine; promote private enterprise, and to establish a Jewish army.

Though Betar was considered the youth movement of the Zionist Revisionist party, it had full autonomy and operated independently from its parent organization. By 1931, the principles and goals of Betar were firmly outlined – members were devoted to a purified Zionism, the creation of the Jewish state, compulsory army training, immigration to Palestine, commitment to learning Hebrew, and obedience to the institutions of the Betar movement. The movement's branch founded in Goworowo by Matisyahu Mishnayes and Aviezer Shikara had a strong appeal to the youth of the village.

During the 1930s, Betar, with the Aliya Bet project was active in smuggling illegal immigrants from Eastern Europe, primarily Poland and Austria, into Palestine. To a large degree, the Polish government was aware of this operation and, to a certain extent actually co-operated.

By the end of 1938, Betar boasted 90,000 members in 26 countries with the majority of them being from Poland.

Abraham had been dating Rebecca Offenberg since they met in an economics class at Harlem Evening High School in 1936. Marriage was planned, but would not take place until Abraham felt that he had the financial security to properly provide for a wife and family. The tendency for most young couples, at the time, was to live with one set of parents or the other. Abraham was determined that prior to the wedding they would have their own apartment with new living room and bedroom furniture.

Abraham and Rebecca April 1940

Goworowo   *13 June 1939*

Dear Uncle Abraham Itzhok,

I am glad to inform you that I am well. I hope that you are the same. We received your dear letter with the $20. For which we thank you very much.

Now dear Uncle Abraham Itzhok I beg you to send the American Consul the affidavit of support which means that you are taking the financial responsibility of my support until I reach the age of maturity. I beg you to file the paper as soon as possible. Perhaps I will receive a number for my Visa within the six months like the consul has informed you. When the time comes for the American authorities to review my file and if they find some papers missing, they will put the case aside and put it into the next quota year. It may take years for my name to come up again. I beg you again to try to send the American consul the necessary papers as soon as possible. For anyone underage, the requirement for the money assignment is required.

My best regards to Bubbe and Zayde. Regards to Aunt Sylvia, best regards to you my Uncle Abraham Itzhok. Regards to Nettie, Norma, and Dorothy for all of you to be well.

Elka Taus

Once again, Elka reiterates the exact sentiments previously written in her mother's letters.

Goworowo   *4 July 1939*

Dear Parents, Sisters, Brother-in-law, and dear brother, Abraham Itzhok,

I am glad to inform you that we are all in good health, thanks God. Hope to hear good news from you. According to my calculations, it is over six months and we still did not hear from the American consul. My opinion is that the American writes to American citizens differently than to foreigners. To prospective immigrants he writes to the point what he demands. Please let me know immediately if you sent the paperwork. Who knows whether Elka will ever immigrate to the United States if you cannot prove support.

Please let me know how everyone is doing. How is my sister, Sylvia doing? How is every individual doing? How is the weather? Are you employed?

If you would have followed my opinion about Elka, she would have been in the United States a long time ago. The situation is dragging along. One is losing patience. A person does not know where he is at.

Now I am letting you know that Anschel left for Dlugosiodlo in the forest for a few weeks to recuperate. He went to a new doctor who prescribed new medications. He was very sick. I had no choice. I had to send him to the forest to recuperate. Life is hard. I believe if the consul were to see him, what he looks like, he would (not) *have given him the visa.*

All be well.

Ruchel Leah

Ruchel Leah's hopelessness is becoming more apparent. Yet, she still has dreams that she, Anschel, Elka, Surcha, and even Moshe will one day be in America with the rest of the family.

While the Puszcza Biala (White Forest) was 30 miles from Goworowo, the town closest to the forest complex was Dlugosiodlo which offered Anschel the pine scented, crisp air deemed to be beneficial for his health.

Puszcza Biala (White Forest)

With money Ruchel Leah borrowed, Anschel took the train from Goworowo to Przetycz a distance of 11 miles and then rode the remaining 3 miles to Dlugosiodlo by cart.

Przetycz Train Station Waiting Room

In Dlugosiodlo, he probably arranged to stay in one of the numerous rooming houses or small hotels. The air in Dlugosiodlo was fresh – filled with the aroma emanating from the pine trees.

With an improvement in his health, Anschel would be able to work regularly affording the family a better quality of life. Manipulating family finances would be one less burden off of Ruchel Leah's shoulders.

Most people outside major cities like Warsaw, Krakow, and Bialystok used a combination of modern and folk medicines in treating various illnesses. Along with the new medicine prescribed by the doctor in Warsaw, Anschel probably drank Psiwo Kozicowe (juniper berry beer) brewed in the region which had an abundance of juniper conifers. The "berries" are actually fleshy cones, not true berries, which are covered with a white powdery wild yeast. Psiwo Kozicowc was made by fermenting the berries with honey and hops.

In the ethno medicinal cabinet of the region, the low alcohol, fizzy beverage was reputed to have therapeutic properties in treating gastrointestinal problems and beneficial in reducing congestion as well as asthma.

Goworowo   *24 July 1939*

> *Dear Sister Sylvia and brother-in-law, Mates,*
>
> *We wish you a heartfelt Mazel Tov* (congratulations – good fortune) *on the birth of your son. We wish you health, a rich life filled with happiness together with your addition to the family. Let your life be renewed with the best of life.*
>
> *We are very happy for you. We would fly like a bird to get a look at your beautiful son. We cried for happiness while reading the good news.*
>
> *Dear brother-in-law, please, I beg of you, write how Sylvia is doing and how does the baby look. I know you are busy but please take time out and write. About two weeks ago I received your letter for which I thank you very much. Your correspondence is very dear and precious to me. We wish you should raise him without problems. When he gets a few months old. Please send me a snapshot of him. I am anxious to see what he looks like. I am putting the order ahead of time.*
>
> *Please write telling me about everyone. Everyone sends their heartfelt regards. Special love and regards to your dear son.*
>
> *Your sister and brother-in-law,*
>
> *Ruchel Leah*
>
> *Excuse me for writing such a short letter. First, it is late at night and secondly, I ran short of writing paper.*

On July 11, 1939, Sylvia gave birth to Nathan Kalman Rubin named after his maternal great grandfather, Nussin Kalman Solka (died 1916 Kozlov, Russia)

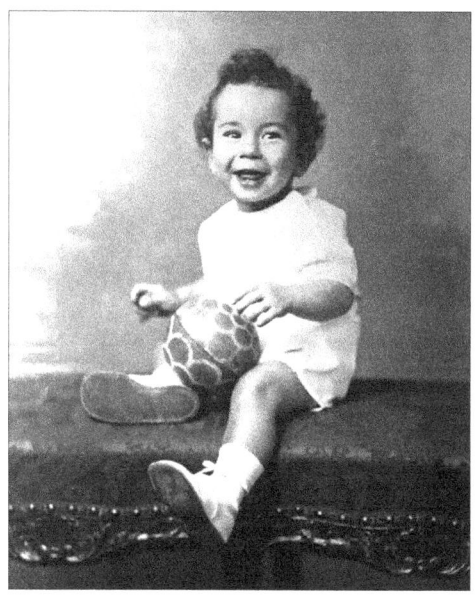

Nathan Kalman Rubin

Goworowo   *27 July 1939*

Mazel Tov

Dear Parents, Sisters and Brother and Brother-in-law,

We wish you a heartfelt Mazel Tov on the birth of the new born boy. We hope he will bring us happiness and contentment. I can hardly describe how happy we were when we heard the good news. I wish you dear parents nachas (pleasure and enjoyment) *from your children and grandchildren. I am so happy for my dear sister, Sylvia of the birth of a son and that she is well. I hope to God that the child will grow up healthy and the mother will be in good health to raise him.*

Anschel has returned from Przetycz where he spent four weeks. He looked good, rested. You can hardly recognize him. He was sunburned. In short, one would not believe that he is a sick man. The air in the forest did him a lot of good. However, after

THE SPIRIT OF RUCHEL LEAH

being in Goworowo for only three days, he got sick again. I hope he gets to feel better. In short, the climate here is not good for him.

Your idea about Anschel staying in Przetycz sounds good but it is impossible to accomplish at this time. Here I have a mother-in-law who works her head off. I can depend on her for some help. Here I am not a stranger in town. I get things on credit. I am always in debt; however, in a strange town you have to pay cash. Who will trust me? For instance, when Anschel left for the forest, I had to borrow money for his trip. I could not possibly do that in a strange town.

The house is worthless. It is rotten in spite of the fact that, a few years ago, I invested money in repairs. It would be easier to sell the house if I could get a clear title to it. However, if Elka immigrates to the United States, I would make every effort to sell it one way or the other. The only relief I receive is what you send me. It is not enough to live on in spite of the fact that I am not extravagant.

Anschel has two brothers (Fishel in Paris and Zisket in Brazil). *One would think that they would help now and then. The truth is that they do not even find time to write a few words to him. That is how they treat their brother who is in need of help. I find myself all mixed up and bewildered. I do not know what action to take. The options are limited.*

Dear parents, you write that you heard from Washington that Elka will receive the number this year. It seems to me that they said that before and nothing happened. I do not think anything will happen until you furnish them a financial statement. Had you written that you furnished them with the right document, I would have believed that Elka has a chance but, without it, there is no chance. It seems to me that you do not follow up what I have suggested to you. Anyway, try your best in helping Elka get her visa. Helping Elka will result in a recovery for Anschel. I can assure you that Elka will not shame you. She is a very fine young lady. Do not get the impression that I want to get rid of her. Believe me I will suffer plenty after she leaves here but, I think that it is the best for her.

We pray to God first for peace in the world; second for good health for all of us; third that we should be able to see each other. I shed lots of tears when I think that Baruch's (Kuperman) *daughter and her family left for America to be with her parents. She is through with European pain and suffering. Perhaps it is not time for us. We must have patience to suffer longer.*

Our heartfelt regards to my dear parents, my dear sister, Sylvia, her husband. It has been a long time since I heard from you. And heartfelt regards to my brother, Abraham Itzhok. Best regards to my sisters. My sister-in-law (Feige Taus Frydman) *sends regards. Your grandchildren send regards. Moshe sends his regards.*

Your daughter, sister,

Ruchel Leah

Please respond promptly.

While it was acknowledged by everyone in Goworowo that the house on Long Street belonged to Anschel and Ruchel Leah after the family's immigration to the United States in 1930, she did not possess a clear title to the property.

When Hilda's sister, Hannah and her husband, Meir Walberg immigrated to the United States in 1913, they sold the house and property to Shalom Joseph (Ruchel Leah's father). If the change of title was registered, it disappeared when Goworowo was burned during World War I. It was known throughout the village that Meir Walberg was the owner of the property. The sale was a family transaction so it was not necessarily common knowledge.

Shalom Joseph contacted Meir's heirs – Hymie, Mordechai, and Rose, his three children by his first marriage to Hannah's half-sister, Tslove, regarding a title transfer to Ruchel Leah to enable her to sell the house. Greed prevailed with their request for payment of $500. ($9,500. current value) to execute the title transfer.

According to the United States Department of Labor, a worker in the Shoe/Allied Industries in 1939 earned an average of $1,005.16 a year. The requested sum amounted to almost half of Shalom Joseph's yearly income. Financially it was impossible. The half-cousins refused to assist the family in Goworowo without payment. The title was never transferred to Ruchel Leah.

Shalom Joseph – New York Shoe Repair Shop

Goworowo   Date Unknown

Dear Bubbe, Zayde, Aunts, and Uncle Abraham and Mates,

Just to let you know that I am in good health. And now my Auntie Sylvia, how do you feel? How is your little one doing? I am sending you a Mazel Tov from far away. I am very disturbed that we are not together. I wish we could be together which would enable me to see your child in person. I am sending regards and kisses to each one of you and wish you good health.

Your grandchild,
Surcha Taus

Goworowo Date Unknown (Portion of the letter is missing)

…and she should study in school to become somebody yet, you are not willing to send her money in Poland (to attend school here).

You must write to the American consul continuously and question him by what right did he reject the application. He may wait another year and again reject her application. You now realize how the consul mistreats immigrants. However, if you bombard him with numerous letters, you may succeed in convincing him to issue Elka a visa. Proof of that is that Kuperman's daughter received her visa and she is already in the United States for six months. She started the proceedings about the same time as we did. It seems that they had a competent macher (influential person/big shot), *not like the one you hired. In his letter the consul writes that he will not issue any numbers for the rest of the year. Not to write him for the balance of the year, to wait for next year's quota. Meanwhile you should try to prepare the financial papers so when the new quota is declared, he may consider the application.*

I am not blaming you but your "macher" who misleads you all along. Do not neglect this matter. That is all. Not much more to write.

You all stay well. Anschel, I, and the children send their heartfelt regards and kisses. Separate regards for my dear sister and brother-in-law and their dear child. We send them lots of kisses.

And now, what should I do with Elka? Should I have her learn a trade?

I am enclosing with this letter the papers I received from the American consul. I predicted such a reply from him. I foretold that he would wait six months, look over the papers and reject them. That is exactly what happened. I begged you to file with the consul opiekuństwo (guardianship papers – referring to the financial support) *but, you failed to do so. I wrote you numerous times about it but you never answered me on this subject. You seem to trust your consultant too much. I assure you that he is an opportunist. He is only interested in your money. That Mr. Linder does not have the faintest idea about the subject.*

United States Entry Visa # 1219918 / 1225580 was issued to Malka Kuperman, age 25, on October 25, 1938. She departed from Gdynia, Poland aboard the M.S. *Batory* arriving in New York on January 15, 1939 to join her father, Baruch and siblings. At the time of Ruchel Leah's letter, Malka had been in the United States for about 6 months.

Goworowo   *July and August, 1939*

Original letter is in a deteriorated condition. The following is a translation of what can be deciphered:

I must write truthfully that Elka's inability to travel is your fault. I had the opportunities for her travel but, only if you had sent me the proper papers. It is not hundreds (of papers) *after all. Her travel would have already been taken care of. I knew in advance that in … six months from now, nothing will be….*

The package has not arrived yet…Now I have a week time…not…only must…I am letting you know…nothing to write about…since everything would have been better…like…what the few weeks without Anschel was like, you cannot image.

At this point, I should have a job and earn money, then it would be better, but now it is bitter for me. I need to wait for him.

Anschel greets you with love and wishes you happiness with your new born grandchild. Elka greets you all and Surcha greets you also.

I greet my…best health, Your son, Moshe…Your daughter Ruchel

We greet, with love our dear brother, Abraham. A greeting with love for Nettie, she should not forget to write a few letters since Sylvia has…no time. A greeting with love for Norma and Dorothy.

Dear Mother, you should be happy and content that you lived to see another grandchild. I wish you, dear parents that you should live to see more grandchildren from your youngest daughter, Dorothy and from all children with good…money. Marry off your children with good…mother-in-law wishes a mazel tov, you should…should marry her off…Nettie with great happiness. And you…should live to…Sura Necha (Solka Sierota – Ruchel Leah's 1ˢᵗ cousin) *told me to write a mazel tov.*

121

Be well, dear parents, my letter shall find you healthy and happy.

Your daughter and son-in-law and grandchildren
Ruchel Leah

Goworowo   *15 August 1939*
Dear Parents, Sisters, Brother-in-law and brother Abraham Itzhok,

Be content and happy with your new additional grandchild, let him be well. Today we received $20. which you mailed to us. It took a lot longer getting here than when you sent money through the Danzig Bank. The parcel you sent has not arrived yet. It has already been three weeks since I mailed the papers. I will let you know as soon as I get a reply.

You promised you would write as soon as Sylvia returns home from the hospital but as of yet, I have not heard from you. I am anxious to know how my sister is doing. Please write. Also how is the child doing and what name was given to the child?

(Page 2 is missing)

…my Elka would have been in the United States a long time ago if not for your macher. He does not seem to understand what the counsel's requests are. Even the paper I sent you last year states that you have to file an affidavit of support for Elka for a certain length of time. This is the meaning of assignment of money. Yet I know that you do not have that kind of money. Therefore, we have agreed not to give him any money in advance, but will pay him his fee when everything will be accomplished. The person is not from Goworowo but a local man is acquainted with him. It is quite possible he would have succeeded with his task but, you did not do

what I asked for or did not want to send.... Now, because of the rejection, I can hardly do anything. Now it is your turn. Try to send the required papers about the support telling the consul that you have been trying for the last two years to comply with their request.

Located in the Free City of Danzig which had been established by the Treaty of Versailles of 1919, the Bank von Danzig opened in 1924. The bank had the status of a joint stock company and the right to issue banknotes which were the Danzig gulden. In September 1939 when the Free City of Danzig was incorporated into the German Third Reich, the Bank von Danzig was transformed into a branch of the German Reichsbank.

Ruchel Leah is referencing an intermediary she contacted to help obtain a visa for Elka. It is unknown who this man was or how she contacted him other than an unnamed local man was acquainted with him. This man was the second person with whom Ruchel Leah communicated to facilitate Elka's immigration. Was the person real or was she exerting additional pressure on the family to execute what she assumed would accomplish the issuance of a visa?

Goworowo   *24 August 1939*
Dear Parents, Sisters, Brother and Brother-in-law,

The scare of war is in the air. I am writing these few words with tears in my eyes. Even on Yom Kippur (Day of Atonement – Jewish Holiest Day) *I did not shed as many tears as I did today. There is great turmoil. I do not have much more to write. Right now Anschel is at home but one cannot tell. They may induct him into the military. They continue to draft everyone.*

Yesterday I received the parcel you sent us. God knows if we will have a chance to use any of it.

You promised to write when Sylvia returns home but I have not received any word of it.

Heartfelt regards to all and with God's help I hope to be able to write you good news. Be all well. Your unfortunate children are in great danger.

Be well.

Your daughter

Ruchel Leah and your grandchildren and son

The tears in my eyes makes it impossible for me to write.

For months, the entire country was experiencing a "calm before the storm". The air was still but there was a unique sense of foreboding. Hope traversed the general public that the storm would by-pass Poland. Yet, as the days, weeks passed, everyone began to prepare for the inevitable – war.

Most young men were required to register for military service. The Army Department in Warsaw set up additional draft commissions where all men up to age 50 had to report to submit their military status. If deemed fit for induction they would receive notification from the Army Department. Anschel fell within the criteria to be considered for military service.

Poland's allies, Great Britain and France, confirmed their commitment to Poland with British Prime Minister, Neville Chamberlain's speech to the House of Commons on July 10th and France having delivered fifty Renault R-35 tanks to enhance the Polish arsenal on July 22nd. One month later, Poland declared a state of alertness in its military offices and ordered emergency mobilization of the border forces. Fortified positions were created at Mokra, Wegierska, Gorka, and Mlawa (Mlawa Line).

After Poland's categorical refusal to acquiesce to Germany's demand for Polish territory, the Nazi regime believed that the best method to acquire Poland was via a pact with the Union of Soviet Socialist Republics (USSR). The German-Soviet Nonaggression Pact (Molotov-Ribbentrop Pact) was signed on August 19, 1939 by the Soviet Foreign Minister, V.M. Molotov, and the German Foreign Minister, Joachim von Ribbentrop, with subsequent clarifications being signed on August 23rd by Molotov and Friedrich Werner von der Schulenburg, the German ambassador to the USSR.

Part 1 of the pact was an economic agreement which stipulated that Germany would exchange manufactured products for Soviet raw materials. A ten year nonaggression pact was outlined in Part 2 where each country promised not to attack the other.

Within the nonaggression pact was a series of secret appendices. Borders for the spheres of influence were delineated to run

Molotov-Ribbentrop Pact

approximately along the Pisa, Narew, Vistula and San Rivers. Under this agreement, the USSR would gain control over Latvia, Estonia, and Finland while Germany would have control of Lithuania and the Free City of Danzig. Poland would be divided into three areas. The Wartheland area which borders Germany would be annexed to become part of the German Reich. All non-German inhabitants (Poles and Jews alike) were to be expelled to the east. Eastern Polish land amounting to over 77,000 square miles would become Soviet territory. The central area of Poland would emerge as a German protectorate named Generalgouvernement under a German civil authority.

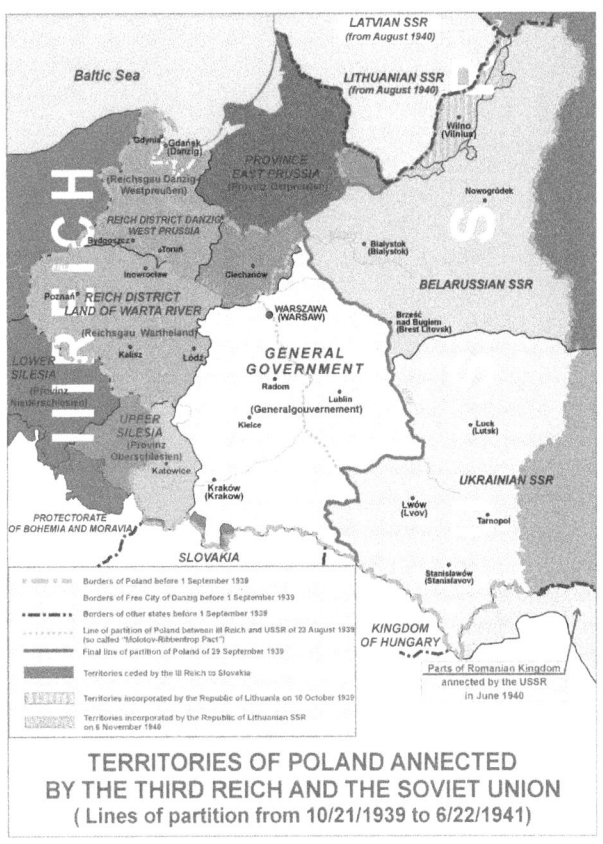

Annexed Territories October 21,
1939 to June 22, 1941

"Article II. In the event of a territorial and political rearrangement of the areas belonging to the Polish state, the spheres of influence of Germany and the U.S.S.R. shall be bounded approximately by the line of the rivers Narev, Vistula and San.

The question of whether the interests of both parties make desirable the maintenance of an independent Polish States and how such a state should be bounded can only be definitely determined in the course of further political developments.

In any event both Governments will resolve this question by means of a friendly agreement."

The provisions contained in the Molotov-Ribbentrop Pact were responsible for the acceleration of the outbreak of World War II.

Even with this agreement between two powerful European nations, most democratic countries and the Jews in Poland were in denial that war was imminent. The general belief was that if Hitler dared to attack Poland, he would be defeated immediately. It was believed that Marshall Rydz-Smigly, Commander-in-Chief of the Polish armed forces, had prepared adequately the Polish military and would either defeat Germany or be able to defend the line long enough for Great Britain and France to fulfill their treaty agreements by entering the war on Poland's behalf.

The darkening storm clouds prevailed. Ignacy Mościcki (1867-1946), President of the Second Polish Republic, ordered general mobilization on August 30, 1939. The entire population was ready and willing to defend their country against an invasion by the German Reich. On September 1, 1939, German troops invaded Poland one week after signing the Molotov-Ribbentrop Pact and the day after the pact was approved by the Supreme Soviet of the Soviet Union. World War II had begun.

The German invasion of Poland was a classic example of the "blitzkrieg" (fast and intense military attack) strategy in which five waves of extensive bombing throughout the day destroyed the

New York Times September 1, 1939

civil and military airport in Okecie, a suburb of Warsaw, railroads, communication lines and munitions dumps.

The Luftwaffe attacked civilian targets and refugees along the roads, terrorizing the people and destroying Polish morale. It is estimated that the Luftwaffe bombings killed between 6,000 and 7,000 people during those few hours.

The aerial bombardment campaign continued for the next few days targeting cities with considerably large Jewish populations. The incendiary bombs landed in Bialystok, Wielun, Lublin, Chelm, Tarnow, Szczuczyn, Gdynia, Lodz, Krakow and others causing death, destruction, and disorientation of the entire populace. In conjunction with the air attacks, the Wehrmacht (unified armed forces of Nazi Germany) launched a massive land invasion with an overwhelming number of troops, tanks and artillery.

The German troops marched across Poland towards Warsaw with precision and efficiency. They entered and destroyed villages leaving in their wake Death and Destruction. Hundreds of thousands of both Jewish and non-Jewish refugees fled in advance of the army into eastern Poland with the hope that the Polish army would halt the German advance. The people packed what few belongings they could and ran, without a specific destination in mind, to a "safe"

The Forward *"Nazi Armies Deep in Poland" September 1. 1939*

place deeper in the country. *"The people ran. This running away was instinctive and without any definite plan or destination....Many families were separated during the panic....The tidal wave of ruined life rushed like a raging torrent that overflows its banks in the springtime."* The *Destruction of Polish Jewry* American Federation for Polish Jews 1940

With a force of over 1 million men, the Polish army was severely under equipped with antiquated equipment. The command made some erroneous strategic military decisions. The Polish army was no match for the modern, formidable Wehrmacht. On September 3, 1939, France and Britain declared war on Germany but failed to provide any meaningful support.

Within days, the German invasion escalated to one of monumental proportions. The population of Goworowo swelled tremendously during those first few days of the war with an influx of refugees from many of the nearby villages. The people of Goworowo became unwilling participants in a horrific living nightmare.

Fear and confusion were the order of the day. The invasion was unprecedented and forced people to make instantaneous, last minute decisions. Ruchel Leah, Anschel, Elka, Surcha, Moshe, Schwartza Dvora, Itche Yosel, Feige, Chaim, and Razal fled Goworowo along with hundreds of others mere days ahead of the tsunami of the German onslaught. Residents including non-Jewish political leaders who believed they would be targeted by the Nazis began fleeing east towards Bialystok, for safety, by any means, with only the possessions they could carry.

Many of these decisions were based on their previous war experiences. Since Ruchel Leah's family had fled into Imperial Russia during World War I and managed to survive until their return to Goworowo in 1918, it was a logical decision for the family to flee east hoping for the same ultimate outcome.

By September 5th the Wehrmacht marched into Goworowo. The streets became deserted as those remaining in the village sought shelter within their homes or went into hiding. Late in the evening into the early hours of September 6th, fighting erupted between the German and Polish troops. The Polish troops withdrew in defeat and the German army marched on.

The next day, the Einsatzkommando (mobile killing squads) arrived. The soldiers broke into shops – both Jewish and Christian – stole all the merchandise. The Einsatzkommando, for no apparent reason, terrorized the Jewish population, plundered and threatened to burn homes. They randomly shot or brutally beat to death many men in the streets including Yankev Roszberg from Ruzan, Leybl Berliner, Mordkhe Trushkevitsh, a shames (sexton) of the synagogue, Betsald Yosef Kavrat, a Talmudic teacher, and Tslave Kruk.

The Jews were accused of killing a German soldier during this murderous tirade. In retaliation, the Einsatzkommando executed seventy-two of the shtetl's most prominent residents. Among those slaughtered were Velve Yagodnik, a Talmudic teacher, his wife and Lazar Korn from Krementshug.

Troops continued to arrive and pass through Goworowo. The infantry was followed by the Panzerveband Ostpreuben (Panzer Group East Prussia) also known as the Panzer Division "Kempf" (armed combat vehicles – tanks) under the command of Major General Werner Kempf. The division was composed of regular army personnel and members of the Schutzstaffel (SS – paramilitary organization).

After the war, Kempf recalled that SS men under his command had spread the rumor that the Jews in Goworowo had taken part in the Polish combat operations and therefore posed a threat to the German military. This rumor fueled further retaliation and murder of the Jewish population.

During the time the Panzer Division was in the village, soldiers from the SS-Artillerie-Standarte and a few soldiers from the Army Feldgendarme (military police unit) randomly executed, by gun fire, 50 Jews in the village. The local German Army commander ordered a court martial with the prosecutor demanding the death penalty. One soldier from the SS-Artillerie-Standarte was sentenced to three years in prison and one officer from the Army Feldgendarme to nine years for taking part in the massacre. The sentences were later overturned in an amnesty ordered by Heinrich Himmler, Reichsfuhrer of the SS.

On the notorious Friday night of terror, the Einsatzkommando arbitrarily went into homes murdering the residents. Chaim Dovid Shran and his wife, Chaya Beyle were among those killed in this brutal tirade.

"The same Friday night, my mother lit the Sabbat candles at our home, covered the windows, and told us… that we had to leave. We left and took our grandparents with us to a mikvah far away from our home. By morning, the Nazis find us and pushed us out to the marketplace. In the market, on the way, we witnessed people lying wounded in the streets, people we knew personally. The marketplace was filled with old people, women, children. The German soldiers surrounded us with their guns pointed. I will never forget my mother's face. She was white and trembling. I could read her lips reciting the Shema." Sonia (Sura Cymerman) Wasserberger 2010 Interview University of South Florida

At 3:30 on Saturday morning, September 9th, the German troops began firebombing three sides of the market which was surrounded by Jewish homes. *"The story of the burning down of Goworowo was such: in the town there was one German, his name was Jung. When the war was about to break out, Goworowo gave money (to the Polish authorities) to buy arms. When the Germans came in, that Jung said that the Jews were traitors. So the Germans spilled gasoline all over the town. A lot of people were shot then. The Germans were going from one house to another. In our house they shot everyone who slept downstairs* (That means the refugees from other towns to whom the Grynberg's family had offered refuge. The owners who slept upstairs were not shot.) *Those who slept upstairs were saved."* Icchok Grynberg Interview September 2004

"In the background, we could see our city being set on fire. Smoke was everywhere." Sonia Wasserberger

Goworowo In Flames ©Imperial War Museum HU 8063

The Germans ordered everyone to leave their homes and congregate in the center of the market. Those who were found in hiding or could not run fast enough in the opinion of the soldiers were shot. *"Dvoyre Tsinaman, a woman of 45… When she appeared on the doorstep to see what the commotion on the street was and heard: Get out!, she turned to the living room to take her six-month-old child with her. A German shot her in the back and she fell dead in the entryway with her child in her arms."* Testimony of Jewish Woman X for the Committee for Collecting Material on the Destruction of Jewish Communities in Poland in 1939, December 1939

A total of 60 people were shot while the round-up was taking place.

About 2000 Jewish residents and refugees were gathered into the market square while three sides of the market were engulfed in flames. *"Now the Nazis decided to kill us in a quick way. We were thrown into our synagogue, where people were sitting motionless on the ground. Many were shot and wounded. They frantically handed out their names with hopes of being remembered, as well as pleas of saying Kaddish for them* (prayer recited in memory of the dead). " Sonia Wasserberger

The Germans intended to incinerate the synagogue with everyone in it prior to completely destroying the village.

"When I entered the courtyard of the synagogue, I saw murdered children there ..... In addition, old people were lying there, 60-year-olds, 70-year-olds and older, some murdered, some wounded, all victims of revolver shots.... The courtyard of the synagogue was locked, and German soldiers with revolvers and fire bombs in hand stood guard so that no one would escape through a crack or something.

We were held there for about 5 to 6 hours. Everyone was in their undergarments and just shirts because we came straight from bed and there was no time to get dressed. There was nothing to eat and nothing to drink. Meanwhile, the last (fourth) side of the market next to the synagogue was burning mercilessly. And we assumed that the synagogue would also burn and that we would be burned alive. Everyone shouted: 'Shema Yisroel!' ... Their voices rose to heaven.

During the time that we were there, Germans came in a few times and took men from the synagogue and the courtyard and led them away. A total of 100 men were taken away. We were sure that they were being led to their deaths. ...

At a certain moment, the Germans took a group of men from of the synagogue and ordered them to collect the shot and wounded Jews from the streets and the market and throw them

into the burning ruins of the houses. They warned them that those who did not obey would also be shot. The Jews were forced to carry out this dreadful command....

When we had been standing in the synagogue and the court-yard for about six hours, a German officer arrived in a car (some said it was a colonel) and asked the soldiers what was going on. The soldiers told him that they were planning to burn the synagogue with all the Jews soon. The Colonel replied: 'This can't happen, there are too many people.'

About half an hour later, the soldiers broke apart a board from the market, creating a passage 15-20 inches wide, and ordered all men to go out through the narrow hole into the meadow on the other side of the creek that runs behind the synagogue. The soldiers hurried people to go faster. Everyone fell over each other, it was a terrible scramble. Those who were in the synagogue jumped through the windows (from way up) straight into the creek." Testimony of Jewish Woman X for the Committee for Collecting Material on the Destruction of Jewish Communities in Poland in 1939, December 1939

Since the Germans did not allow anyone to use the bridge to cross the creek, people were forced to walk through the water to the meadow beyond. The Panzer Division continued with the destruction of the village making sure that the shtetl was completely engulfed in smoke and flames.

The German military held about 2000 people in the meadow without food or shelter for three days. Afterwards they herded everyone to the courtyard of a mill located outside of Goworowo. After taking photographs of the entire group, German military

*Patrolling the Bridge ©Imperial
War Museum HU8059*

authorities instructed the people to vacate German controlled territory. Panic ensued. Many were paralyzed with fear and some, despite
the order, returned to the burnt out ruins of Goworowo. Most people
fled in the direction of Ostroleka. They dispersed like chaff before the
wind to seek safety from the murderous hordes of German soldiers;
not knowing where they were going or what would become of them.

Destruction of Goworowo ©Imperial War Museum
HU8065, HU8062, HU8060

137

"Your unfortunate children are in great danger." Ruchel Leah

Goworowo In Ruins

GOWOROWO

My mother, may she rest in peace, was born in Goworowo town

To Grandpa, Nathan-Kalman, bless his memory, and Grandma, Deborah, may she rest in peace,

She was sent to Beit Yaakov School, where she studied Torah.

She grew up under those circumstances, she grew up and met father – her husband.

The town lay next to the river

There Jews lived under difficult conditions and it was horrible.

Small businessmen and craftsmen barely could make ends meet.

The Learning House was not far from there where Jews were quick to open in prayers.

People affiliated with different parties, Zionists and Bund, were gathering and participating in endless discussions.

The "market" was in the center of town

There people could buy and sell and also barter.

So lived the Jews until war broke in 1939, when Hitler raised to power, may his name be blotted out, and the murderers arrived.

Jews escaped to the fields and forests, literally like terrorized animals.

They locked all the Jews in the Learning House and were going to set them on fire while still alive.

Babies, women and old people were crying, shouting "Hear O Israel" and hoping for a heaven sent miracle.

Suddenly, without any reason, an SS officer ordered those in charge to open the doors and so they were saved.

Shabatai Chrynovizky (1916-2022 Ruchel Leah's first cousin) translated by Michael Chorev (Shabatai's nephew)

January 2005

The Run To Nowhere

A nd they ran!

The roads east were jammed with old and young, men, women, and children, everyone carrying whatever they could wrapped in sheets, in tattered luggage, some pulling handcarts while others just moving forward step by step. The air was filled with the explosive sounds of bombs and artillery, the smell of smoke and fear.

Fleeing East

Along with hundreds of other desperate Goworowo villagers, Ruchel Leah, Anschel, Elka, Surcha, Moshe along with Schwartza Dvora, Itche Yosel Taus, Feige Taus Frydman, and her children, Chaim and Razal, fled. They joined the throng of people from the surrounding villages heading east to escape the Nazi terror that was beginning to unfold. They became refugees in their own country.

They ran immediately to the small village of Brzezno, 2 ¼ miles from Goworowo. Dating from 1428, the village was originally a szlachta (noble estate) owned, since the 1840s, by the Marchwicki family. In 1900 Stanislaw Marchwicki built the imposing March-wicki Palace situated on a small hill in the center of the village.

Marchwicki Palace, Brzezno

Since Ruchel Leah, Anschel, Elka and Surcha could travel at a faster pace than the others, they left Moshe in Brzezno with the Taus family. They continued their escape from the German onslaught, the only way they could, on foot, to Ostrow Mazowiecka another 16 miles away; they left the others to follow.

On September 10th just three days after the Nazis arrived in Ostrow Mazowiecka, an order was given that all Jewish men were to assemble at the City Hall. They were instructed to run from there to the Gymnasia Square. Those who could not keep up were maliciously run down by soldiers riding motorcycles. Upon arrival in the square they were commanded to sit still or be shot. Finally, in the evening the men were allowed to return to their homes while the German soldiers randomly fired their rifles at them. Many men were murdered. The events of the day were a clear indication of the unfortunate future for the residents of Ostrow Mazowiecka.

Ostrow Mazowiecka

"Day to day it became more difficult, they seized us for forced labor and did not give us any food. The Nazis tore the beards off the old Jews and threw them in the water. The nights were filled with terror and tragedy. The Nazis went around at night to houses robbing, beating up Jews…

September 20, 1939 an order was issued that all the Jews without exception, children, old, and sick, must stand in the street and leave the houses open. If they find anyone in the houses, they will shoot them. And when everyone was gathered in the streets, the murderers told us that there was no reason for us to be here as there will not be any bread for us and that we can leave Ostrów and go to the Russians… About five hundred sixty Jews stayed in Ostrów and their situation became more difficult. A short time later, the five hundred sixty Jews were gathered together and they were ordered to dig a large trench outside town. There they were buried alive." Eyewitness account of Noach Laska translated by Judie Ostroff Goldstein *Memorial Book of the Community of Ostrow-Mazowiecka* 1960

Terrified, Ruchel Leah, Anschel, Elka, and Surcha, along with hundreds of other refugees, again ran from the Nazi terrorism. They ran with nothing – perhaps some toast, no bedding, no extra

143

clothing, just themselves. How could they survive? They must have scavenged for food and been repeatedly assisted by strangers along the route with scrapes of food and temporary shelter otherwise they would not have survived the journey.

Ultimately they arrived in Soviet controlled Bialystok, 62 miles further east. They were physically and mentally exhausted. The city was overcrowded with the influx of refugees from all parts of Poland. There were 33,000 refugees in Bialystok by November 1939 with hundreds more arriving daily.

Fleeing Ostrow Mazowiecka

The refugees as well as the local population experienced a sense of abandonment. It was difficult for Jewish organizations to provide aid, food distribution, and rescue efforts with the dramatic surge in the city's Jewish population. The organizations were relying on their pre-war strategies which were no longer realistic or viable. The only available place for the family to secure shelter was in one of the local synagogues. A decision was made to continue fleeing east. The family traversed through Poland until they reached Kartuz Bereza in Belarus which was 110 miles from Bialystok.

The Soviet army crossed the Polish border early in the morning on September 17, 1939 taking possession of north-east Poland.

The formal line of demarcation between German occupied and Soviet administered territories, roughly along the Bug River, was formalized on September 28th when a new Soviet-German pact was signed validating the secret protocol included in the appendix of

Chicago Tribune *September 17, 1939*

the Molotov-Ribbentrop Pact. This pact gave Germany all Polish territory west of the Bug River with the Soviets taking everything to the east. Germany now had 22 million Polish "slaves of the Greater German Empire" at its disposal while the Soviets gained a western buffer zone.

The Jews in Bialystok lived in constant fear after the German forces entered the city on September 15th. With the defeat of the last remnants of the Polish army, the German military began to withdraw, to the pre-determined lines of the Molotov-Ribbentrop Pact which then left Bialystok completely under Soviet control.

On September 21st, Soviet planes dropped leaflets announcing that Soviet forces were about to arrive and liberate Bialystok from German occupation. A welcoming committee was organized to embrace their "savior". During the six days that the German army had been in Bialystok, they killed more than 100 Jews, vandalized and looted more than 200 Jewish factories, businesses, and homes. The Soviets were deemed to be a welcome respite from the crimes perpetrated by the German Nazis.

"Around 1.5 million Polish Jews were gathered, along with non-Jewish Poles and Ukrainians, within the redrawn Soviet borders after the Germans crossed into western Poland in early September. The majority of them had become Soviet subjects.... Others had fled the advancing Wehrmacht into those parts of eastern Poland that had become Soviet after the Molotov-Ribbentrop Pact of August 1939. Families faced wrenching, difficult, often split-second decisions about whether or not to flee, about who should go or who should stay. Grandparents often insisted on staying behind, whether because they genuinely expected the Germans to leave them unharmed or because they did not want to be a burden to the younger and stronger. In some cases, parents pushed their youth to run while they could; in others, young people defied the pleas of their parents to stay with them and instead headed for the riverbanks that carried them to the Soviet side. All these moves were made 'in panic and uncertainty,' within moments, days, or occasionally weeks, depending on the changing progress of the battlefront, without any possibility of knowing the full situation, much less any inkling of what would soon transpire under Nazi control. Families expected that they would be reunited."

Shelter from the Holocaust Rethinking Jewish Survival in the Soviet Union **Edited by Mark Edele, Sheila Fitzpatrick, and Atina Grossmann 2017**

Kartuz Bereza   *18 December 1939*

Dear Parents, Sister Sylvia, Husband,

and dear child and dear Sisters and Brother,

    This is to let you know that we are well.

    Be well and write us at the following address.

    Kartuz Bereza

    Byelorussia

    UL Koshchushka #88

    Ancil Taus

    c/o Yenia Porodovskaya

    Your daughter and son-in-law, grandchildren and son

Ruchel Leah Taus

The Soviet army moved into the ancient town of Kartuz Bereza in September 1939 supplanting the German occupation.

The town, Kartuz Bereza, was first mentioned in historical records as early as 1477. For more than 300 years it was known as Bereze Kartuskaya. The name was derived from Bereza for "birth" and Kartuskaya which referred to the monastery built by the Catholic Carthusian monks.

Along with the Soviet occupation of the "former" Polish territory came a complete revision of government to conform to that of the Soviet Union.

In 1940 Kartuz Bereza was declared to be part of the Central District of the *Belarusian Soviet Socialist Republic* which included eight villages. Veteran communists arrived from the Soviet Union to administer all offices. A bank, network of cooperatives, committees of the communist party and the secret police of the Soviet Union (NKVD) were established in Kartuz Bereza.

All independent political and social institutions were closed by the Soviet authorities. Homes and businesses were nationalized. The Jewish schools were closed while the Tarbut schools were transformed into Soviet Yiddish language schools. Tarbut schools had traditionally been a network of secular, Hebrew language schools affiliated with the Zionist movement in parts of Poland and the Pale of Settlement where Kartuz Bereza was situated.

Life was difficult, particularly for the newly arrived immigrants. Many, like Ruchel Leah, arrived with virtually no possessions, a minimal amount of funds, and nothing of value which could be sold. The family managed to secure a room in the home or boarding house of Yenia Porodovskaya at Koshchushka St. #88. The lack of money and availability of food items created another set of issues. Anschel needed to work so the family could survive.

Provisions – salt, candles, and chicory (from the dandelion family; the root when roasted was used to make a coffee-like beverage) – had to be purchased from a centralized location controlled by the Soviet government. There was a definite shortage of kerosene and groceries. Long lines formed daily in front of the bakeries for the limited supply of bread.

Historically, many Jews in Kartuz Bereza were involved in the lumber industry – felling timber, working at sawmills, crafting furniture or trading in lumber and wood products.

The new arrivals from German occupied Poland tried to get work in sawmills, offices, or at the train stations. The number of positions was extremely limited. The Soviet nationalization of businesses coupled with the heavy tax burden harmed many Jewish operations. The businessmen gathered themselves into cooperatives to resist being absorbed into a "state" business.

Kartuz Bereza   *11 February 1940*

Dear Parents, Sisters, Brother-in-law, and Brother,

    I wish to receive from you an answer to my letter.

    We are now in a small town by the name of Kartuz Bereza in Belarus.

    We are well and are making a living. Do not send us any money but please do write us letters telling us about everyone and also about Sylvia's child.

    Stay well.

Best wishes from your daughter Ruchel Leah Taus

Your son-in-law and grandchildren send their love.

Kartuz Bereza   *12 February 1940*

Dear Parents,

    This is to inform you that we are alive and healthy. We live very happily.

    Regards from everyone.

    Your daughter,

Ruchel Leah Taus

The Soviet authorities were highly suspicious of all international communication, particularly to anyone in the United States. In contrast to all her previous letters, Ruchel Leah sarcastically conveyed a sense of happiness and optimism with the assumption that the family would be able to read the underlying message. With an eye on survival, Ruchel Leah rapidly adapted to living under Soviet rule. In some of her correspondence, she began communicating in Russian. This not only facilitated a rapid passage of the postcards through the censor system, but also demonstrated her loyalty to the Soviet regime.

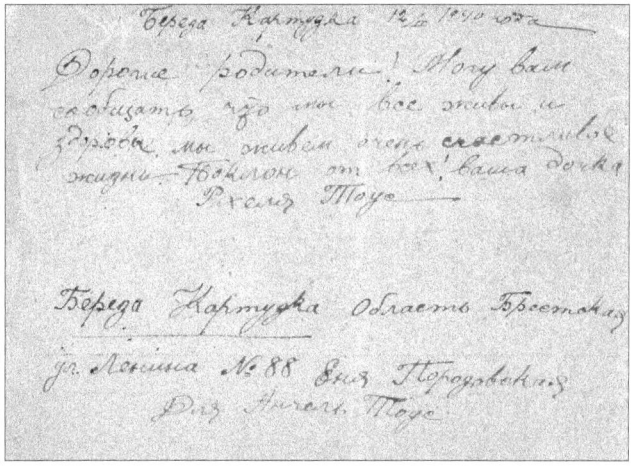

Russian Letter February 12, 1940

Kartuz Bereza   *5 April 1940*
Dear Parents, Sister and Brother Abraham,
    Why are you not writing to us? I do not know what to think about what happened to you.
    We are doing well.
    Regards to all of you.
    Your daughter and sister,
Ruchel Leah Taus

Receiving letters was a life line by which Ruchel Leah was able to maintain her spirit of hope and courage particularly at a time when the curtain seemed to be drawing to a close on her world. Hearing any news from the family in the United States helped allay her anxieties.

Once she arrived in Kartuz Bereza, Ruchel Leah continued to send multiple postcards at the cost of 30 kopeks ($.06) each for regular international mail. The postcards went via train/ship to New York which took approximately three to four weeks. At an increased

150

rate of an additional 1 ruble ($.20) the cards could have been sent airmail, but Ruchel Leah chose to save the extra ruble to spend on the necessities of life.

Kartuz Bereza   *19 April 1940*

Dear Parents, Sisters, Brother-in-law and dear Brother,

Today I received your letter. I cried reading the letter because you did not mention Papa's name not once throughout the letter. You signed the letter from "me, your mother". It made me sad.

Thank you for the regards from your new grandchild. Let him grow up in good health with his parents.

Dear family, I cannot write more. We must move on – where to, we do not know. It is three days before Passover (begins April 22, 1940). Where will we have Passover, we do not know.

We do not know where Mendel Chaim (Rubin) and family are. We believe they are in a town nearby.

If I did not remember your address by heart, I could not have written to you.

There is nothing to write about our condition. As soon as we settle down in our next destination we will write to you. I suppose it has to be that way.

My dear family, be well. I end this letter with warm kisses.

Anschel's health is about the same. Our package of troubles arrived before we got here. He works and I stay at home. Our children go to school.

Your daughter,

Ruchel Leah

A hearty sincere regards from your grandchild, Surcha Taus

Be happy and contented. A hearty regards to Nuskale (Nathan Kalman Rubin) *without even knowing him. Regards to everyone wishing them good health.*

Your grandchild,

Elka Taus

My in-laws (Schwartza Dvora and Itche Yosel Taus) *are in Bialystok as of today but, they will not remain there.*

With this postcard, Ruchel Leah reverted, once again, to writing in Yiddish. Perhaps this was so the Soviet censors would not have a complete understanding of the content of the correspondence.

In 1940, the Soviets delivered identity documents to all the inhabitants of Kartuz Bereza. During the process, they tried to expel many of the Jewish residents under the pretext that they were bourgeois – members of the capitalist class who owned most of society's wealth. Leaders of the Jewish communists testified that most of the Jews in the town were refugees and had lost all their possessions, so they were definitely not bourgeois. The Soviets nullified the expulsion decree.

Even though Kartuz Bereza was not occupied by German troops until June 23, 1941, Ruchel Leah and Anschel felt that they had to move on – further east into Soviet Russia for safety.

Along with thousands of others on September 9, 1939, Mendel Chaim, his wife Michala, daughter Bejla Leja Rubin Cymerman, her husband Moszek Cymerman and two daughters – Sura and Etka escaped the synagogue in Goworowo to the "safety" of the meadow on the other side of the creek while the Jewish section of the village along with the synagogue was consumed by flames. After three days, the Germans rounded up those who were remaining in the meadow. They marched them to the courtyard of a mill outside of Goworowo where they remained until the German military authorities advised that the Jews had twenty four hours to vacate German controlled territory. Mendel Chaim and his family fled east to Soviet occupied Bialystok.

Refugees arrived in Bialystok in the thousands. There was no place for the family to stay so the decision was made to move on. A friend of Moszek Cymerman's, who lived in Hancewicze, offered his home as sanctuary. Hancewicze was 83 miles from Kartuz Bereza further east into Soviet territory. *"We settled there for a while, but our future remained unknown."* Sura Cymerman Wasserberger 2010

The tremendous influx of refugees taxed Bialystok's infrastructure. Daily life was a struggle for mere survival. Food was scarce, work basically non-existent, and people were forced to sleep in any open space they could find with minimal sanitary conditions. In early 1940, the surge of refugees ceased.

According to Felicja Nowak, a refugee from Warsaw who joined her grandmother in Bialystok:

"At first they slept in fields and forests. Afterwards they found temporary shelter in railway stations, empty trucks…synagogues, schools, and pioneer collectives…Here they lived for months like herds of animals, hungry and unwashed.

Severe overcrowding led to a deterioration in sanitary conditions. Any available space was packed, and with the onset of winter, masses of refugees had to move to the already overcrowded train station. They were forced to take shelter in synagogues, schools, and public buildings…The Jewish refugees…were a burden on the Soviet authorities and the local inhabitants alike. Frieda Zerubavel, a refugee from

Lodz, described the scene upon her arrival at the Bialystok train station: 'The station is full of refugees. Whole families are sprawled on blankets. The children cry, the adults quarrel. People slouch on benches, or huddle together in groups. Hundreds of refugees hang around the station concourse, eagerly scanning new faces...'" The Jews of Bialystok During World War II and the Holocaust Sara Bender 2008

This was the city of Bialystok – a city in which Schwartza Dvora, Itche Yosel, Moshe, Feige, and her children were residing in a synagogue – endeavoring to survive.

Kosow   *13 May 1940*

Dear Parents, Sisters and Brother,

We are now in this small town. Everything is in the best of order. You cannot ask for anything better. We received your letter. It took three months for the letter to reach us. Please send post cards. Please have Papa himself write to us. Do not worry about us. We are supplied with everything.

Continue trying for Elka. Perhaps something will develop. Thanks to Mr. Linder for misguiding us. My opinion from the beginning was that he would not succeed. I suppose it has to be this way.

I do not know where Mendel Chaim and his daughter (Bejla Leja Rubin Cymerman) *are at.*

Your children wish you well.

Ruchel Leah

Heartfelt regards to Nuskale. I cannot write anymore. I beg you, please write to Fishel and Zisket that their parents and we are alive.

The family had traveled approximately 24 miles from Kartuz Bereza to Kosow Poleski. Over the course of history, the village of Kosow Poleski was considered part of Imperial Russia, Poland, the Soviet Union, and now, Belarus. The name of the village had also changed over time and language depending upon the controlling country. During the interwar years, the village was renamed Kosow Poleski (currently Kosava).

Jews arrived in Kosow Poleski as early as the 16th century constituting, for centuries, the largest segment of the population. They were engaged in commerce and worked small farms. Kosow Poleski was a typical Jewish community with an old and new synagogue, schools, and political organizations ranging from Zionists to Bundists.

Ruchel Leah, Anschel, Elka, and Surcha settled in at the home of M. Chernihov (Czernichow in Polish) 21 Sovetskaya Street where they tried to recreate a "normal" life. Under Soviet rule, life continued to be difficult. Again, Ruchel Leah praised the Soviets for they were *"supplied with everything"* hoping the family would understand her cryptic messages.

Postcard from Kosow Poleski

With all that the family was enduring, Ruchel Leah still pleaded for efforts to continue on behalf of Elka's visa application. The family proceeded on her behalf, however in 1940, additional roadblocks were placed in the application process. Visa requirements were in a constant state of flux. The State Department issued a report from the Visa Division to Polish, German, and Czechoslovakian consuls that there was no additional space to fill for the required financial support affidavits. HIAS was advised to cease sending the financial documents.

The consuls were advised that new regulations would be forthcoming which would stipulate that the financial sponsors needed to establish escrow accounts with sufficient funds to demonstrate that the immigrant would be supported for one year.

Complicating the situation further, three new requirements were added with expiration dates: certification that the immigrant was not a member of the Communist party or any group working against the United States to include a statement of loyalty to the United States; proof of permission to leave the current country of residency; and a confirmed means of transportation to the United States.

With new quota numbers enacted in March 1940, the United States Assistant Secretary of State, Breckenridge Long wrote a memo which described the options of controlling the rate of immigration during emergencies, *"Delay and effectively stop for a temporary period of indefinite length the number of immigrants into the United States. We could do this by simply advising our consuls to put every obstacle in the way which would postpone the granting of visas."*

Each consulate office operated under their own guidance to comply with Long's directives. Any and every excuse was given **not** to grant a visa. According to *The Jews Should Remain Quiet: Franklin D. Roosevelt, Rabbi Stephen S. Wise, and the Holocaust* by Rafael Medoff,

2019 *"Some applicants…ran into trouble when they presented a ketubah, the traditional Jewish religious wedding certificate, as evidence of their marital status. …had been married in a religious ceremony only, and not according to civil law; or they found it impossible to obtain evidence of their marital status from a Nazi government office; or they married in Russia….and could not enter the USSR to retrieve the necessary documentation. U.S. consular officials refused to recognize a ketubah as proof of marriage and therefore deemed the applicant's children 'illegitimate' and rejected them on the grounds of low moral character."*

By the summer of 1940, Long helped the State Department formulate rules which would cancel ALL existing visas, requiring the applicants to reapply. These laws were never implemented.

Kosow   *10 June 1940*

Dear Parents, Sisters, Brother-in-law and Brother,

In all this time we received only one letter from you. We have written to you many times. What I am worried about and upset is the fact that you do not mention anything about Papa. I believe that with all the problems and pain that we are experiencing here, I do not need any additional worries. Please be sure to write about our dear father and also about everybody in the family.

We are alive and in this town. Anschel's health is as it was. Imagine that Anschel is the breadwinner. That is good. Yet, we hope that we might get to see you. It is wonderful thinking – swimming across the Atlantic.

Many thanks to Mr. Linder for the big favor he did for my child. I will never forget him. My heart foretold me what is awaiting us. I had hoped that we might succeed in rescuing one from the family but, we failed.

Heartfelt regards to all of you from all of us. I miss you very much. I do not have a photograph of you to look at or any photographs of us to see how we looked before the catastrophe.

Each and every one send their love and kisses with blood and tears.

Your never forgetful daughter and sister,
Ruchel Leah

We do not know where Mendel Chaim is. My mother-in-law (Schwartza Dvora) *is in Bialystok. So is Feige* (Anschel's sister).
Lazar is … (Lazar Frydman – Feige's husband)

The Soviets wanted Polish refugees to register as Russian citizens. Mendel Chaim and his family refused to register. The Soviets considered a refusal to be an admission that they were spies. Since they could not be returned to German occupied Polish territory, the Soviets sent those who refused citizenship registration en masse to labor camps in Siberia.

"They took us to Siberia. It was a terrible trip. My family was herded into a train, along with many other people. It was a cargo train. When we entered the car, the doors were closed, locked behind us. And the car was crowded, filled to overflowing with refugees, cramped and uncomfortable, no facilities. After about two days of hard travel, we were taken into a big open field.

Then we were placed in boats. The journey was very dangerous. It seemed to take forever… We were given cups to bail out the water of the Northern Dvina River. Finally, we reached an area of many islands (Solovetsky Islands). *Our journey ended at what seems to be the end of the world, the cold land of Siberia* (an archipelago 100 miles from the Arctic Circle).... *they took us to another nearby island, which was heavily forested. The tall trees towered over us. ...Each day the men were taken into the forest to chop down trees, while the women cleaned the trees. This was manual labor, hard labor. Our people were mainly educated professionals; they were not accustomed to chopping trees.... Our island was populated by criminals, who had been sent there for many years."* Sura Cymerman Wasserberger 2010

It was difficult to survive. Many older people could not adapt to the climate and life. Housing was a large one room barracks which held about thirty individuals. There was no heat, beds were simple wooden planks with no mattresses, and food was subsistence at best. After a year of constantly being in bed, Michala Rubin passed away.

When war between Germany and the Soviet Union began on June 22, 1941, all the island overseers and Soviet citizens who were imprisoned on the island were called up for military service. The labor camp was essentially closed and the Polish refugees were stranded.

Using cut logs, the men fashioned rafts to take everyone to the mainland. Moszek Cymerman, Mendel Chaim, and Etka Cymerman took one of the rafts for a test. Mendel Chaim fell overboard and drowned. The body was retrieved by a gentile Polish man with whom the family was acquainted. Mendel Chaim was buried *"in Siberia, far from home; only a stick marked his grave. My grandfather did not live to see freedom."* Sura Cymerman Wasserberger 2010

The refugees managed to get to the mainland, hired a small boat to take them down the Northern Dvina River and traveled south. Their destination was the war free area of Uzbekistan, settling in the city of Bukhara.

With the end of the war, the family managed to receive papers to allow them to emigrate, as Polish citizens, from Soviet Russia back to Poland. Goworowo had been destroyed so the family moved to Szeczcin. One of Moszek Cymerman's cousins put the family in touch with representatives from the American Joint Distribution Committee (JDC) who helped with food, necessities, and transported them to a Displaced Persons (DP) camp in Berlin.

When the Berlin camp was closed in 1948, JDC flew the refugees to the Augsburg DP camp in Bavaria. It was at this camp where Sura met and in December 1948, married Alfred Wasserberger, a dentist, prior to immigrating to the United States on July 9, 1949.

It is inconclusive where Lazar Frydman was in June 1940. From Ruchel Leah's letters, it does not appear that Lazar left Goworowo with his family. According to testimony given to Yad Vashem item ID number 1140984 by his daughter, Shoshana (Razal) Frydman Vievorka on July 8, 1999, *"Lazar (Eliezer) was murdered in the Shoah (Holocaust) in 1940"*.

It was common practice for the Germans to kidnap men off the street to become part of the slave labor force. *"Rounding up Jewish passer-by in the street, packing them like cattle into a military truck and taking them to work somewhere in Poland, has become a daily occurrence. …They are just 'lost', as if the earth swallowed them, and their near and dear ones never learn what happened to them." The Destruction of Polish Jewry* – American Federation for Polish Jews 1940

The Lodz ghetto Registration Card No. 730 indicated that Lazar was interred in the ghetto in 1940 as part of the forced labor team working in multiple industries in the region. Lazar lived at 17 Jewish Street, worked as an assistant baker, piekarz czeladnik, at Opas located at 8 Garden Street in Lodz.

Lodz Ghetto Registration Card
#730 Lazar Frydman

Feige states, in a letter dated March 30, 1948, that Lazar was actually killed in 1944. Perhaps he survived the four years of forced labor. To a child of two, Shoshana possibly equated her father's disappearance to his having been murdered.

Kosow   *25 June 1940*
Dear Parents, Sisters and Brother,

Today we received two letters from you. We were glad to read that you are all well and that Papa is alive. My only hope is that I shall have the privilege to see you someday. It is very hard to believe that it could possibly happen. It is hard to believe that the grounded ship will ever reach the shore.

What can I tell you about our life? The fact that I am writing to you proves that we are alive. We ran away from home with only what we had on our backs. Moshe was with us as we ran until we reached the village of Brzezno. There he remained with my in-laws and Feige and her children. Anschel, the children and I continued our journey on foot to Ostrow Mazowiecka. There was no way to get any kind of transportation.

Moshe could not keep up with us. The great tragedy affected him greatly. We never met up again. We got to every town ahead of my in-laws and Moshe. When we reached Bialystok, we could not find a place to stay except in the Synagogue. We decided to continue running until we reached Kartuz Bereza.

Once there, we got the news that my in-laws, Moshe, Feige and her children are in Bialystok in the Synagogue. After a few weeks there, they took some people to the hospital. Included in the transfer was Moshe. My mother-in-law did not know where they took him and has not seen him since. That is how it happened.

We came here naked and barefoot with only the clothing on our back and one pair of shoes. No bedding. We suffered greatly from the cold this winter. I am without strength or energy to get up at 4 am to stand in line to obtain some bread. We get used to everything. The only good thing is that Anschel works. His health is not very good. He is weak. He lost 18 kilos (39.7 lbs.) *and I lost 20 kilos* (44 lbs.).

That is how we changed from the better times. Do not worry about us. As long as we are alive.

Stay well all of you.
Ruchel Leah, Elka, and Surcha

It is not known what prompted the Soviet authorities to enter the synagogue in Bialystok let alone remove some of the refugees to a hospital. Perhaps, Moshe had become increasingly erratic, boisterous, and uncontrollable due to his condition or became seriously ill due to the lack of food, severe winter cold, and inadequate sanitation facilities thus necessitating his transfer to a hospital. Moshe had evanesced.

Kosow   *26 July 1940*

Dear Parents, Sisters, Brother-in-law and Brother,

I am informing you that we are in the best of health, strong as steel (an idiomatic expression meaning that they are able to take all the suffering).

It has been quite a few weeks since I have heard from you. I would appreciate hearing from you more often. I would like to know what is going on in all respects.

We have nothing extra to write about. We are alive. Anschel works. He looks awful, bad. Elka studied the entire winter and is now looking for work. That is the only way we can make it. It would have been a good idea if I could go to work also but then who would prepare the food (if you can call it so)?

I had hoped to reach my goal. I would have liked to write you more but, what is the point? That is how it has to be.

My in-laws are not in Bialystok anymore. They (NKVD – The People's Commissariat for Internal Affairs) *are relocating them and also Feige and her children to some place but I have no knowledge to where. Perhaps they will send us a note telling us their whereabouts.*

It is very sad what has happened to Schwartza Dvora lost in a strange land.

We do not know what will happen to us. Anschel worries about his parents, their loneliness. He worries about who will help sustain them. They may die of hunger.

We do not know anything about Lazar. No doubt, he is dead by now.

Be well, these wishes from your lost children. With heartfelt kisses for the entire family and Nuskale.

Ruchel Leah

Less than two weeks after the Soviet invasion of Poland, on October 22, 1939, the Soviet occupation administration organized elections for the People's Assemblies of Western Ukraine and Western Belarus under the control of the NKVD and the Communist Party. The candidates backed by the Soviet Union received 90% of the votes.

The NKVD – The People's Commissariat for Internal Affairs was originally created as an agency to conduct routine police work and oversee the country's prisons and labor camps.

During the National Assembly session on October 30, 1939, a decision was passed for Western Belarus of which Bialystok was considered to be part, to join the Union of Soviet Socialist Republics (USSR) and to be unified with the Belarusian Soviet Socialist Republic (BSSR). The proposal was accepted by the Supreme Soviet of the USSR on November 2nd and the Supreme Soviet of the BSSR on November 12th.

Following the incorporation of Bialystok and the surrounding territory into the BSSR, a policy of Sovietization began. In 1940, an emphasis was made on the migration of local Belarussians to the city designed to "improve" the ethnic base. This increase in the Belarusian population gave the BSSR additional control of the region.

The NKVD forced the deportation of over 100,000 ethnic Poles, Belarusians and Jews who were dubbed "enemies of the people" to the eastern part of Soviet Russia, mainly Siberia. There was a major change in the ethnic structure of the city. The Poles and Jews lost their dominance.

After July 1940 nothing further is known regarding the whereabouts of Ruchel Leah's in-laws. Feige and her children had been separated from them in March 1940 and sent to Ostrowiec-Kielecki (renamed Ostrowiec-Swietokrzyski) in southeastern Poland, 230 miles from Bialystok. It is conceivable that Itche Yosel and Schwartza Dvora were among those in the general deportation eastward, further into Soviet Russia.

Bialystok was occupied by German forces, once again during Operation Barbarossa, from June 27, 1941, known as "Red Friday", to July 27, 1944. There were still about 50,000 Jews living in Bialystok and 350,000 in the province. On the day following the occupation, the Jewish quarter including the Great Synagogue in which approximately 2000 people had been interred was burnt down with everyone inside. Exterminations took place in rapid succession – on Thursday, July 3rd, 300 of the Jewish intelligentsia were taken to Pietrasze, a field outside the town and murdered; on Saturday, July 12th over 3000 Jewish men were slaughtered in the field.

Firing Squad

The actions of the German forces were universal throughout the occupied towns. The Jewish population was terrorized and murdered.

165

As described by Berl Manperl in "How I Read Yiddish Literature to an S.S. Captain" *Mezritsh Book – In Memory of the Martyrs of our City* translated by Jack Kugelmass and Jonathan Boyarin *From a Ruined Garden – The Memorial Book of Polish Jewry* 1983

"...the German murderers terrorized their defenseless Jewish victims with all the dark force of their fiendish power. They tortured, beat murderously, ridiculed, degraded, and outraged our deepest and most intimate human sensibilities. Whoever was 'blessed' with a bullet and redeemed from agony was considered lucky. Our only friend was Death; we ate from the same plate as Death; the only one whom we had ceased to fear was Death.

...All these dark forces had one goal; to eliminate us from the face of the earth, to eradicate us so thoroughly that not even the least remnant would remain.

...It was a mere sport to them, a way of quenching their thirst for blood. Sensing the approach of the two-footed beasts, we used to escape with our last ounce of strength, each to his own hiding place...in order to conceal our tortured bodies and souls....

...the Hitlerite beast ruled, sowing murder and destruction among our people."

Detaining Jews

Between the end of July and the beginning of August 1941, the Bialystok ghetto containing 50,000 Jews was established. Confined to a small area of the city, the ghetto was split into two sectors by the Biala River. Most of the ghetto inmates were put to work in slave labor enterprises supporting the German war effort – textile, shoe, and chemical companies.

In November 1943, the ghetto was liquidated with the transportation of its inhabitants to the Majdanek concentration camp and Treblinka extermination camp. Only a few hundred residents of the ghetto survived the Holocaust.

Assembly

Kosow   *14 February 1941*
Dear Parents,

We received your post card. We did not receive the food package you sent us. Perhaps you worry about us. The truth is, we are not short of anything. We have everything. That is why you sent us a container of fat, condensed milk, cocoa, tea, sugar, etc. If you send us a gift, we will accept it, but we are not short of anything. We can get everything here.

Your question whether we see Shalom Pras…. The answer is we did not see him since we left Goworowo. We do not know where he is.

Such is life. We work and make a living.

I close with regards to Sylvia, her husband and their child. My children send their love. Elka feels pain and disappointment that she could not attend Itzhok's wedding ceremony.

Regards to Mr. Linder. Regards to my sisters. Dear parents, do not worry about us. We write to you often but, you seldom write. Stay well.

Anschel sends his regards. We had word that Moshe is in a hospital in Smolensk.

Ruchel Leah Taus

A food shortage existed throughout Belarus due to the Soviet economic policy, introduction of collective farming, and the tremendous influx of refugees from Poland. The items listed would have been considered luxury items and were not readily available to families of Ruchel Leah's economic status. By mentioning those items, Ruchel Leah was transmitting a subliminal message for the family to send them to her.

Times were not easy for the family in New York. Abraham (Itzhok) contributed half his weekly salary to the household. With the balance of his salary, he had to support himself – transportation to/from work, lunch, clothing, extra in the pushke for Ruchel Leah, and a little each week for his savings. Finally, he felt he had saved enough money to get married. He and Rebecca were wed in a civil ceremony on October 14, 1940 with only their mothers, Hilda Blum and Clara Offenberg, in attendance. A religious ceremony and reception, which they paid for, subsequently took place on January 12, 1941.

Rebecca and Abraham Blum

Situated in Western Russia on the Dnieper River was Smolensk, one of the oldest Russian cities, with a Jewish presence dating back to the late 13th century. The total population in 1939 was 157,000 with 14,812 being Jewish. The city was a major railroad junction 378 miles north of Bialystok.

The Smolensk State Medical University, founded in 1920, had a contingent of hospitals under its jurisdiction. (Today there are 31 hospitals under the umbrella of the Smolensk State Medical University.) In 1930, the University was reorganized into two independent institutes: the Smolensk State Pedagogical Institute of the People's Commissariat of the USSR and the Smolensk State Medical Institute of the People's Commissariat of the USSR. Moshe could have been transported to a hospital in Smolensk operated by one of these facilities.

Kosow 2 *March 1941*
  Dear Bubbe and Zayde, Aunts and Uncle Itzhok,
  The situation here is about the same as ever.
  I am in the fifth grade in middle school in the town of Kosow. Not far off the third quarter of the year will end. I will be 12 years old on March 4th.
  How are you? What is new? My hope is to get to see you in person. I have no more news to write.
  I close with best wishes for your good health.
  Regards to Sylvia, Mates, and the child,
  Regards to Itzhok and wish him happiness in his life.
  Your grandchild,
Surcha Taus
Please reply. Regards from all.

There is a maturity evident in Surcha's note. Unlike today, children were forced, by circumstances, to abandon their childhood at an earlier age. It is hard to imagine the world in which these children lived, what they saw and experienced. Despite it all, Surcha expresses hope for tomorrow.

Kosow 2 *April 1941*
Dear Parents, Sisters, Brother, Sister-in-law (Rebecca) *without meeting and knowing her and Brother-in-law,*
  Wish you all good health and happiness. During the whole winter season I received just one post card from you with the news about Abraham Itzhok's wedding. That is all the news I had from you. I am anxious to know what is going on with all of you.
  Winter season is almost over. Spring will be here soon. It is two weeks before Passover. Everything is in the best order.

Anschel's health is about the same. In fact, it gets worse as time goes on. One cannot write a lot about it. But as long as there is life, there is hope. He had so many attacks this winter that I thought he would not make it through the winter.

Please write us whether you received the two letters from us which included two tchotchke (small item of interest). *It seems that you are too lazy to write us. Elka works in an office. Surcha goes to school. She is in the fifth grade. Not much more to write.*

Stay well. And heartfelt regards for my sister, Sylvia, her husband and child. Why does she not write? Not a word from her for a long time. Regards to my brother, Abraham Itzhok and his wife. Regards to my sisters. Each one of you please write to us. Keep us posted about your life and health, etc.

I wrote you before that Moshe is alive. He is in a hospital in Smolensk. I was informed that his sickness is not curable.

I wish my dear parents good health and have lots of nachas from your children.
Ruchel Leah

Months passed and the family did not receive any additional letters from Ruchel Leah. "…*nachas from your children.*" How could there be "nachas" when Ruchel Leah, Anschel, Elka, Surcha, and Moshe had vanished like a wisp of smoke into the abomination today known as the Holocaust.

During the winter of 1939 and early spring 1940, the German High Command and the Reich Security Main Office arranged for the deployment of the Einsatzgruppen behind the front lines to initiate mass murder operations of primarily Jews, Communists, and other individuals opposed to the establishment of German occupation of

Soviet territory. The Einsatzgruppen were Schutzstaffel (SS) paramilitary death squads who were responsible, primarily by shooting, for mass killings.

Nazi Germany launched a surprise attack against Soviet Russia, its one time ally, on June 22, 1941. Code name Operation Barbarossa (originally known as Operation Fritz) was driven by Hitler's ideological desire to destroy the Soviet Union as outlined in his 1923 manifesto, *Mein Kampf* (My Struggle) which characterized all Eastern Europeans – Jews and non-Jews alike as "sub-humans." The manifesto was an autobiography which outlined Hilter's political strategy and future plans for Germany.

Hitler had regarded the German-Soviet nonaggression pact of August 23, 1939 as a temporary tactical maneuver. The destruction of the Soviet Union by military force, thus eliminating the perceived Communist threat to Germany and the seizure of Soviet land for permanent German settlement, had been core objectives of the Nazi party since the 1920s. On December 18, 1940, Hitler signed Directive 21 – Operation Barbarossa, as the first operational order to invade Soviet Russia.

Operation Barbarossa was a carefully orchestrated invasion of the Soviet Union in June 1941. Three army groups composed of more than three million German soldiers supported by 650,000 troops from Finland and Romania, later augmented by divisions from

Operation Barbarossa

other Axis (German allies) countries – Italy, Croatia, Slovakia, and Hungary attacked on a broad front stretching from the Baltic Sea in the north to the Black Sea in the south.

The Soviet armed forces were initially overwhelmed. The air force was almost completely destroyed while on the ground; the Soviet soldiers were surrounded by German units who cut them off from both supplies and reinforcements. They had no option other than to surrender.

At the onset of Operation Barbarossa, the small area of Kosow Poleski, a Soviet controlled territory, was almost entirely surrounded by German forces. The displaced people from the surrounding region caused the Jewish population of Kosow Poleski to swell to about 2,250 from the recorded population in 1921 of 1,473. After bombarding the town in late June, on July 1, 1941 the German army took complete control of Kosow Poleski. A reign of terror was immediately instituted. They demanded a ransom of 4 pounds of gold from the Jewish community knowing that it would be virtually impossible to achieve, formed a nine member Judenrat (an administrative agency representing the Jewish community), enforced the wearing of yellow stars, instituted forced labor, and engaged in sporadic killings, merely for sport.

In late July, with the arrival of significant reinforcements, the SS (Schutzstaffel) and police supported by locally recruited auxiliary units began to physically annihilate entire Jewish communities in Soviet Russia.

During Operation Barbarossa, Smolensk was captured by the Germans on July 16, 1941 during the first Battle of Smolensk. Near the village of Magalenschina 2000 Jews were annihilated by gassing or firing squads. The Jewish ghetto was established in late July.

The Soviet military launched an unsuccessful counteroffensive in August 1941. As a result of the fighting and the rampaging German forces, Smolensk was 93% destroyed. According to oral history, the hospital in which Moshe was a patient was bombed during this offensive.

As the German army advanced deeper into Soviet Russia, the Einsatzgruppen (SS paramilitary death squads) closely followed, eradicating thousands in their wake. With the assistance of the German army, the Einsatzgruppen concentrated the Jews in ghettos and holding facilities, killing many of the elderly, young and placing able-bodied men and women into forced labor for the benefit of the Third Reich.

With the success of both the military operation and the extermination of thousands of Jews, Hitler decided to commence deportation of German Jews to German occupied Poland commencing on October 15, 1941. This was the initiation of the Final Solution – the annihilation of European Jewry.

The Soviet Union mustered their forces and launched a major counterattack against the center of the front on December 6, 1941. The German forces were pushed back from the outskirts of Moscow, aided by their historical enemy – the harsh Soviet winter for which the German army was not prepared. The Germans managed to stabilize their battle front in the area east of Smolensk.

After the United States Congress, in a joint resolution formally issued a declaration of war with Germany, on December 11, 1941, the German Reich restricted all mail in or out of German occupied territory to the United States or any Allied Nation – Great Britain, France, or the Soviet Union. It would have been impossible for Ruchel Leah to continue communicating since the German forces controlled Kosow Poleski since July 1941.

Three ghettos were established in June 1942 in Kosow Poleski. One was in town, enclosed by barbed wire, where the skilled workers and their families were confined. The second, set up at the Puslowski Palace in Mereczowszczyzna, was for the unproductive including the old and infirm. The third, known as the "Court" ghetto, was created on the adjacent Biernacki estate for the families of labor camp workers. Between the hours of 6 a.m. and 6 p.m., residents of the last two ghettos could move freely between the ghettos.

Living in a German occupied and controlled town was completely demoralizing. Thousands of men, women, and children, young, old, disabled and sick were crowded into the ghettos – all struggling to merely survive. Refuse and garbage was thrown in the streets. Disease was rampant. Housing and sanitary conditions were deplorable. Hunger was the order of the day. Residents were allowed to purchase only a small amount of bread, potatoes, and fat – if it was available. Some residents had smuggled money or valuables into the ghetto which they used to trade for contraband food. Others had to beg or even steal food in order to stay alive. People were weakened by hunger and exposure to the weather.

On July 19, 1942, the Jews were no longer allowed to leave the ghettos. Less than a week later on July 25th, the first and main slaughter of about 1200 people occurred.

"On the morning of that day two Ukrainian policemen came to 'The Court' ghetto. One of them pointed his gun at the Jews and threatened them and the other one went through the rooms and took everything he could lay his hands on.... The policemen there went wild until nine o'clock in the morning. At about that time, the policeman who was standing at the crossroads

announced that a German was approaching on his horse. That was the Oberwachmeister Pertz and with him also arrived Jarmolowski, the head of the police. They both gave instructions to the policemen, most likely regarding the slaughter.

An hour later they saw three small cars and seven trucks approaching…most likely these trucks went directly to 'The Castle' and only after they slaughtered all of 'The Castle' ghetto Jews did they go to 'The Court' ghetto.… 'The Court' ghetto was composed of a few sections. Some lived at the Biernacki's and the rest.…in the barracks that the Soviets built. In that ghetto there were about six hundred people, in 'The Castle' ghetto there were about 500 people, and the rest were in 'The City' ghetto." Translation of *Pinkas Kehilat Kosow Poleski* (Memorial Book of Kosow Poleski) 1945 project coordinator Bob Fitterman

The ghetto inhabitants were lined up and skilled craftsmen – shoemakers and tailors – were asked to step forward. Local troops kicked and tortured the remaining Jews who were then ordered into the awaiting trucks. They were stacked into the trucks in a prone position, several layers deep – everyone laying face down towards the truck bed. The screams of terror must have been deafening as people were piled into the truck. Many of those on the bottom layers suffocated to death during the short drive to the Puslowski Palace where the survivors were directed out of the trucks.

Leaving the dead in the trucks, the Jews were herded to an area where they were summarily murdered. As they were being executed the air echoed with the sound of gunshots and cries of the words of the Shema. The sounds of supplication rescinded as the last shots were fired. The bodies of the dead were dumped, along with the previous victims, into open potato storage pits which remained uncovered for several days until the police instructed local residents to cover the bodies.

The Shema is a prayer, recited three times daily, which affirms one's faith in Judaism and is a declaration of the belief in one God. It is tradition for Jews to recite the Shema as their "last" words.

Shema Yisrael – Hear O Israel

Hear, O Israel, the Lord is our God, the Lord is One.

Blessed be the name of the glory of His kingdom forever and ever.

You shall love the Lord your God with all your heart, with all your soul, and with all your might. And these words which I command you today shall be upon your heart. You shall teach them thoroughly to your children, and you shall speak of them when you sit in your house and when you walk on the road, when you lie down and when you rise. You shall bind them as a sign upon your hand, and they shall be for a reminder between your eyes. And you shall write them upon the doorposts of your house and upon your gates… (Shema – 1st stanza)

On August 2, 1942, Soviet partisans attacked the German forces in Kosow Poleski. After a four hour battle, the partisans prevailed. A few dozen young Jews were selected to join the partisan forces. When the Germans regained control, the police ordered the remaining 200 Jews to dig a trench. One cannot begin to fathom the fear and terror these people experienced as they prepared their own graves. They were all murdered.

The skilled craftsmen who survived the first onslaught were sent to the Smolensk ghetto where they were to work in their profession

Kosow Poleski Memorial
Monument

for the benefit of the Third Reich. All but one man, Meir Kuliszewski, were subsequently murdered or succumbed to disease.

The Soviet 19th Mechanized Brigade of the 28th Army liberated Kosow Poleski on June 11, 1944. There were only 26 survivors.

After months of no communication from Ruchel Leah, the entire New York family was distraught upon the realization that the letter dated April 2, 1941 was the final communication.

Goworowo Salvaged Headstones

GOWOROWO (Continued)

So parted the Jews from their sacred and holy souls

They had neither a chance nor a choice

May their souls be bound up in the bond of everlasting life.

The survivors from the horrible terror will remember and remind all their lives, what happened to them.

They will tell and pass their whereabouts to the following generations

And will never forgive!!!

Shabatai Chrynovizky (1916-2022 Ruchel Leah's first cousin) translated by Michael Chorev (Shabatai's nephew)

January 2005

Desaparecidos

When the dark clouds of war lifted with the unconditional surrender of Germany on May 8, 1945 and with the subsequent liberation of German occupied territories, the search, in the Holocaust milieu, for Ruchel Leah, Anschel, Elka, Surcha, and Moshe commenced. The quest for information during the years after Ruchel Leah's final letter dated April 2, 1941, was stymied by the war. With Abraham serving in the United States Army from 1942-1945, there was no one in the family directing the pursuit for their whereabouts. It was virtually impossible to obtain information from any authority or relief agency pertaining to people who had been displaced from their pre-war locations.

Upon his discharge from the military on October 18, 1945, Abraham, along with his sister, Norma, launched the family's search for the lost ones – Los Desaparecidos – those who disappeared.

Thousands were lost or homeless. Were they dead or alive? Had they been exterminated in the concentration camp gas chambers; slaughtered in the forests; or murdered on village streets? Did they survive in hiding; were they in a displaced persons camp; had their names been changed to escape and survive; or were they alive in the frozen tundra of Siberia?

These were questions that needed to be answered.

"The dead don't go anywhere, they're all here. Every man is a cemetery, an actual cemetery, in whom lie all our grandmothers and grandfathers, the father and mother, the wife, the child, everyone is here all the time." Isaac Bashevis Singer, author (1903-1991)

Norma and Abraham July 4, 1945

No one will ever know the complete truth regarding Ruchel Leah, Anschel, Elka, Surcha, and Moshe's fate. There are conflicting accounts of what actually transpired.

Natan Kalman Khrunovitzki (Ruchel Leah's first cousin) submitted testimony to Yad Yashem (World Holocaust Remembrance Center in Jerusalem, Israel) on November 16, 1956 in which he stated that Ruchel Leah, Anschel, Elka, and Surcha had perished at the Treblinka extermination camp. Their names do not appear in the Treblinka records. Names of those who were murdered immediately upon arrival were not recorded by the camp officials, so it is conceivable that their names would not have been recorded.

Natan spent the war years as a refugee in Siberia, therefore he did not have first-hand knowledge of what became of the Taus family.

The report was based on hearsay. There were few survivors from Treblinka with no one reporting having seen the family or actually witnessing their deaths.

According to the *Goworowo Memorial Book*, Anschel had been sent to Majdanek, a concentration camp near Lublin. How and when did he get picked up and sent there from Kosow Poleski? Where were Ruchel Leah and their daughters?

Feige Taus Frydman states in a letter dated March 30, 1948, *"My brother, Anschel and your sister, Ruchel Leah and both girls – Elka and Surchale were killed in Auschwitz in 1944. I know because I was not too far from them. Therefore, I can relate what happened. I could not believe my eyes. After liberation I went to someone of authority and informed myself. I could not rest."* No additional information was forthcoming. Where did she go to obtain the information? Who was "someone of authority"?

The Germans were fastidious in recording names of the inmates at Auschwitz. No family member's name appears in the Auschwitz records. However, if they were killed immediately upon arrival, as in Treblinka, their names would not have been recorded.

Kosow Poleski was the last confirmed location of the entire family with the exception of Moshe. The history of the German occupation of Kosow Poleski does not include records of deportation to any concentration camp. Unless they moved to another location after the final correspondence of April 2nd, it can be reasonably assumed that the family perished in the mass extermination of the town's ghettos in July/August 1942.

The search for the truth of Los Desaparecidos began…

Paris   *the 19ᵗʰ of January 1946*

Dear Friend (Abraham),

    What a joy it was for me to receive your letter today. It is a wonderful feeling to know that someone is interested in my well-being.

    In reality, I am one of the only ones who were able to escape the grip of Hitler. In 1942, I was deported with my entire family to Germany. It was only in 1945, after a cruel martyrdom of three years that I was rescued. What I suffered there, I cannot tell you for it is unbelievable. Unfortunately, I returned home alone. My wife (Richla Frydman Taus) *and my two daughters* (Resla and Claudine) *disappeared, burned in a crematory furnace.*

    My sister (Elka Taus Ter) *who lived in Paris was also deported with her husband* (Leibel Ter). *Her three daughters escaped at that time. One of my nieces* (Lucienne), *a young lady of twenty three, was killed by a dismantled bomb. The older daughter* (Rachel) *was married. She is now single with a ten year old son* (Claude Roger Zaliman) *as her husband* (Abraham Zaliman) *was also deported. The youngest daughter* (Helene) *is going on seventeen.*

    And that is what Hitler did to a large family who were very close and only asked to live honestly.

    I am now alone, very alone. During my captivity, my apartment was emptied entirely by the Germans and I have absolutely nothing except my hands to work with but without a lot of courage to do so. Indeed you must understand this.

    At forty-six years old, I have to start completely over from A to Z and that is hard. How does one forget a wife and two daughters, one of who was supposed to be married and the other, a child of ten?

Your offer to help me touches me deeply. I thank you for it. To be truthful, I lack everything.

You asked me about news of my brother and your sister (Anschel and Ruchel Leah). *Since 1940, I have not known anything that happened there. I have learned from Zisket* (his brother in Brazil) *that they all took refuge in Russia but, I fear now the worst, because their safety has not been confirmed to me.*

On your side, do you have news from Zisket? I do not have his address and I would very much like to correspond with my brother since I do not have anyone other than him.

How are your parents and sisters doing? Tell me everything in your next letter with a lot of details. I would also like to have the address of my cousin Leon (Leiba). I am writing in today's mail to Mrs. Schulmann to thank her for her help. I embrace you both very affectionately.

The person who is actually writing to you is my oldest niece. She beseeches you to believe in the assurance of her best sentiments.

My uncle is with us for the moment, as I do not want to leave him completely alone. Our family has become so much smaller that I am content to have found my uncle again. I have my son and my younger sister with me and we are all trying to live the best we can.

Several letters have been sent to Goworowo but all have come back stamped "Unknown".
R. (Rachel) *Zaliman*

Mr. Taus
60 rue de la Chapelle
Paris

The bonds of friendship often transcend both time and space. Apparently prior to immigrating to the United States in 1921, Chava Yidis (Ida) Leviton was close friends with members of the Taus family and by extension, because of Anschel Taus' relationship with Ruchel Leah, the Blum family. In 1923, Chava Yidis married Peisach Truchnowski, who had arrived in the United States from Goworowo in 1920. As with many immigrants, his name was changed. He became legally known as Paul Cohen. Upon his death in 1939, Chava Yidis was alone with two teenagers – Jeanette (15) and Herman (14). She subsequently married Harry Schulmann in 1945 thus becoming Mrs. Schulmann. Apparently, she maintained contact with the friends from her youth, the Taus family.

Letter Dated January 19, 1946 from Fischel Taus to Abraham Written by Fishel's Niece, Rachel Zaliman

16 March 1946

Dear Friends,

I am very touched to have received your nice letter and happy to hear of your good news.

186

I thank you for having sent me the address of my brother. I wrote him and am awaiting a response. I would truly be so pleased to correspond with him for he is the only close relative who remains alive.

I am happy to know that you and yours are all in good health.

You told me that you were a soldier for three years (United States Army 1942-1945). *It is such a pity that you did not come to France. As for me, I became a soldier in 1939 at the declaration of war and returned to my family a year later. Then in July, 1942, there was a general deportation which lasted for three years of which I alone survived.*

I came back and once again began my profession as a tailor and am working a little. It is very hard at this time for I am lacking many things, which I need.

Thank you for the parcel you said you were sending. I am not hiding the fact that it is welcome and that it will bring happiness. I will let you know as soon as it arrives.

I send warm thoughts to your parents, your wife, your son, and your sisters.

With warmest wishes to you all,
Fishel Taus

On May 19, 1939, a mutual military aid convention, the Kasprzycki-Gamelin Convention was signed by the Polish Minister of War Affairs, General Tadeusz Kasprzycki and the Commander of the French army, Maurice Gamelin. The convention obligated both countries to provide military support in case war erupted with Germany. France promised a "bold relief offensive" within three weeks of a German attack.

Since the convention was a military agreement, it was not enforceable until it was ratified by each of the respective governments. France ratified the treaty on September 4, 1939 after Germany's initial invasion of Poland.

Five million reservists were mobilized by France to add to the standing army, based on conscription, of 900,000 men. As per the law revised on March 16, 1935, the period of compulsory military service was for two years instead of the original one year time period due to the increased threat of a resurgent Germany under Hitler's dictatorship.

France declared war on September 3, 1939. The French troops marched in support of Poland's fight against the German invasion. Faced with a strong resistance from the German military, the French army ceased their aggressive attack. France's failure to adhere to the terms of the treaty was considered to have been a contributing factor to Hitler's rapid conquest of Poland.

With Germany's invasion of and success in Poland, a fog began to obscure the City of Light – Paris. Germany turned its attention to the Western European countries and attacked France on May 10, 1940. The French army was rapidly defeated. A French delegation signed the Second Armistice agreement imposed by Germany on June 22, 1940 in a railroad car on the outskirts of Compiegne, France. This was the same railroad car in which Germany had signed the capitulation to the Allied forces in November 1918 which ended World War I.

The newly formed French State, Vichy France was a pro-German puppet government lead by Marshall Philippe Pétain. Vichy France maintained nominal sovereignty over the entire country as defined by the armistice with full control in the unoccupied southern free zone and limited authority in the Wehrmacht occupied northern zone. In November 1942, the free zone became occupied territory with Germany closely supervising all French officials. The Vichy government actively participated in rounding up Jews and other "undesirables", which turned France into a quasi-police state. To guarantee French cooperation, the Nazi government kept two million French soldiers in Germany as forced laborers.

Upon the surrender to Germany in June 1940, the French troops were sent to prisoner of war camps or forced labor camps in Germany. Some soldiers were repatriated to the Vichy government and others, Fishel among them, were released from service. A large number of soldiers escaped and joined the new Free French forces which were units of resistance founded by Charles de Gaulle (President of France 1959-1969) who had rejected the armistice concluded by Marshal Pétain. Based in London, Free French forces were designed to continue France's struggle against Germany and her allies.

German forces marched into Paris, occupying the city on June 14, 1940. A governing force was established which was composed of the German military and approved French officials under the Vichy regime. The occupation initiated a series of prohibitive rulings and shortages. A curfew was enacted from 9 p.m. to 5 a.m. Rationing of food, tobacco, coal and clothing was imposed. One million Parisians left the city to seek refuge in the provinces.

Parisian Jews were harshly treated. The Ordonnanance de' Aryeni-sation (Aryanization Ordinance) was decreed on October 18, 1940 which barred Jews from certain professions – doctors, lawyers, professors, shop owners; it also included restrictions regarding dining and frequenting public places. Seizure of private property commenced.

Using a billet vert (green postcard), the Paris police summoned Jewish men who were not French citizens, 18-40, to present themselves to the authorities on May 14, 1941. More than 5,000 men, mainly of Polish extraction, were taken into custody. The prisoners were sent to the transit camps of Pithiviers and Beaune-la-Rolande in the Loiret Region of the Loire Valley.

> *"They wake them from their sleep at six o'clock in the morning, and at seven o'clock they get a kind of unsweetened coffee and no bread. These people, who have committed no crime and will not stand trial, suffer from a well-organized hunger."* from the diary of journalist Jacques Bielinky (1881–1943)

Billet Vert Roundup May 14, 1941

The eradication of French Jewry had begun with the full cooperation of the Vichy France government. Secret orders of Jewish deportation of French citizens as well as non-citizens to the Auschwitz concentration camp were issued on May 23, 1942 by Adolf Eichmann, head of the Anti-Jewish sector of the Gestapo.

By the end of May, all Jews over the age of six were required to wear the identifying yellow star. Designed to isolate the Jews from the general French population, further restrictions were enacted in July. Basic citizen rights were denied the Jews: being forbidden to be on all main streets, movie theaters, libraries, parks, restaurants or cafes, public places and also required to ride in the last car of the metro trains.

On July 16-17, 1942 Eichmann's deportation orders were implemented. The French police under orders of the German military began the Vélodrome D'Hiver Roundup which was part of a series of assemblages code named Operation Vent Printanier (Operation Spring Wind) that occurred during the spring/summer 1942. After dark, the French police arrested 13,152 Jews. They were held for five days in the Vélodrome d'Hiver stadium famous for having hosted the 1924 Summer Olympics. They were crowded together in the summer heat with hardly any food or water and no proper sanitation facilities prior to being sent to internment camps at Drancy and Pithiviers. From the internment camps, the majority of the prisoners were deported to Auschwitz.

Vélodrome d'Hiver Stadium

Fishel, his wife, Richla Frydman Taus and their daughters, eighteen year old Resla and ten year old Claudine were arrested in the roundup and deported to Pithiviers on July 16, 1942. Often families were separated and sent in different convoys to concentration camps. The train cars for the convoys were supplied by the Societe Nationale des Chemins de Fer Francais (SNCF), the French national railroad system, under the direct approval of the Vichy government.

Registration at Pithiviers

Fishel and Richla were transported to Auschwitz on July 31, 1942 on Convoy 13. An Auschwitz prisoner registered Fishel as prisoner number 55702 under the name of Fritsch Tous, who was then assigned to be one of the camp's forced laborers. Richla was originally selected for forced labor, but was murdered at the camp on August 5, 1942.

There are no records attesting to the length of time Fishel was actually incarcerated in Auschwitz.

He was transferred, at some point, to the Sachsenhausen-Oranienbourg Concentration Camp about 22 miles north of Berlin. The camp, which primarily held political prisoners, Jehovah's Witnesses,

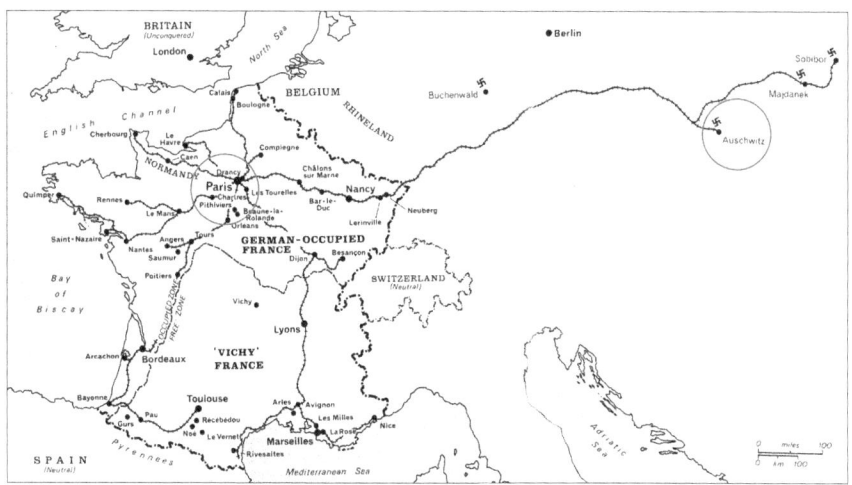

*Train Route from French Internment
Camps to Concentration Camps*

Soviet prisoners of war, Poles, homosexuals, Freemasons, and Jews, was organized as a labor camp. Large work forces worked in the nearby brickwork factories and for the aircraft manufacturer, Heinkel, who built the He177 bombers. Prisoners were "lent out" to other prominent German firms, AEG (Allgemeine Elektricitäts-Gesellschaft AG) and Siemens, to work manufacturing electronic equipment.

From Oranienbourg, Fishel was sent to the Flossenburg Concentration Camp entering the camp on February 6, 1945 under prisoner number 47034. Located in the Fichtel Mountains of Bavaria close to the Czechoslovakian border, Flossenburg was the third largest concentration camp in Germany. The camp had been established in 1938 primarily for the exploitation of forced labor. There, Fishel was assigned to Platting's Kommando (detachment of concentration camp forced labor prisoners). The camp's original purpose was to produce granite for Nazi architectural projects. The inmates marched back and forth to the quarries with minimal protection from the weather

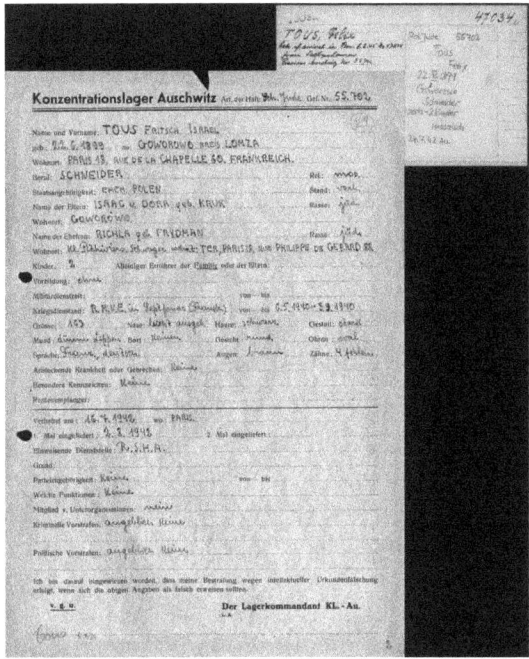

*Fishel's Auschwitz Registration / Transfer Document
to Flossenburg Concentration Camp*

working twelve hours a day in the quarry, moving rocks, digging and other menial physical tasks. They had one break a day when they were fed a small bowl of broth. Many did not survive the ordeal of the quarry.

By 1943, the bulk of the prisoners were shifted to produce the Messerschmitt Bf 109 fighter planes in support of the German war effort.

With the advance of the Allied forces in April 1945, the command hierarchy at Flossenburg, in keeping with Reichsfuhrer-SS Heinrich Himmler's goal: *"not a single prisoner must fall alive into enemy hands"*, ordered around 16,000 inmates on a Death March to avoid their being discovered at a concentration camp. The prisoners went on a brutal march deeper into Bavaria. On May 3, 1945 the United States Army released Fishel from imprisonment at Traunstein,

Forced Labor Flossenburg Concentration Camp

Aircraft Factory Flossenburg Concentration Camp

approximately 175 miles south of Flossenburg. He was repatriated to Paris on June 24, 1945.

Resla Taus was placed on Convoy 14 Train 901-9 on August 3, 1942 from Pithiviers at 6:15 a.m. bound for Auschwitz. She was one of 974 women out of the 1034 Jews deported on that convoy. She did not survive the concentration camp.

Young children were often taken from their mothers, left alone, and ultimately transferred to Drancy for further deportation to Auschwitz. This was Claudine Taus' fate when she was sent from Drancy to Auschwitz on August 24, 1942 in Convoy 23 aboard Train 901-18.

Cousins – Helene Ter, Claudine Taus, Lucienne Ter 1936

Rachel Ter (Fishel's niece), her husband, Abraham Zaliman, a butcher, along with their 5 year old son, Claude Roger lived at 13 rue Jacques Kable. During the roundup, the French police only arrested Abraham, number 50719 du dossier juif (of the Jewish file). He was sent to the internment camp at Drancy for deportation to Auschwitz aboard Convoy 23 – the same convoy as his wife's young cousin, Claudine, on August 24, 1942. Upon arrival at Auschwitz, they were among the 908 out of 1000 people on the transport who were sent to the gas chambers.

Both Elka (Fishel's sister) and Leibel Ter were interned in Drancy on January 1, 1944. According to the original deportation list from Drancy, Card Number AN F9 5734 and the Préfecture de Police Card Number AN F9 5628 and AN F9 5665 they were deported by Convoy 66 which left Drancy on January 20th bound for Auschwitz. Elka and Leibel were among the 864 people out of the 1155 transported who were selected for extermination upon arrival on January 25, 1944.

Deportation From Gare d'Austerlitz to Drancy

Drancy Internment Camp

In January 1942, the Office for Jewish Affairs under the Vichy government dissolved all Jewish community institutions with all their assets being "donated" to the replacement organization, the Union Générale des Israelites de France (UGIF) which had been created by the anti-Semitic politician, Xavier Vallat (1891-1972), the Commissioner-General for Jewish Questions. The purpose of the UGIF was to represent Jews before all authorities particularly in regards to

197

assistance and welfare. All Jews living in France were required join the UGIF. The funding for the UGIF came from a fund generated by the confiscation of Jewish property, from the Commissariat-General for Jewish Affairs, and from the required membership dues.

UGIF Membership Cards
(courtesy YIVO Institute for Jewish Research)

Juliette Stern (1893-1963), who had been the director-general for the French branch of WIZO (Women's International Zionist Organization), was appointed to the UGIF's leadership. She took it upon herself to manage Branch Number 5 of the UGIF which administered dormitories for children "stuck" at Drancy meaning they could not be transferred to a different location or they were homeless children. Branch Number 5 had more children than dormitory capacity. A plan was devised, in direct violation of specific German orders, where former members of WIZO and social workers found hiding places for these additional children with non-Jewish families and institutions.

By 1944, the rescue system had become a well-orchestrated means of saving children destined for deportation. A social worker at the Lucien de Hirsch School, Rachel Ida Lifchitz worked clandestinely as "social assistance" at the UGIF under the direction of Juliette Stern. Rachel Lifchitz accompanied the children selected from Drancy to the train station where she entrusted them to non-Jewish escorts to deliver them to their places of hiding.

After the deportation of her parents to Auschwitz in January 1944, Helene Ter, 15, was taken to Drancy, where she was handed over by the German authorities to the UGIF. Under the tutelage of Rachel Lifchitz, Helene was placed into hiding in Paris.

To ensure the welfare of the hidden children, Juliette Stern manipulated funds to pay a monthly fee for their lodging. Suspicion was cast upon the accounting practices of Branch Number 5. After an investigation conducted by the Gestapo's Jewish department headed by Heinz Rothke, the Gestapo arrested all the employees of UGIF Branch Number 5 except Juliette Stern who avoided being arrested as she was attending a funeral. She then collaborated with members of the underground to kidnap the children from the dormitories.

While 250 children were deported at the end of July 1944 from the dormitories, WIZO was responsible for saving more than a thousand children in total by either placing them in hiding or "kidnapping" them from the dormitories. These children, dispersed to 31 locations, were under the direct care of Rachel Lifchitz.

On the night of April 21, 1944, British/American bombers targeted the La Chapelle marshalling yard to destroy the facility. Marshalling yards are a network of tracks and switches used to sort railroad cars, putting them together to form an entire train with different destinations. The yard was targeted to make it difficult for the Germans to move their Panzer battle tanks by rail to the Normandy coast. The bomber units were instructed not to drop the bombs if they could not readily identify the target in order to avoid killing civilians. However, the entire area was destroyed with 641 people killed and another 377 wounded. Lucienne, Elka and Lieba Ter's daughter, died on April 29, 1944 as a direct result of the bombing.

The deportation of French Jews continued until the last convoy from Drancy to Buchenwald Concentration Camp on August 17, 1944. Approximately 77,000 Jews were deported into locations in Eastern Europe. Most of the deportees perished in the concentration camps, mainly Auschwitz or at other killing centers. Only 2,500 French concentration camp inmates survived the war.

Fishel survived the concentration camps, but at what cost? He returned to Paris, staying with his niece, Rachel, her son, Claude Roger and her younger sister, Helene, instead of living in his pre-war apartment at 60 rue de la Chapelle 18th arrondissement. He had become a mere shadow of the man he had been prior to the invasion of France by Nazi Germany. He was drained, physically and mentally, apparently suffering from depression and loneliness.

Fishel at Rekindling the Flame Ceremony,
Arc de Triomphe, Paris ©Memorial
de la Shoah/coll.UEVCAJ-EA

16 August 1946

Dear Sir and Friend,

I have no other way than to write to you in French for it is the only language that I know.

I am congratulating you on how well you express yourself in French. I would like to be able to do as well in American.

My uncle is in good health. He works a little without too much energy, of course.

You are completely caring to ask about him, which gives him pleasure.

He fixed up the apartment that he had occupied before the war but, continues to stay with me. This is not ideal since I work outside the home and I am already taking care of my little son and my younger sister. But for my uncle, it is better than solitude.

I look forward to hearing from you, dear Sir and about those close to you.

I send you my best wishes.

R. Zaliman

After finishing his studies at the cheder (Jewish primary school for boys), Abraham felt that going away for secondary religious studies at a Yeshiva was not something he wanted to pursue. He wanted to have a secular education to augment his religious education.

The public primary schools in Poland were free and accessible for all children. However, it was not common for Jewish males to attend public school in the small villages. With his desire for further education, Hilda managed to fund hiring the public school principal's son to tutor him in written Polish and secular studies during the summer. After taking an examination, Abraham, at about age 14, was placed into the 3rd grade of Polish public school. At that time, he was one of only three Jewish males to attend public school in Goworowo. Among other courses, languages were a part of the curriculum. Abraham studied French and became relatively fluent.

The family's journey to the United States in 1930 was planned with a departure out of Cherbourg, France. It was common for Polish immigrants to travel by train to depart from either Hamburg or Bremen, Germany, but even as early as 1930, there was a distrust associated with the German people and blatant German anti-Semitism. In order to leave from France, the family had to obtain special

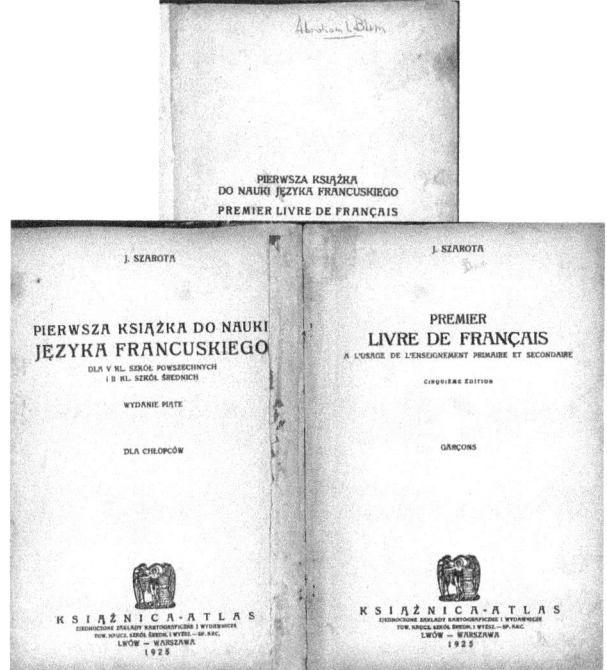

Abraham's Polish French Primer

permission from the Polish immigration authorities. The excuse given to travel via France was that someone who had immigrated to Paris years earlier owed Shalom Joseph money for shoes and the family needed those funds to proceed to the United States. With a few well-placed zloty, the permission was granted.

Departing from Warsaw on Saturday night, June 14, 1930, they traveled by train across Germany into Paris. Upon arrival in Paris, Hilda, Abraham, and Dorothy left Sylvia with the other girls at the Gare du Nord train station for several hours while they went by taxi to visit Fishel at the apartment where he lived with his sister Elka – 88 rue Philippe de Girard. Upon returning to the station, they boarded a train to continue the journey to Cherbourg. Abraham's knowledge of French made the travel through France and visit with Fishel possible.

While pursuing his high school diploma at Harlem Evening High School (graduated January 30, 1936), Abraham continued studying French; knowledge of which he used, once again, in the correspondence with Rachel Ter Zaliman.

Report Card Harlem Evening High School 1932

Union of Russian Jews, Inc.
55 West 42nd Street Suite 952-953
New York 18, NY

Jan. 18, 1946

Miss Ann Blum (Norma)
1451 Wilkins Ave. Apt. 11
Bronx 59, NY

Dear Miss Blum:
We are in receipt of your inquiry regarding the locating of your relatives.

There is now a possibility of locating relatives in Soviet Russia and in places under Soviet occupation, through the Information Bureau of the Soviet Red Cross in Moscow. A separate inquiry should be made out for each person, according to instructions from Moscow. (If inquiry is about family, consisting of husband, wife and children, living at the same address, inquiry can be made in the name of either husband or wife, giving full information about them and, under additional information, mentioning names, ages of other members of family.)

If you want us to make out the inquiry for you in Russian and to mail it (twice) by airmail, registered, with return receipt, to Moscow, please let us have detailed answers to the following questions:

Full first and last name and detailed address in U.S.A. of inquirer.

Information regarding the person sought:

1. *Relationship*
2. *First and last name*
3. *First and last name of father and mother*
4. *Where and when born*
5. *Citizenship*
6. *Profession*
7. *Former address: please state last known address before the outbreak of the war; also later address if the person sought was evacuated or heard from:*
8. *When was the last news received*
9. *Additional information: if any kind of additional information that can help to contact the person sought is available, such as information received through third parties, etc.*

Upon receipt of your answer, enclosing the amount of $1.50 – by check or postal note, covering translation and postage for each inquiry (we repeat: for each person separately), we shall mail you the Russian text in triplicate for your signature and then shall forward it to Moscow.

The Red Cross is supposed to send the answer directly to you and we cannot assume any responsibility for results of inquiry. Sincerely yours,

UNION OF RUSSIAN JEWS, Inc.

The Union of Russian Jews, Inc. was a fraternal organization established in 1945 (to 1960). The main function of the organization was to provide relief for one's relatives in the Soviet Union after World War II. They also provided assistance to those seeking to find their lost ones as evidenced from the correspondence.

1451 Wilkins Avenue
Bronx 59, NY

January 21ˢᵗ, 1946.

Union of Russian Jews, Inc.
55 West 42ⁿᵈ Street
New York 18, NY

Gentlemen:
Thank you for your letter of January 18ᵗʰ, 1946.
Herewith are the answers to your questions required in locating relatives in Soviet Russia.

Inquirer: Miss Norma Blum
*   1451 Wilkins Avenue*
*   Bronx 59, NY – USA*

Information regarding persons sought:

1. *Relationship* — *Sister*
2. *First and last name* — *Rachel Taus or Toja or Blum*
3. *Father and Mother* — *Joseph and Hilda Blum*
4. *Where & when born* — *Goworowo, Poland, 1906 (approximately)*
5. *Citizenship* — *Poland*
6. *Profession* — *Housewife*
7. *Former Addresses:*
   Before the war — *Goworowo, Woj. Bialostok (Province)*
   County of Ostrolenka, Poland

Later address —

8. *When last news received* – *February, 1941*
9. *Additional information:*

Anciel — *40 years* – *Shoemaker* – *husband*
Elka — *20 years* – *Office* — *daughter*
Sara — *16 years* — — *daughter*
Moshe Blum – *34 years* — –*brother*

The last named was last heard from in Feb. 1941 at the Smolensk Hospital.

Thanking you for your prompt attention herein,

Very truly yours,
(Miss) Norma Blum

Union of Russian Jews, Inc.
55 West 42nd Street Suite 952-953
New York 18, NY

Jan. 28, 1946

Dear Mrs. Blum:

We received your letter, mailed on Jan. 22, 1946, with inquiry about your sister. – You forgot to include your check for $1.50.

Please sign the enclosed applications, in ink, in the right hand corner of each sheet, near your typewritten address and return them all to us. We will then send you the number of these applications and the receipt for $1.50 – when we get it from you. Be sure not to make any written remarks on these applications. If necessary, please make them in your letter to us.

It is understood that we do not guarantee results of these inquiries. The answer, if any, will be sent to you directly from Moscow.

Awaiting the return of the signed applications and your remittance for $1.50, we are
Sincerely yours
UNION OF RUSSIAN JEWS, Inc.

1451 Wilkins Avenue
Bronx 59, NY

January 30th, 1946

Union of Russian Jews, Inc.
55 West 42nd Street
New York 18, NY

Gentlemen:

Herewith are the three applications which I have signed as requested by you. Please note that I am "Miss" Blum, and not "Mrs." Blum.

Herewith also find express money order in the sum of $1.50. Thanking you for your attention herein.

Very truly yours,

enc.

Union of Russian Jews, Inc.
55 West 42nd Street Suite 952-953
New York 18, NY

February, 1946
Miss Norma Blum
1451 Wilkins Ave.,
Bronx, 59, NY
Dear Miss Blum:

We received your letter of Jan. 30, 1946, with signed applications, regarding inquiry about your sister. Your applications are #2365; your receipt is #14272, for $1.50.

We noticed that you are Miss and not Mrs. Norma Blum and changed it accordingly.

We mailed these applications to Moscow, on Febr. 2, 1946, and are sure they will reach the Soviet Red Cross. We do not, however, guarantee results of these inquiries. Should you receive a reply, please let us know it, referring to the number of your applications and to the number of your receipt.

Sincerely yours,
UNION OF RUSSIAN JEWS, Inc.

UNITED STATES SENATE
Committee on Military Affairs

March 29, 1946

My dear Abe:

I have your letter of March 25th relative to endeavoring to contact individuals in Poland to see if they are still alive. Unless they are American citizens that cannot be accomplished. It would be my suggestion you write directly to the American Red Cross or even UNRRA here in Washington and it may be possible they have some means of locating the individuals. Our state government will not take any actions whatsoever on alien citizens.

Always cordially,

A.B. Hermann

Abe Linder, Esquire

90 Adams Street

Hoboken, NJ

Abe Linder had been contacted to use his Republican political connections to assist in resolving the enigma of the family's disappearance. Linder approached Howard Alexander Smith (1880–1966), who served as Senator from New Jersey from 1944-1959. Senator Smith was on the Committee on Military Affairs.

The Congressional Directory volume for the 79th Congress, 2nd Session (1946) lists Albert B. Hermann as Senator Smith's secretary. In his official capacity as secretary, Hermann signed the letter on behalf of the Senate's Committee on Military Affairs.

A. B. Hermann had organized the Young Republicans of New Jersey, ran successful campaigns for governors and United States

Senators in New Jersey, and, in 1949, joined the staff of the Republican National Committee where he served as the executive director.

Initially the United States Army command assisted in the administration of the displaced persons camps (DP camps) in the American sector of Germany. If Ruchel Leah, Anschel, Elka, and/or Surcha had been in one of those camps, the Committee on Military Affairs might have been able to obtain the records.

On October 1, 1945, the United Nations Relief and Rehabilitation Administration (UNRRA) took over the responsibility for the administration of the camps with the military continuing to play a role in providing transportation, supplies, and security.

UNRRA was established by a 44 nation conference in Washington on November 9, 1943 to address reconstruction during and after World War II. It was originally created as a branch of the United Nations, but in 1945, became an international organization, originally headed by New York's former governor Herbert H. Lehman, under the jurisdiction of the Supreme Headquarters of the Allied Expeditionary Forces in Europe.

While the activities of the UNRRA were diverse, ranging from administering displaced persons camps to relief for those affected by the war, aid for the recovery of the agriculture industry, and social services, it also allocated funds to deal with the widespread European dislocation. UNRRA was responsible for the repatriation of millions of displaced persons during the war years and, immediately, thereafter.

DAyton 3-4128

1451 Wilkins Avenue
Bronx 59, NY

April 11th, 1946.

U.N.R.R.A.
Washington, D.C.

Gentlemen:

I, Joseph Blum, residing at 1451 Wilkins Avenue, Bronx 59, NY, am a citizen of the United States and was naturalized at the Supreme Court of the State of New York, County of Bronx on September 17th, 1929.

I hereby appeal to your body for any information which you may be able to obtain regarding the whereabouts of my family. I am enclosing herewith a copy of the names and addresses of my family.

Thanking you for your kind attention herein,
Respectfully yours,
enc.

Inquirer: JOSEPH BLUM 1451 Wilkins Avenue Bronx 59, NY

Information regarding persons sought:

10.	*Relationship*	*– Daughter*
11.	*First and last name*	*– Rachel Taus or Toja or Blum*
12.	*Father and Mother*	*– Joseph and Hilda Blum*
13.	*Where & when born*	*– Goworowo, Poland, 1906 (approximately)*
14.	*Citizenship*	*– Poland*

15. *Profession*   – *Housewife*
16. *Former Addresses:*
Before the war   – *Goworowo, Woj. Bialostok*
                                (providence)
                                County of Ostrolenka, Poland
Last known address   – *M. Chernihov*
                                21 Ovetskaya Street
                                Kosow CCP
17. *When last news received*   – *February, 1941*
18. *Additional information:*
Anciel   – *40 years*   – *Shoemaker*   – *husband*
Elka   – *20 years*   – *Office*   – *daughter*
Sara   – *16 years*   –   – *daughter*
Moshe Blum – *34 years*   –   – *brother*
The last named was last heard from in Feb. 1941 at the
Smolensk Hospital, in Russia.

AMERICAN RED CROSS
New York Chapter
315 Lexington Avenue
New York 16, NY

MUrray Hill 4-4455

FOREIGN INQUIRY SERVICE
205 East 42nd Street
New York 17, NY
Room 1201

MUrray Hill 4-4455

April 25, 1946

Mr. Joseph Blum
1451 Wilkins Avenue
Bronx, NY
Re: Family in Poland

Dear Sir:

Your letter of April 11, 1946 addressed to our National Headquarters, Washington, D.C. has been referred to this chapter for reply.

In reply to your request, we regret to advise that the American Red Cross no longer accepts inquiries for any formerly enemy or enemy occupied country in Europe. The Central Location Index, Inc., have taken over these problems.

If you have not already done so, we suggest that you contact one or more of the following agencies of the Central Location Index, Incorporated:

> *World Jewish Congress, 1834 Broadway, New York City*
> *"HIAS" 425 Lafayette Street, New York City*
> *International Migration Service, 122 East 22ⁿᵈ Street N.Y.C.*

We regret our inability to be of service in this instance.

Very truly yours,

GEORGE FELL

Asst. to the Executive Director

By Correspondent, Foreign Inquiry

In 1943, it was recognized that there would be a need for a comprehensive location service with information sharing when the war ended. The Central Location Index (CLI) was established on May 27, 1944 to consolidate data regarding refugees and those still missing. The CLI, a non-government organization (NGO) was a membership corporation which was an amalgamation of various relief organizations – The American Christian Committee for Refugees, Inc., American Friends Service Committee (AFSC), American Federation of International Institutes (AFII), American Jewish Joint Distribution Committee, Inc. (AJDC), Canadian Location Service (CLS), Hebrew Sheltering and Immigrant Aid Society (HIAS), International Rescue and Relief Committee (IRRC), International Migration Service (later called the International Social Service), National Refugee Service, Inc., Service for New Americans, and Unitarian Service Committee (USC). All organizations financed the operations of the CLI with AJDC being the largest contributor.

The CLI charter stated, *"The purpose for which the corporation is formed is to provide a central index for registering the names of, and other information concerning, people displaced as a result of war or other catastrophic causes, and to ascertain the whereabouts or otherwise locate such people so that they, their relatives or friends, or others who may be interested in them may establish mutual contact, all without charge or cost to such person, and to do everything which may be advisable or necessary therefor." History of Central Location Index, Inc.* memorandum by Etta Deutsch, Executive Director Central Location Index May 1949

The World Jewish Congress (WJC) was established in 1936 under the leadership of Stephen S. Wise and Nahum Goldmann. The primary purpose of the organization was to unify the Jewish community and strengthen Jewish political influence to assure the survival of World Jewry. Creating a Jewish state was part of the WJC goals.

At the end of the war, the emphasis of the WJC activities shifted to rebuilding the European Jewish communities. They assisted displaced persons, advocated restitution and reparations from Germany, assisted in punishment of war crimes / crimes against humanity, and were involved in the creation of the State of Israel.

The International Migration Service was an international non-governmental organization founded in 1924. The Service was designed to assist children and families confronted with the problems of migration.

The end of World War II brought in its wake the largest population migrations in European history. Hundreds of thousands of Jews, survivors of the Holocaust, sought secure homes outside their native countries. Many of these people found their way to the displaced persons camps in Germany, Austria, and Italy.

Staff members of the International Migration Service worked in the DP camps assisting the unaccompanied minors and provided tracing services to contact family members in other countries. Reports were regularly issued in an effort to improve the living conditions in the DP camps.

Cooperation among the various components of the CLI was basically non-existent as each organization continued to act as an independent entity.

There are no existing records to indicate that any of these agencies were contacted.

Cyprus Staff Special
Camp 65 D9 Coordya
Frydmann Feige
A.I.G. – C.I.D.
Jerusalem

1948. 30 March

Cyprus

Shalom (idiomatic Hebrew expression for Hello), *my dear friend Neshkale* (Nettie), *you should live and be well,*

Today, I received your letter dated March 15ᵗʰ. Imagine the happiness I felt when I started reading and realized that you were taking such a warm interest in my well-being. I also received the $1 (equates to $11. today) *in your letter for which I am very thankful.*

Dear Neshkale, I will try to answer each of your questions. I also want to thank your husband (Bernard "Bernie" Berliner) *for showing an interest in me, your childhood friend, even though he does not even know me. I am very happy that you are writing about your six-week-old child.*

Neshkale, my life is not describable. I have lost everything. I am so lonely. When a dear friend writes me, I feel proud and reassured of everything in life. I am thankful to Chava Yidis (Mrs. Shulman) *for giving you my address. I wish her all the best that I could possibly wish for myself.*

Neshkale, you asked about my husband, Lazar. Unfortunately he died in 1944 and up to this day I am a widow with two children. One is a ten year old girl, Razale who has grown into a tall girl. My boy, Chaim is fifteen years old and is very handsome.

I do not know anything about the whereabouts of my parents or your brother, Moshe because they took me away from them. In 1940, your brother was together with my parents. When they disappeared, so did he. I find it difficult to describe all of it. But to whom do I have to open my heart and relate all of this?

My brother, Anschel and your sister, Ruchel Leah and both girls – Elka and Surchale were killed in Auschwitz in 1944. I know because I was not too far from them. Therefore, I can relate what happened. I could not believe my eyes. After liberation I went to someone of authority and informed myself (looked for information). *I could not rest.*

A world destroyed – six million people both young and old. The murderers did not spare anybody. How my two children and I survived I cannot describe on a piece of paper. This was the work of God.

The children were with a Christian family and took them out of the German concentration camp. They went through a lot. It was God's will. It is heavy on your heart to be reminded however; the eyes are not dry from crying. When I write to you, I feel as if I am pouring my heart out. I do not have anyone to talk to about this.

What you asked me about what kind of help I need; I do not know what to tell you. I have been in Cyprus now for twelve months, a whole year. I think that my ship, Theodor Herzl will start transporting in about three months.

I am not going to ask you for help while I am in Cyprus. Letters, yes. I will send you the address of my children in the Land of Israel where I can use the things you are going to send me. I can use everything, as I have nothing.

My children left for Israel five months ago. I hear that they are studying well and they are not wanting for anything. The correct address for my children –

> *Frydman Chaim*
> *Kiryat Motzkin*

Beit Yeladim (Ahava)

P.O. Box #4

Palestina

What you have written me about not being lonely and that you are going to help me, I thank you with all of my heart. God will repay you double for your good heart and for giving help to a lonely person.

I am closing this letter. Stay well and strong. From me, your lifelong friend.

Feige Frydman

My children and I send regards to you Neshkale, your husband, and child. Please continue to write us.

Nettie and Bernie Berliner

Like pawns in a game of chess, the NKVD – The People's Commissariat for Internal Affairs moved people to areas which served both the Soviet ideology and war effort. In March 1940,

Feige, Chaim, and Razal were transported to the industrial town of Ostrowiec Kielecki (renamed Ostrowiec Swietokrzyski) in southeastern Poland.

After being captured by the Wehrmacht on September 8, 1939, the town remained occupied by the Germans and was incorporated into the Radom District of the General Government which had been created in German occupied central Poland. While they resided at Rybacka 6 in Ostrowiec, Feige might have worked at the Jeger Works, a brick factory or at the steel mill.

Ostrowiec was a center of a Polish resistance movement against Nazi occupation with an underground production of weapons and a Polish press. The Germans conducted mass arrests, executions, and massacres of Polish citizens to stop the activity of the resistance.

Two ghettos, known as the "Large" and "Small" ghetto, were established in April 1941. By September 1942, Chaim and Razal had left the ghetto. It is conceivable that it was at this time that the children were with the Christian couple Feige refers to in her letter. If we examine her statement *"The children were with a Christian family and took them out of the German concentration camp"*, she may have been referring to the ghetto as a concentration camp or we can look at it more metaphorically in that the children were spared from being prisoners of the concentration camp. In a nation filled with anti-Semites there were honorable and righteous people who risked their own lives to save others.

Liquidation of the large ghetto as part of the Einsatz Reinhard (Operation Reinhard) began on the night of October 11, 1942. Einsatz Reinhard was the codename of the secret German plan to exterminate the Polish Jews in the General Government district of central Poland which was governed by German civil authorities.

This deadly phase of the Holocaust marked the introduction of extermination camps.

The Jewish police ordered everyone in the ghetto to assemble in the Market Square where approximately 15,000 people gathered. A group of Lithuanian Einsatzkommandos (mobile killing squads) wearing JVB armbands (Juden Vernichtungs Bataillon – Jew Extermination Squad) went through the ghetto shooting anyone they found in hiding. They were particularly sadistic when murdering children.

The head of the Gestapo, Bottcher was *"standing at the main square…he was shooting at them with a revolver. Several elegantly dressed women were standing next to him. Bottcher handed the revolver to one of them and taught her to shoot Jews."* Aron Frydenthal, eyewitness

Around 1,000 people were killed during the operation, 1,570 were selected to work and over 10,000 were selected for the death camp in Treblinka. A labor camp was established in the area of the former ghetto. Feige had been selected to work.

On January 16, 1943 there were additional relocations. About 1,000 people were deported to the labor camp in Sandomierz, 150 to the camp in Blizyn, and the balance, Feige among them, to Camp Czenstoszyce to work in the sugar factory which was about ½ mile from the ghetto along the Kamienna River, a tributary of the Vistula River.

Feige with a group of younger Jews managed to escape and join the Polish partisans. She succeeded in July 1944 to reach the village of Podegrodzie about 45 miles southeast of Krakow. It is unknown whether she was betrayed by the partisans who had a reputation of betrayal and murder or if she was picked up in a German roundup. Regardless of the cause, Feige was sent to Auschwitz.

Miraculously, Feige survived. After liberation from Auschwitz by the Soviet Army during the Vistula-Oder Offensive on January 27,

1945 she managed to travel back to Ostrowiec to be re-united with her children.

In later years, Chaim told his son, Sandro Gilboa that he spent his teenage years in a labor camp in Siberia. How did he get to the labor camp if he was with a Christian couple in German occupied Poland? Did the Christian couple flee to Soviet territory and were deported to Siberia? Where was Razal? How did both children get back to Poland and locate their mother? These questions remain unanswered if that were the case.

Feige felt that she had lost her entire family and friends during the war. Other than her children, she had no one with whom to speak about the horrors she had endured. Many other survivors did not want to be reminded about their experience, so she was basically alone with her horrific memories.

With no assets, no home to which she could return, no family to rely upon and the responsibility for the safety and health of her two children, Feige was at a loss as to her next steps. Recognizing that many Jews had been deported as refugees by the Soviet government to Kazakhstan SSR (Soviet Socialist Republic) during the war years, she felt that going to Kazakhstan would be viable option.

According to Document #210187 of the International Committee of the Red Cross, International Research Service in Arolsen (Waldeck) Germany dated September 4, 1959, Feige, Chaim, and Shoshana (Razal's Hebrew name as she was then called) lived in Kazakhstan until 1946. "Mother worked in a bakery. Chaim went to a Russian school. Shoshana was not well."

Postwar Poland was a dangerous place for Jewish survivors. Many who returned to their hometowns were murdered by Poles who feared reclamation of property or homes. Violent acts were perpetrated on other Jewish survivors by anti-communist groups who adhered to the concept that the Jews supported the new Communist regime. During that period Jews were randomly pulled off trains and shot. Forty-two Jews were killed during the Kielce pogrom on July 4, 1946 which broke out after a rumor circulated that a Polish child had been kidnapped by Jews.

By October 1946, Feige joined thousands of Jews who were repatriated from the Soviet Union, those who survived in hiding during the war years, other concentration camp survivors, and those who traveled from central Poland to escape the anti-Jewish violence. They traveled to Reichenbach (Dzierzoniow) in Lower Silesia in western Poland, a former German territory that had been deeded to Poland in the Potsdam Conference of July 1945.

One of the three major towns in the region was Pietrolesie, later named Pieszyce, south of Wroclaw, which had a predominately Jewish population. The region had the reputation of being a hub for survivors where they might reunite with relatives or friends from their original villages. Housing, work, and welfare were provided by various Jewish institutions.

The area was also a center of Zionist activity organizing Habricha (the escape) which was designed to help the survivors escape post-World War II Europe to Palestine which was still under the British administration mandate of July 24, 1922. The escape to Palestine was in direct violation of the British government's White Paper of 1939. The 1939 mandate restricted Jewish immigration to Palestine to 75,000 people over a five year period and had limitations on Jewish land purchases. As a response to the White Paper, there was a tremendous increase in "illegal" immigration to Palestine.

Habricha was conducted with the aid of Jewish agents sent from Palestine, former partisans, and Jewish Brigade soldiers already in place in Italy and Germany. The purpose was singular – to lead the survivors out of the ashes of Europe into the safety of the "Promised Land"- Israel.

With Lower Silesia being close to the Czechoslovakian border, the Habricha worked swiftly to smuggle people out of Poland through Czechoslovakia to the displaced persons camps (DP camps) located in Germany, Austria, and Italy to begin the journey to Palestine.

Both Chaim and Razal were registered as orphans by Feige, as their mother, in the education department of the Central Committee of Jews in Poland (CKZP) in Pietrolesie on October 1, 1946. In Jewish culture, if one parent was deceased, the child was considered to be an orphan.

Frydman Children's Registration in the Education Department of the CKZP

Feige entered her last name on the registration forms as "Kruk", her mother's maiden name. As anti-Semitism was rampant in post-war Poland, she possibly speculated that the use of the Polish surname, Kruk meaning "raven", would be advantageous to her and the children who were listed with their proper surname – Frydman.

Established on November 12, 1944, the CKZP was a state sponsored political organization that represented Polish Jews. Providing care and assistance to Holocaust survivors, the CKZP legally represented the Jews in their dealings with the new Polish government and its agencies. The Committee was also instrumental in working with the Habricha to organize and implement the illegal immigration efforts to Palestine.

There were several calculated advantages to registering Chaim and Razal with the education department of the CKZP. First of all, the registration gave the family access to assistance – housing, schools, care packages from the UNRRA, and day care centers. Secondly, it was via the CKZP that families in western nations and relief organizations could search for Holocaust survivors.

Clandestine missions smuggled thousands of Jews from the area with the ultimate goal of illegally entering Palestine. The illegal immigration was given the code name of Aliyah Bet. Aliyah means "going up", in this case referring to "going up to Jerusalem". Bet, the second letter of the Hebrew alphabet, was used to distinguish it from the limited legal immigration to Palestine permitted under the British White Paper mandate referred to as Aliyah Aleph – the first letter of the alphabet.

The Habricha provided the refugees with false documents, food and shelter while transporting them from town to town and country to country. They crossed borders illegally at night, climbed the high passages of the Tetra Mountains into Austria or the Alps into Italy. They smuggled and bribed in order to succeed. Some groups of refugees were composed of children organized by the Jewish youth movements and Aliyat Hanoar – Youth Aliya (a project of Hadassah Organization).

The organization workers did not collect money for their activities and received no monetary compensation. All funds were used to support the escape from Europe which had become viewed as a "cemetery" of the devastated Jewish community and culture.

Once the immigrant was in a DP camp, generally in Germany or Austria, they were smuggled to an Aliyah Bet transit camp in France or Italy. These camps were often administered by members of the Mossad L'aliyah Bet, a branch of Haganah, to await a ship in an attempt to reach Palestine. The Palyam, a marine branch of the Palmach, the elite fighting force of the Haganah was responsible for the command and sailing of the ships.

The Haganah was an underground military organization in Palestine which, after World War II, among other functions, participated in the illegal transportation of refugees to Palestine. The ships used were small, crowded craft that sailed along the Palestinian shore seeking remote locations to off load their precious cargo – refugees. Most of the ships were intercepted by the British fleet. The passengers were diverted to internment camps on Cyprus, a British colony which was only a day sail from the port of Haifa. Only a few ships managed to penetrate the British blockade and bring their passengers safely ashore.

Recognizing that she and the children had no viable future in Poland as their lives had been destroyed, Feige reasoned that the only alternative for a better life would be to immigrate to Palestine. Under the auspices of the Koordynacja (known as the Coordinatsia – Zionist Coordination for the Rescue of Jewish Children in Poland), Feige, Chaim, and Razal began their "escape" out of Poland.

From Pietrolesie, they were transported to Eschwege, a former German air force base located in the Frankfurt district of American occupied Germany that had been transformed into a DP camp. As children, Chaim and Razal were placed in a branch of the Eschwege camp at the Wolfsbrunnen Castle which was under the administration of the UNRRA while Feige probably stayed in the main Eschwege camp.

Chaim and Shoshana Displaced Persons Camp Cards

In early 1947, David Szirman, a counselor for the Coordinatsia, brought a group including Feige, Chaim and Razal from Eschwege to the Dornstadt children's DP camp near Ulm in southwest Germany. The American military administration in 1946 had given a barracks located on a former German Luftwaffe airfield to serve as the Dornstadt children's DP camp. While Chaim and Razal went to school at Dornstadt, Feige was employed as a kitchen helper.

On the Registration Supplementary Record-Face Sheet for Chaim, dated January 21, 1947, the preparer, R. Reinman recorded *"Chaim is*

Chaim and Shoshana at Dornstadt

a nice boy, quite intelligent, but very thin and pale, Shoshana (Razal) *is rather backward and relies too much on her brother, who tries very hard to hide the fact by making excuses for her."* With all that the children had endured since leaving Goworowo, it is understandable that Chaim would be protective of his younger sister and that Shoshana would rely upon him. Was Shoshana mentally challenged or was she merely a frightened 9 year old little girl facing a stranger speaking to her in a language that she may or may not have fully comprehended?

After having been separated from her children during the war, it must have been a heart wrenching decision for Feige to send her children alone on the journey to Palestine. Yet, she knew life in "the Promised Land" would afford them a future they would not have if they remained in Poland.

In many cases, the trains that originated from DP camps in the American sector of Germany were assisted by the United States military police who guarded the train cars and helped in the disembarkation process by providing truck transport to the transit camps in the area.

The United States Army cooperated with the clandestine operation because the DP camps in the American Zone were overwhelmed past capacity by the thousands of survivors. Whenever there was an opportunity to alleviate the situation by transporting groups of refugees to other destinations or countries, the American forces provided transportation without greatly scrutinizing the presented documents.

On March 22, 1947, the children along with their teachers, as guardians, boarded a train at Ulm for the two hour trip to Munich thus commencing their journey to Palestine. In Munich, the group was transferred to a train bound for France. Their destination was the Chateau des Rhuets near Vouzon in the Loire valley.

At the end of the war, the Chateau welcomed Jewish children from all over Europe who came for refuge and education prior to immigrating to Palestine. Most of these children had lost their entire families during the Holocaust and others had been separated from their families for many years. Chaim's name appears as #137 on a list from the Organisation Internationale Pour Les Refugies as having been at the Chateau des Rhuets. Since his name is the last one on that page we can assume that Shoshana's name appears on the following page. The children departed almost immediately for the 375 mile trip south to Sete, France where they would board the *Theodor Herzl* bound for Palestine.

With the help of members of the ex-French underground, the 1,768 ton metal ship, *Theodor Herzl* (originally a cable laying ship, *Guardian Ex-Ceibar* sailing under the Honduran flag), was made ready for a clandestine voyage to Palestine. Both Chaim and Shoshana's names appear as numbers 96 and 97 respectively on a list designating authorized passengers to Palestine under the authority of the Third Batch of Special Children's Quota dated December 1947.

Sailing with an entirely Spanish crew, the vessel left Sete on April 2, 1947, despite British efforts to prevent her departure. Aboard ship were 2,641 Ma'apilim (illegal immigrants) from two transit camps – one in France and the other in Belgium. The ship was overcrowded with 1800 people accommodated below deck and over 800 on deck. It was scheduled to add an additional 1,000 passengers from Italy but because of technical problems, it was decided to bypass Italy to sail directly to Palestine. A further rendezvous with the ship, *Shear Yashuv* was planned off the coast of Turkey, but this, too, was cancelled because of communication difficulties.

On April 13, 1947, the ship was intercepted by two British Royal Navy ships, destroyer HMS *Haydon* and anti-aircraft frigate HMS *St. Brides Bay*, approximately 16 miles from the coast at Tel Aviv. One of the most intense battles of the Aliya Bet operation ensued with three of the immigrants being killed and 27 wounded. The captured *Theodor Herzl*, surrounded by five British destroyers, was brought into Haifa Bay.

Theodor Herzl

Banners were hung on the ship's hull which read "YOU JOINED THE NAVY TO CHASE ORPHANS" and "THE GERMANS DESTROYED OUR FAMILIES & HOMES DON'T YOU DESTROY OUR HOPE". The sick and wounded were interned at the Atlit detention camp about 12 miles south of Haifa. The remaining passengers disembarked, went through a disinfection procedure, and were herded on a British ship for immediate deportation to the Cyprus detention camps.

The *Theodor Herzl* remained in Haifa harbor as part of the "shadow fleet" (commandeered illicit immigration ships) until the creation of the State of Israel in 1948 when she was put back into service to legally transport immigrants to Israel.

Ma'apilim from Theodor Herzl

It is inconclusive as to the exact route Feige took to board an illegal ship bound for Palestine. Leaving Dornstadt approximately the same time as the children, Feige traveled with the Habricha to a transit camp near Metaponto in Southern Italy where she boarded the *Moledet* as one of 1,577 Ma'apilim (1023 men, 513 women, 41 children). Formerly a 749 ton cargo steamer built in 1876, as the *San Felipe* she had previously plied among the fjords of Norway. The *Moledet* known also as the *Patria,* meaning Homeland, had been fitted for this voyage in Sweden and in Marseille, France. The name commemorated the original *Patria* who lost hundreds of immigrants in a drowning in November 1940 while in the port of Haifa during a Haganah sabotage mission intended to save those immigrants from deportation.

Under the command of Palyam member, Fabi Gever, with additional Palyam members aboard as escorts to assist the immigrants, the *Moledet* sailed under a Panamanian flag on March 23, 1947. It became apparent, immediately upon departure that the vessel was

listing to one side due to the stormy weather and the overcrowded decks. On March 29th, a British reconnaissance plane spotted the ship. When the *Moledet* was about 30 miles off the coast of Palestine on March 30th, she began sending distress signals – water was penetrating the ship after a severe engine failure and the ship was in danger of sinking. British destroyers, HMS *Haydon* and HMS *Charity*, along with the mine sweep ship, HMS *Octavia*, and the anti-aircraft frigate, HMS *St. Brides Bay* arrived. An engineering crew was sent aboard to correct the engine failure. The British evacuated half of the passengers taking them via their ships to the port in Haifa. The remaining refugees stayed on board the *Moledet* while the ship was towed into the port on March 31st.

The immigrants, after showing passive resistance, were loaded onto the deportation ships, HMT *Empire Rival* and HMT *Ocean Vigor*, for transport to the internment camps on Cyprus.

The frustration level of seeing the Promised Land yet, like Moses, being denied entry must have been astronomical. In Deuteronomy 34:4 God said to Moses, *"I have let you see it with your eyes, but you will not cross over into it"*. To be turned away, particularly after all that the refugees had endured, created feelings of anxiety, fear, and hopelessness beyond our comprehension.

Navy News Moledet *May 2008*

The Cyprus internment camps were run by the British government to detain those who had illegally attempted to immigrate to Palestine. There were 12 camps on the island which operated from August 1946 to January 1949 holding 53,510 people. Operated similarly to POW camps, the British imposed military rule and surrounded each camp with barbed wire, watchtowers, armed military police and over 2,000 British personnel.

Cyprus detainees were legally allowed into Palestine at the rate of 750 per month. During 1947-48, additional special quotas were allocated for pregnant women, nursing mothers and the elderly. Following Israeli independence on May 14, 1948, the British began to deport the Cyprus detainees to Israel at the rate of 1,500 per month.

Camp conditions were deplorable. The inmates were packed in tents, huts and shacks which were designed to accommodate no more than 10,000 people. They suffered from the extremes of weather, had poor sanitary conditions, and little fresh water.

The Joint Distribution Committee (JDC) became involved in the welfare operations of the camps. Medical and welfare teams were recruited from Palestine to run nurseries and clinics. JDC improved the quality of the food rations and supplemented the basic food supplies, catered to religious requirements, and set up a bureau to assist in searching for missing relatives. JDC in partnership with Youth Aliya took on the task of providing educational facilities with teachers recruited from among the refugees.

Hotel Cyprus

234

There were two types of camps on Cyprus – "summer camps" of which there were five where the detainees were housed in tents and seven "winter camps" composed of tin huts and some tents. Most children were placed in the winter Camp 65 known as the Children's Village located at Dekalia. When Chaim and Shoshana arrived in Cyprus about a month after Feige's arrival, there is evidence from a Camp listing that they were living in Camp 65. The name "Feige Frydman" does not appear on any available list, but she gave "Camp 65" as the return address on her letter.

By December 1947, Feige was, once again, separated from her children who had been cleared for immigration to Palestine. Reference card #23988 indicates that they "left for Palestine from Cyprus in Dec. 1947". In 1947, the British decided that they would no longer finance the passage of released refugees from Cyprus to Palestine which forced outside agencies to pay for the transport. The Jewish Agency leased a few ships among which was the *Andrea*. A debarkation list from the ship dated

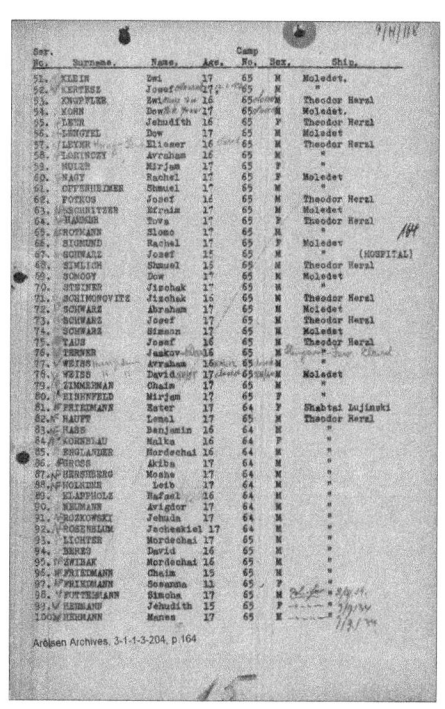

*Cyprus Internment Camp
Listing #96 &97*

December 12 1947 verifies that Chaim and Shoshana were transported to Palestine as unaccompanied orphans. Upon arrival in Haifa, they were taken about five miles north of the city to Kiryat Bialik, part of the Haifa District. They lived in the Ahava Beit Yeladim (Children's House of Love) – a facility for children coming from distressed family backgrounds which included orphans.

Founded in Berlin in 1914, originally as a soup kitchen for Jewish children, Beit Ahava for Children and Youth evolved, by 1922, into a residence for children located in the backyard of the Great Synagogue. Beate Berger, a nurse from Frankfurt, accepted the responsibility of establishing the care facility. With the rise of anti-Semitic assaults in Germany by 1933, Beate Berger was among the first to recognize the dangers for the Jewish community. She collected donations to enable the transition of Beit Ahava from Berlin to Palestine. The first group of children departed for Palestine in April 1934. Construction of the facility began immediately at Kiryat Bialik in the Zevulun Valley. Ahava Beit Yeladim formally opened in 1935.

In 1938, Beate Berger managed to transport the remaining staff and children from Beit Ahava in Berlin to the safety of Palestine. Between 1934 and 1940, Beate Berger saved the lives of 300 children by bringing them out of Germany, Austria, Italy, Lithuania, and Poland to Ahava Beit Yeladim. At the institution, the children lived in social groups, received psychological and social assistance, and education – traditional, cultural and agricultural farming. The facility, after the war, continued to admit orphans and Holocaust survivors under the auspices of Youth Aliyah. To this day, Ahava Children and Youth Village continues to operate as a facility to care for children ages 6-18 whose life circumstances have led them to live outside their family homes.

There is an inexplicable error in the children's address as written by Feige and the accurate address for the Ahava Beit Yeladim. While P.O. Box #4 is correct, she listed the town as Kiryat Motzkin. Located

5 miles north of Haifa, the four Krayot (townships) – Kiryat Motzkin, Kiryat Bialik, Kiryat Yam, and Kiryat Ata were in a cluster in the Haifa Bay area. The Ahava Beit Yeladim facility was in Kiryat Bialik which is located approximately 1½ miles away from Kiryat Motzkin. The P.O. Box currently in use is the same #4 as when the facility was originally established in Palestine.

After the multiple periods of separation, by the end of 1948, Feige was permanently reunited with her children in Haifa, Israel.

3 February 1949

Haifa, Israel

My dear friend,

I received your letter of 4 January 1949. Thank you very much. I am trying to respond promptly. When I re-read your letter, I was encouraged by your positive words for the future. All of the hope and encouragement is more than a mother would give.

I want to clarify something for you. Namely – parcels that come from the United States are inspected and the money that you included in the package was not there. Neshkale, do not include money in the packages. In regards to the food parcel, I did not receive it as of yet. I believe that it will arrive soon and will be a great help to us. For this, I thank you very much.

I am happy to tell you that I now have a room where the children and I can live together. I work in a factory where I earn one pound a day ($4.03 a day). It is a small amount of money but I manipulate to get by.

I really did not want to burden you with my situation but you expressed interest in how I live and under what conditions. Therefore, I am describing it for you.

While I sit and write this letter, I am looking at the picture you sent of your parents. It reminds me of many pleasurable occasions and I thank you for sending it. I wish them a long, healthy, happy life. Thank you for all the help you are giving me.

I am puzzled as to why you do not look healthy and robust in your picture. When you left Poland, you had more weight. You have to improve your health. Sylvia does not look bad. Norma appears to be undernourished. Your husband is handsome and looks kindly. Why was Itzchok not in the picture? Your mother is looking very good. Also why is Dorothy not in the picture? I would like to see a current picture of those not in the one you sent.

Accidentally I found out the news that Malkie Kuperman (Baruch Kuperman's daughter) *will be coming to Israel. You may want to send me a letter with her.*

With this I am ending this letter. I wish you all good health and happiness.
Your best friend,
Feige and children

I completely forgot – why is Sylvia's husband not in the picture?

I am including my daughter, Shoshana's (Razal's Hebrew name) *picture. In my next letter, I will send you a picture of my son.*

Shoshana Frydman

Dorothy, Abraham, Norma, and Nettie

Hilda and Shalom Joseph Blum

28 April 1949
Ramla, Israel
(Lamedstrasse 6, Ramla)

My dear Neshkale, husband, and daughter –
may you live and be well,

I, with my two children, thank you very much for the food parcel. It arrived in time for Passover (April 13-21, 1949). Such parcels always come in handy however, for the holidays, it is even better.

Neshkale, you can believe me that I never anticipated that I would live in such abnormal times. I never imagined that in Eretz Yisrael (Land of Israel) *there would be a shortage of food. I received the package when I was not feeling well so it was impossible for me to send a reply. Today, I feel fine so now I am writing this letter. May God repay you for all you have done.*

There is no new news right now. I have received from you three large containers of meats and one small can of meat, three cans with fish, two packages of cheese, two tins of butter, one can of milk, two kilos of sugar, two boxes of raisins and one kilo of dried milk.

Neshkale, when we receive a package, we have to pay a fee so please pre-pay the fee. It will make it easier for us.

Regards to your parents, sisters, and brother.

From me, your friend, I thank you a lot,

Feige Frydman

I wish you good health and financial success.

Do not forget us in the future.

Neshkale, you may wonder why I am in Ramla. The reason

is that I am supposed to do lighter work. I work in a barbershop in Ramla. We hope it will work out.

Please reply and do not forget my children and me.

During the years of the Holocaust, the symbolism of Passover, the holiday commemorating freedom from Egyptian slavery, was an important milestone in the calendar for all Jews throughout occupied Europe. They were alive. They prayed for redemption from the yoke of death.

"...The urge to observe the generations-long tradition was also great; it became a symbol of the existence of the Jewish people for me...It seemed to me that the souls of my nearest and dearest would come to me, the souls of those who had been torn away from me and killed in such a terrible way....I wanted to ask their pardon for clinging so tightly to life when they were no longer with me, for forgetting them in moments of my own physical pain and torture....It was the first Seder since the aktsyes (roundup of Jews), *the deportations, and selections of 1942."* Binyomin Ornshtayn –"Passover: Under the Rule of Hitlerite Tyranny" *The Destruction of Otvotsk, Falenits, Kartshev* translated by Jack Kugelmass and Jonathan Boyarin *From a Ruined Garden – The Memorial Book of Polish Jewry* 1983

The food package from Nettie must have been like "manna (miraculous source of food) from heaven" for Feige. Passover 1949 was particularly significant for the Frydman family being, for the first time united, in their new home – Israel. As written in the Haggadah (the text that recounts the events of the Exodus and the order of the Seder -Passover meal), *"next year we will be in the land of Israel; this year we are slaves, next year we will be free people."* Feige and the children had been released from the horrific terror of Nazi bondage, British internment, the uncertainty of post-war Europe and were now free in the Land of Israel.

Immediately after gaining independence, the newly established State of Israel faced many economic challenges. The country while recovering from the aftermath of the War of Independence had absorbed a tremendous increase in population due to the influx of European refugees, had a limited supply of food and hard foreign currency.

In April 1949, the government announced that food, clothing and all essential provisions would be rationed. The plan called for a reduction in the cost of living and an effort to use local produce thus saving foreign currency. Nutritional experts developed a balanced diet of 2700–2800 calories. Ration books with coupons were issued. The monthly coupons allowed for: 9 lbs. of potatoes; 2 oz. of beets; 5 eggs per child and 2 per adult; 3.5 oz. of coffee; 2 oz. of tea; 9 oz. of chicken/meat. The rationing bolstered a flourishing Black Market which traded in food products.

Gifts of food products from overseas were cherished. The government imposed an import fee on these gifts.

Ramla is located in Central Israel between Jerusalem and Tel Aviv about 74 miles south of Haifa.

5 December 1949

Ramla, Israel

My dear friend Neshkale, husband, and child,

I wonder why I did not receive a letter from you. What is the reason for it? Why are you mad at me? I have done nothing I am aware of – I owe nothing to anyone, only my soul to God.

Everything is the way it was. May God make it possible for things to improve. So many different times I have lived through and now we have to suffer again as a widow with children. You have to worry about everything and you cannot find suitable employment. I am broken and sickly from the tragic war. Everything hurts. Every now and then something else hurts. I do not get any help from my brothers (Fishel and Zisket). *They have forgotten their sister.*

A heartfelt regards to your parents, sisters, and brother. My children send their regards.
Feige Frydman

Feige, while she survived the Holocaust, was a victim of the Holocaust. She lived but, at what toll – both physically and mentally? While her children gave her the will to survive, her spirit had been broken!

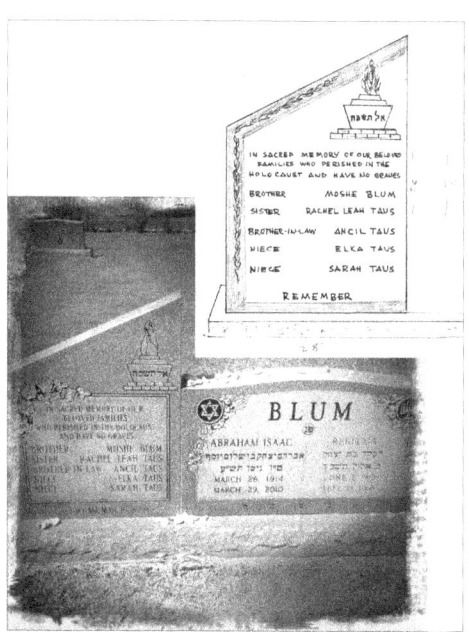

Memorial Monument Corpus Christi, Texas

They were all Desaparecidos, victims of the Holocaust. Ruchel Leah, Anschel, Elka, Surcha, Moshe, and millions of others had fallen into a deep crevice, disappearing forever.

They will always be remembered.

Coming from obscurity to a position of ultimate power, Adolf Hitler galvanized an entire nation with his rhetoric of hate which culminated in the commitment of mass genocide.

Holocaust survivor, author Primo Levi (1919-1987) warned that *"it happened, therefore it can happen again: this is the core of what we have to say. It can happen, and it can happen everywhere."*

Mankind must never allow a repetition of the Holocaust.

El Maleh Rachamim (God Full of Compassion) – Prayer for the Soul of the Departed
Transliteration:

Al molay rachamim, shochayn bam'romim, ham-tzay m'nucha n'chona al kanfay Hash'china, b'ma-alot k'doshim ut-horim k'zo-har haraki-a mazhirim, et nishmat Ruchel Leah bas Shalom Yosef, Anschel ben Itche Yosel, Elka bas Anschel, Sura bas Anschel, Moshe ben Shalom Yosef, kol hanosfim b'shoah she-halach l-olomo, ba-avur shenodvu tz'dakah b'ad hazkarat nishmata. B'Gan Ayden t'hay m'nuchata; la-chayn Ba-al Harachamim yas-tire-ha b'sayter k'nafav l'olamim, v'yitz-ror bitz-ror hacha-yim et nishmatah, Ado-nay Hu na-chalatah, v'tanu-ach b'shalom al mishkavah. V'nomar: Amayn.

God, full of compassion, who dwells in the heights, provide a sure rest upon the Divine Presence's wings, within the range of the holy, pure and glorious, whose shining resemble the sky's, to the soul of Ruchel Leah daughter of Shalom Joseph, Anschel son of Itche Yosel, Elka daughter of Anschel, Surcha daughter of Anschel, Moshe son of Shalom Joseph, and all who perished in the Holocaust for a charity was given to the memory of their souls. Therefore, the Master of Mercy will protect them forever, from behind the hiding of his wings, and will tie their soul with the rope of life. The Everlasting is their heritage, and they shall rest peacefully upon their lying place, and let us say: Amen.

Through the myriad of narratives which presented a microcosm of the Holocaust, in *The Spirit of Ruchel Leah*, we are honoring the legacy of all who were victims. We are ALL the descendants of *The Spirit of Ruchel Leah*. We will continue to carry the heritage of hope, courage and perseverance.

We will never forget!

Appendix A

Major United States Immigration Laws
1790-1965

YEAR	NAME OF LEGISLATION	HIGHLIGHTS OF LEGISLATION
1790	Naturalization Act of 1790	The country's first naturalization law that provided citizenship to "free white persons" after two years of residence if they would demonstrate good moral character and swear allegiance to the Constitution. Note: this law addresses only naturalization not immigration
1798	Alien and Sedition Acts	Four laws contained numerous immigration enforcement provisions such as: residency requirement for citizenship increased to 14 years (appealed in 1802); authorized the President to deport any resident immigrant considered "dangerous to peace and safety of the United States" (2 year expiration date); authorized the President to apprehend, restrain and deport resident aliens if their home countries were at war with the United States (this provision is still in force)

1864	Immigration Act of 1864	This act established the Commissioner of Immigration under the auspices of the Secretary of State. It confirmed the enforceability of labor contracts made by immigrants outside the United States
1870	Naturalization Act of 1870	The naturalization process was extended to aliens "of African nativity and to persons of African descent"
1875	Page Act of 1875	The first Federal immigration law which prohibited the entry of undesirables such as Asians entering the United States as contract laborers; it imposed fines on those imported laborers from oriental countries "without their free and voluntary consent, for the purpose of holding them to a term of service"
1882	Chinese Exclusion Act	This is the first attempt at regulating immigration along racial lines; it was a "response to racism and to anxiety about threats of cheap labor from China". It restricted immigration of Chinese laborers for 10 years and prohibited Chinese naturalization. It also provided deportation procedures for illegal Chinese
1882	Immigration Act of 1882	This law imposed a 50 cent head tax upon arrival of non-citizens to fund expenses of regulating immigration by the Treasury Department. It is also the first time that the concept of likely to become a public charge was promulgated to restrict immigration

1891	Immigration Act of 1891	This law established the Bureau of Immigration within the Treasury Department. It empowered the "superintendent of immigration to enforce immigration laws" and allowed deportation of unlawful aliens
1903	Anarchist Exclusion Act	Those deemed inadmissible to the United States were increased to include anarchists, people with epilepsy, beggars, and importers of prostitutes
1907	Immigration Act of 1907	This act increased those restricted from immigration to certain classes of disabled and diseased people
1917	Immigration Act of 1917	This law established an "Asiatic Barred Zone" (Barred Zone Act) Asiatic Barred Zone" and expanded the list of grounds of inadmissibility to include those previously deported and a literacy test for those 16 and older
1921	Emergency Quota Act	This act limited immigration based on admission quotas based on nationality of those in the United States as per the 1910 census
1924	Johnson-Reed Act	This law imposed the first permanent numerical limitation on immigration at 165,000 as well as changed the national origins formal and the reference year from 1910 to 1890. Students, nationals from the Western Hemisphere countries, members of certain professions, wives and children of United States citizens were exempted from the quotas

1942	Magnuson Act	This act appealed the Chinese Exclusion Acts and allowed Chinese nationals to become US citizens; a quota of 105 new Chinese immigrants were allowed in the United States per year
1948	Displaced Persons Act of 1948	This act allowed over 200,000 individuals displaced from their homelands by Nazi persecution to immigrate and granted permanent residence status to those already residing in the United States who met the definition of displaced person
1952	Immigration & Nationality Act (Hart-Cellar Act)	While maintaining the national quota system, it consolidated several immigration laws. It set a quota for aliens with skills needed in the United States and assigned quotas to Asian nations. It reverted control of visa authorization to US consular officers. It increased the ability to deport those suspected of Communist sympathies national origins quota system and replaced it with a system based on relationships to a US citizen, lawful permanent resident, family member or a US employer. Though there were caps on overall immigration, no limits were imposed on the number of "immediate family members" admitted annually. Immigrants from Western Hemisphere were capped at 120,000 annually
1965	Immigration & Nationality Act	This act replaced the national origins quota system (Hart-Cellar Act)

Appendix B

The Immigration Act of 1924 (Johnson-Reed Act)
May 26, 1924

Sec. 1. That this Act may be cited as the "Immigration Act of 1924."

Sec. 2. (a) A consular officer upon the application of any immigrant . . . may . . . issue to such an immigrant an immigration visa which shall consist of one copy of the application provided for in section 7, visaed by such consular officer. Such visa shall specify (1) the nationality of the immigrant; (2) whether he is a quota immigrant (as defined in section 5) or a non-quota immigrant (as defined in section 4); (3) the date on which the validity of the immigration visa shall expire; and (4) such additional information necessary to the proper enforcement of the immigration laws and the naturalization laws as may be by regulation prescribed.

[The act then goes on to prescribe photographs, notation on the passport of the number of visa, when such visas are not to be issued, the fees for visas.]

[Sections 3, 4, and 5 then define the terms "immigrant," "non-quota immigrant," and "quota immigrant."]

* Enumeration of Preferences within quotas: time for giving preferences; percentage of preferences.

Sec. 6. (a) Immigration visas to quota immigrants shall be issued in each fiscal year as follows: (1) Fifty per centum of the quotas of each nationality for such year shall be made available . . . to the following classes of immigrants, without priority of preference as between such classes: (A) Quota immigrants who are the fathers or mothers of citizens of the United States . . . or who are the husbands of citizens of the United States by marriages occurring on or after May 31, 1928 of citizens who are citizens of the United States who are twenty-one years of age or over; and (B) in the case of any nationality the quota of which is three hundred or more, quota immigrants who are skilled in agriculture, and the wives, and the dependent children under the age of eighteen years, of such immigrants skilled in agriculture, if accompanying or following to join them. (2) The remainder of the quota of each nationality for such year . . . shall be made available in such year for the issuance of immigration visas to quota immigrants of such nationality who are the unmarried children under twenty-one years of age, or the wives, of alien residents of the United States who were lawfully admitted to the United States for permanent residence. . .

Sec. 7. [Gives an elaborate description of duplicate application of visas and the form of visas, copies to be kept for records, statements required as to membership in classes of aliens excluded, statements as to exemptions from exclusion and the various verifications as to signatures, ages, fees paid, etc.]

Sec. 8. [Covers when a consular official may issue a non-quota immigration visa.]

Sec. 9. [Covers the issuance of non-quota visas and quota visas to relatives.]

Sec. 10. (a) Any alien about to depart temporarily from the United States may make application to the Commissioner of Immigration and Naturalization for a permit to reenter the United States stating the length of his intended absence, and the reasons therefor.

[Subsections (b)-(g) detail the issuance of reentry permits, their fees, effects, and treaty-merchant reentry permits.]

Sec. 11. (a) The annual quota of any nationality shall be 2 per centum of the number of foreign-born individuals of such nationality resident in continental United States as determined by the United States census of 1890, but the minimum quota of any nationality shall be 100.

[Subsections (b)-(g) detail how national origin is determined, presidential proclamation of quotas, monthly issuances of visa limits, and the issue of visas to non-quota immigrants.]

Sec. 12. (a) For the purpose of this Act nationality shall be determined by country of birth, treating as separate countries the colonies, dependencies, or self-governing dominions for which separate enumeration was made in the United States census of 1890 and which was not included in the enumeration for the country to which such colony or dependency belonged. . . .

[Subsection (b) requires the secretaries of state and commerce, with the attorney general, to issue jointly statements as to the numbers of the various nationalities as of the census of 1890. Subsection (c) covers the effects of changes in the political boundaries of foreign countries; (d) and (e) cover the issuance of monthly statements and the proclamation of quotas available.]

Sec. 13. (a) No immigrant shall be admitted . . . unless he (1) has an unexpired immigration visa . . .; (2) is of the nationality specified in the visa; (3) is a non-quota immigrant if specified in the visa as such; (4) is a preference-quota immigrant if specified . . . as such; and (5) is otherwise admissible under the immigration laws.

[Subsection 13(b) covers such details as readmission of aliens without visas.]

(c) No alien ineligible to citizenship shall be admitted to the United States unless such alien (1) is admissible as a non-quota immigrant under the provisions of subdivisions (b), (d) or (e) of section 4, or (2) is the wife, or the unmarried child under 18 years of age, of an immigrant admissible . . ., and is accompanying or following to join him, or (3) is not an immigrant as defined in section 3. . . . (e) No quota immigrant shall be admitted under subdivision (d) if the entire number of immigrant visas which may be issued to quota immigrants of the same nationality for the fiscal year has already been issued. . .

Sec. 14. [Covers deportation procedures for alien children under age sixteen.]

Sec. 15. [Covers the maintenance of exempt status.]

Sec. 16. [Covers when it is unlawful to bring to the United States by water an alien, including the fines or prison penalties thus engendered.]

Sec. 17. [Covers the commissioner of Immigration and Naturalization's authority to issue rules and regulations to implement the act.]

Sec. 18. If a quota immigrant of any nationality having an immigration visa is excluded from admission to the United States under the immigration laws and deported, or does not apply for admission to the United States before the expiration of the validity of the immigration visa, or if any alien of any nationality having an immigration visa issued to him as a quota immigrant is found not to be a quota immigrant, no additional immigration visa shall be issued in lieu thereof to any other immigrant.

Sec. 19 & 20. No alien seaman excluded from admission . . . shall be permitted to land . . . except temporarily for medical treatment, or pursuant to such regulations as the Attorney General may prescribe for the ultimate departure, removal, or deportation of such alien from the United States.
[Subsequent sections and subsections detail the detention of seamen on board vessels, penalties, evidence of failure to detain or deport, deportation procedures, preparation or use of documents and the offenses in connection with forging, counterfeiting, immigration visas or permits, false statements, and so on.]

[Sec. 21 & 22. Details official documentation and offenses in connection with forgeries, counterfeits, and alterations.]

Sec. 23. Whenever any alien attempts to enter the United States the burden of proof shall be upon the alien to establish that he is not subject to exclusion under any of the provisions of the immigration laws.

[Sections 24 to 32 essentially repeat prior law as to steamship line fines, prevention of alien landings, and so on of the Immigration Act of 1917.] Source: 43 Stat. 153; 8 U.S.C. 201.

Appendix C

Goworowo Memorial Book

Published by The Goworowo Societies in
Israel, United States & Canada

A Walk Through the Shtetl – Excerpts

Translated by Sandra Chiritescu

Goworowo was connected to the big world via two train stations along the Warsaw-Lomza line: Pasek and Goworowo, and also via three main roads which led towards Ostrow Mazowiecka, Rozan, and Ostroleka. The distance from Goworowo to Warsaw was 90 kilometers, and to Lomza 60 kilometers. The Hirsh River, a run-off from the Narew River, cut through the shtetl coming from the southern side and separated it from the village of Wolka (*Wólka Brzezińsk*), which also had Jewish residents.

The Szczawin estate was located at a distance of about 2 kilometers. It belonged to the wealthy nobleman, Glinko. North of the shtetl was the village Goworówek: not far from there was the Rembish estate, which was for a certain period of time was owned by the Jewish noblemen Stein and Fein who were from Jedwabne. Aside from the

257

estates mentioned above, the shtetl was surrounded by the following estates: Zambrzyce, Ponivke, Brzeźno, Suchcice, Gucin, Czernie, Kruszewo, Jawory, Danilowo, Pakshevnitse, and others.

When you entered the shtetl on the main street and crossed the bridge you were greeted on the left side by the impressive, red brick prayer house. …

The Other Side of Long Street

The corner house on the other side of Long Street belonged to Reb Bertshe Viroslav, a wheat merchant who was among the cheerful Aleksander Hasidim. He never earned enough to make a living and loved Kiddush and the meal after the Sabbath *(considered the fourth meal of the day)*.…

There was another house where Reb Itche Yosel Taus, the gravedigger lived with his wife, Dvora. He was a leader of the burial society along with his son-in-law, Lazar Frydman, a baker. A little further, where the street bordered Ratenski's fruit garden, lived Reb Sholem Greyner, a locksmith who with his three sons are today in Israel. Next to them lived Yekl Markus, a peddler.

At the front, in a brick building, lived Reb Avrom Luzim, a smith who raised cows and sold their milk for additional income. Thanks to his efforts with his relative Sura Girl Klas in the United States, she sent large sums of money which allowed the building of the new big synagogue. On the eastern wall of the synagogue, a special plaque was hung in her honor. …

Nest to them, at the front, lived the widow of the shoemaker, Blum, who died in America *(at the time Hilda Blum was living in Goworowo, she was not a widow. Shalom Joseph Blum had immigrated to the United States in 1923. She followed with the minor children in*

1930. Shalom Joseph died in Fort Worth, Texas on May 7, 1959). Her son-in-law, Anschel Taus, a first rate shoemaker, quiet and intelligent person died in a German concentration camp next to Lublin….

…In the neighboring apartments lived Shimen Vaser, a wood turner; the wheelwright, Reb Leybl Karlinski, a Gerer Hasid whose three sons and one daughter were killed by the Germans with one daughter who lives in Israel; and Avzik Rubin, the butcher. They all lived in the house of Reb Yankev Shapse Trukhnavski and his son-in-law Reb Avrom Shafran. Reb Avrom was among the respected men in the shtetl, an Otwocker Hasid, learned, wise, and intelligent man. He had a colonial store which was among the biggest in Goworowo…. Reb Avrom's two other sons, Moshe and Dovid were killed by the Germans. His first born, Binyumen and Mendel, as well as Itche, a student at the Lomza Yeshiva, a pedagogue and leader of the Beit Yaakov School live in the United States today….

In a small house lived Mordechai Sierota a tailor from Makov, the son-in-law of Avrom (*Avromka Solka*), the synagogue sexton. He bought this house from Shmuel Volf Broyner, a soldier in the Polish army who made his way to Goworowo after World War I…

Mikhl *(Max)* Schmeltz who later died in the United States. His children live in America (*Aaron, Hymie, Reuben, and Abe Schmeltz*) and Brazil (*Sura and Rivka Schmeltz*) today….

The Market

… In the neighboring two-story house lived Itche Solka, the son of Avromka, the synagogue sexton, who had returned from Cuba and opened a shoe store; … At the top Reb Avrom Solka had his apartment the last few years. He was the usher of the Rabbinic court. He was a small Jew from Zhvave with a long beard. He was a big

THE SPIRIT OF RUCHEL LEAH

shot, mixed up in the town's affairs and knew everyone's secrets. He was among the most capable matchmakers in the area. Later when his children from the United States generously supported him, he did not forego the post of the Rabbinic court's usher....

Probostwo

On a big square across from the church stood a big brick building where the Polish People's House stood and the first Christian cooperative which was in intense competition with the Jewish merchants. A little deeper into the field was the Christian cemetery....

From the Probostwo a path leads towards the fence of the Christian nobleman, Glinko's residence, a palace in the estate, Szczawin. He was one of the wealthiest men in Poland and many Jews from Goworowo and the surrounding area conducted large business transactions and generated their income from him.

On the way back to the shtetl ...there was the city's post office and next the shtetl's police headquarters. After the house of the Christian town doctor, Glinko stood the big parish church and the priest's palace...

The Other Side of the Market

...In a nice two story building, Reb Moshe Tenenboym had his hotel and restaurant. He was president of the community for many years and an activist in the Mizrahi party....

...In the courtyard there was the new big synagogue that was built in the year 5685 *(1924/25),* the old wooden synagogue, the Talmud Torah, the Aleksander and Gerer prayer houses, the Beit Yaakov School, the interest free loan bank, and the welcoming office *(where strangers to the shtetl were welcomed).* ...

260

Appendix D

Bulletin 1 – The Tragedy of the Shtetl Goworowo
© Wiener Holocaust Library Collections, 532/1.
Translated by Sandra Chiritescu

Committee for Collecting Material on the Destruction of "Jewish Communities in Poland in 1939"
Bulletin   Number I   December 1, 1939

(All materials published in the committee's bulletins have been gathered by responsible community activists, written down during interviews with credible narrators, and strictly fact-checked.)

The Tragedy of the Shtetl Goworowo (Govorove) (Ostroleka District, Bialystok Voivodeship)

A Jewish woman X from Rozan (Ruzshan) on the Narew River narrates.

"On Tuesday, September 5th, at 4 o'clock in the morning, a German plane dropped bombs on the shtetl Rozan where I lived and had a shop. I myself saw two bombs fall. One fell down on Brikgas (Bridge Street), next to the public elementary school which was whitewashed and therefore called 'The White School'. I heard afterwards that this bomb killed four soldiers. The second bomb fell on Kilinskis Street close to house No. 1, not far from the market. The windows were shattered but there were no human victims. More bombs fell on the shtetl, but I do not know anything about the aftermath because I went to Goworowo soon after where my husband had gone on Saturday, September 2nd, with the children and the goods from the shop.

When I went to Goworowo, a mass of refugees was heading there, mostly Christians.

I arrived in Goworowo at 7 o'clock in the morning, on the same day, September 5th.

During the night of September 5th to 6th, a battle broke out between the Polish and German armies. Several (few) escaped from the shtetl. And the people hid where they could. I, my husband and the children hid with 150 other people in a brick house in a terribly cramped space. In the middle of the night, two Jewish soldiers from the Polish army came to us and said: 'Flee! Watch out, the Germans are getting closer!' 25 of us, including me and my two children, quickly ran around the house and away to the village Wasewo (Vonseve).

On Wednesday September 6th, we stayed in Wasewo. The day went by calmly.

On Thursday September 7th at dawn, we (me and my two children) made our way back to Goworowo because a rumor had spread that the Germans were being pushed back by the Polish military. The information, however, turned out to be false: on our way to Goworowo we ran into German patrols on horseback and soon after, half a kilometer away from Goworowo, the German army appeared, advancing from the shtetl to Wasewo. We continued walking and rested by the wayside from time to time. The German soldiers pointed us out to one another: 'Jews! ... Jews! ...' But nothing bad happened.

So we arrived in Goworowo and stayed there.

Throughout Thursday (September 7th) and Friday (September 8th) the German military marched across Goworowo late into the night. It seemed like an entire army.

Thursday (September 7th). Soon after the first German soldiers marched into Goworowo, they broke into all locked-up shops, both Jewish and Christian, and stole all the goods from there. The Germans also broke into and entered the houses that weren't locked, but only looked around briefly without taking anything.

At a certain moment, when the soldiers stopped at the field kitchens to eat, a crowd gathered near the house where I lived. I was just outside the door when a soldier asked me:

'Jews?'

'Yes, we are Jews was my answer.

A soldier replied: 'There aren't any Jews anymore.'

Whereupon I asked:

'What are we supposed to do, if we happen to be Jews!'

'Hang yourself!' the soldier exclaimed curtly.

Other German soldiers shouted to the Jews:

'Go to Palestine!'

Or. 'Go to Hore-Belisha!'*

Or: 'Go to France to your rich Jews!'

Saturday, September 9th, at half-past three in the morning, a

---

* Isaac Leslie Hore-Belisha (1893-1957), British politician.

shooting was heard in town. I lived in a house near the market, near the Brikgas (Bridge Street). I looked through the glass-pane in the door and saw how the Germans were firebombing with a small machine all three sides of the market across from them, and also the street surrounding the market which leads towards the train station.

Only Jews lived by the market and on the streets mentioned above. The Christian quarter only began near the railway.

The targeted houses began to burn.

And soon the Germans were heard exclaiming: Go! That was the order to leave the houses. Frightened people got out of their beds straight away, just in undergarments, and went out onto the street. The Germans ordered everyone to run quickly to the center of the market. They shot those who were hiding or who walked slowly (because of weakness or age). I saw it with my own eyes.

I can list the names of those shot that I knew:

1) Moyshe-Yudl Geltshinski, a man over 60, a merchant, born in Wegrow (Vengrove). He was very fat and heavy and therefore could not run fast, which is why he was killed by a German bullet. As far as I know, he has a son in the United States (he calls himself Avrom Gelkh there) and two children in Cuba (a son Yitskhok, and a daughter Khaye).

2) Khaym Geltshinski, Moyshe-Yudl's brother-in-law, just over 40, a tanner.

3) Shmulke Plotker, aged 45-50, an employee of the 'Standard' gas station. He was with his son Moyshe-Nokhem. When the soldiers chased them faster, the son ran off and escaped without seeing that his father had fainted from weakness. The Germans shot the father!

4) Dvoyre Tsinaman, a woman of 45 (her husband's name is

Shloyme). When she appeared on the doorstep to see what the commotion on the street was and heard: 'Get out!', she turned to the living room to take her six-month-old child with her. A German shot her in the back and she fell dead in the entryway with her child in her arms.

5) Shloyme Doyid Feyntseyg, circa 50, hatter. His wife is now said to be in Lomza (Lomzshe), with their daughter Royzke. Another daughter, Tsirl, was in Warsaw, a son Khaym Leyzer and a daughter Feyge-Leye live in Uruguay.

A total of 60 people were shot, they say all of them Jews. I don't know the names though because I'm not a local.

The Germans slaughtered the *shoykhet* Khaym-Shloyme Batskoyitsh with his own butcher's knife in Bagateles, a village near Goworowo.

They shot blacksmith Yankl Roznberg half a kilometer from Goworowo when he was looking for his family.

I managed to walk safely to the middle of the market with my two children. About 2000 people had gathered there (only Jews). There were not only local residents, but also refugees from Rozan, Chorzele (Khorzshl), Myszyniec (Mishnits), Krasnosielc (Krasnoshelts) and also some from Ostroleka (Ostrolenke). Three sides of the market were burning, the heat was terrible.

After a short while, the Germans forced the whole crowd into the synagogue and the synagogue courtyard (behind the fourth side of the market, which hadn't burned yet).

When I entered the courtyard of the synagogue, I saw murdered children there (5-year-olds, 10-year-olds and older). I myself saw six dead little bodies. In addition, old people were lying there, 60-year-olds, 70-year-olds and older, some murdered, some wounded, all victims of revolver shots. I do not know under what circumstances they died. I also had no opportunity and no desire to pursue the matter and make inquiries.

The courtyard of the synagogue was locked, and German soldiers with revolvers and fire bombs in hand stood guard so that no one would escape through a crack or something.

We were held there for about 5 to 6 hours. Everyone was just in their undergarments and just shirts because we came straight from bed and there was no time to get dressed. There was nothing to eat and nothing to drink. Meanwhile, the last (fourth) side of the market next to the synagogue was burning mercilessly. And we assumed that the synagogue would also burn and that we would be burned alive. Everyone shouted: 'Shmo Yisroel!' The children asked for bread and water and cried; devout Jews said 'Vidui.' Their voices rose to heaven.

During the time that we were there, Germans came in a few times and took men from the synagogue and the courtyard and led them away. A total of 100 men were taken away. We were sure that they were being led to their deaths.

These images are engraved in my memory: the Germans took away Hershl Orlik, a shoemaker (his father's name is Noyekh, and his brother-in-law Noske Kirzshner). A father of six children (the oldest boy is probably 12 years old). Five children ran after a German, they fell to his feet and wept asking him to set their father free. The German brandished his revolver, drove the children away, and took their father with him.

At a certain moment, the Germans took a group of men from of the synagogue and ordered them to collect the shot and wounded Jews from the streets and the market and throw them into the burning ruins of the houses. They warned them that those who did not obey would also be shot. The Jews were forced to carry out this dreadful command. Some of those shot were still alive and conscious, they stretched out their hands and begged for mercy, not to throw them into the fire — it didn't help.

When we had been standing in the synagogue and the courtyard for about six hours, a German officer arrived in a car (some said it was a colonel) and asked the soldiers what was going on. The soldiers told him that they were planning to burn the synagogue with all the Jews soon. The Colonel replied: 'This can't happen, there are too many people.'

About half an hour later, the soldiers broke apart a board from the market, creating a passage 15-20 inches wide, and ordered all men to go out through the narrow hole into the meadow on the other side of the creek that runs behind the synagogue. The soldiers hurried people to go faster. Everyone fell over each other, it was a terrible scramble. Those who were in the synagogue jumped through the windows (from way up) straight into the creek.

The Germans did not let anyone cross the bridge that went over the creek. You had to walk through the water (fortunately it wasn't deep). Afterwards, the Germans also set fire to the synagogue.

For two days and two nights, the Germans held the 2,000 people, old and young, in the meadow without eating or drinking, without letting them go. Among us there were sick people, even wounded people, for example Yosl Tsudiker. His three children were wounded (the Germans had fired into his house through the windows and hit all three children, but only lightly wounded them).

On the third day a German came and drove us from the meadow to the courtyard of a mill behind the town (the mill owner was a Jew by the name of Rits). There we met Jews who had managed to escape from the meadow during the night. The Germans took pictures of the whole group in the mill's courtyard and said: 'Now you can go!' People went into town, not all at once, of course, but one by one.

From the entire Jewish quarter of Goworowo there was not a single house left. Everything had been burned, coldly calculated by the Germans without any reason. The Polish military was no longer in the city. There was no fighting, there was no resistance at all against the Germans, from anyone — and certainly not from the Jews.

Now we began to search for the remains of the burned victims.

Libe Geltshinski asked me to help her look for her burned husband Moyshe-Yudl. In a burnt down wooden house I recognized pieces of his fur coat which were still smoldering. There was nothing left of the body.

Shmulke Plotkern found his son Avrom, also in someone else's burned house, recognizable by his watch and artificial teeth.

Dvoyre Tsinaman was burned alive in the fire with her child and no trace of them has been found."

Appendix E

Goworowo

By Shabatai Chrynovizky · January 2005

| גוברובע |

אמי ע"ה נולדה בגוברובע העיירה
לסבא נתן-קלמן ז"ל וסבתא ע"ה
דבורה,
שם גם למדה אז תורה
בבית יעקב, לשם היא נשלחה.

בתנאים של אז, כשהיא גדלה
כך הכירה את אבא - בעלה.
לעד הנהר שכנה לה העיירה
שם חיו היהודים בתנאים קשים והיה
נורא.

סוחרים קטנים וגם בעלי מלאכה
ובקושי רב היתה להם פרנסה.

גם בית המדרש לא רחוק שם היה
שם יהודים היו ממהרים לפתוח
בתפילה.

מפלגות שונות ואנשים שם היו
מתאספים
כמו הבונד וגם הציונים
וכך היו שם אין סוף ויכוחים.

ה"שוק" היה במרכז העיירה
שם יכלו אנשים לקנות או למכור
וכן להתחלף בסחורה.

עד פרוץ המלחמה כך חיו היהודים
עד 1939 כשהגיע היטלר ימ"ש ואיתו
הרוצחים,
יהודים אז ברחו לשדות וליערות
ממש ממש כמו חיות נרדפות.

בבית המדרש נעלו את כל היהודים
במטרה לשרוף את כולם בחיים,
היו שם תינוקות, נשים וגם זקנים
שציפו אז לנס, שיבוא ממרומים.

לפתע, ללא שום סיבה, קצין ה-ס.ס.
לממונים הודיע
לפתוח הדלתות, וכך אותם הושיע.

כך השיבו היהודים בחזרה
את נשמתם הקדושה והטהורה
כי שום סיכוי להם לא היה, וגם לא
ברירה
תהא נשמתם, בצרור החיים צרורה.

הניצולים שנשארו מאותה אימה נוראה
כל חייהם יזכרו ויזכירו, מה להם קרה.

יספרו ויעבירו כל קורותיהם
לדורות הבאים שיבואו אחריהם.

ולעולם לא לסלוח!!!!

שבתאי
ינואר 2005

תרגום מיידיש: זהבה

Hebrew

269

Yiddish

Appendix F

Locations in The Run to Nowhere

Appendix G

Recipes

*R*ecipes Remembered, a Celebration of Survival* is a compendium of stories and recipes gathered by author, June Hersh through interviews with Holocaust survivors and their families. The recipes represent traditional Jewish cuisine enjoyed prior to World War II or dishes that they felt were representational of their lives after the war. The cherished recipes are authentic, while modernized in some instances, to those that nourished and nurtured generations of Jewish families.

In selecting the recipes for *The Spirit of Ruchel Leah,* June culled her book for recipes that were regionally similar to those Ruchel Leah would have prepared in Goworowo and then, ultimately, in Belarus. Many of the recipes carry the name of the Holocaust survivor who submitted them as an homage to that person's resilience and strength.

These recipes use iconic ingredients which were readily available in Poland. As in all small, impoverished shtetls, Ruchel Leah had to rely on ingredients which were seasonal and abundant. Thus, many dishes were created around potatoes and cabbage with creative variations using root vegetables and starches to replace the expensive meats and chicken.

All recipes have been fully tested and professionally written so you can join in on this culinary journey of Jewish life.

Recipes excerpted by permission of the author from *Recipes Remembered, a Celebration of Survival*, published by Eat Well-Do Good August 2021.

Helen Plasknik's Braised Red Cabbage and Apples

This could very well be the ultimate sweet and sour recipe. Mild, sweet red onions and tangy cabbage meld together with tart, crisp apples, honey, lemon and brown sugar. The result is a mélange of flavors that roll off your tongue. Just like a see-saw, you can tip the balance in whichever direction you please, adding more lemon for a sour flavor or brown sugar to make it sweeter.

Yields: 8 to 9 cups; Start to Finish: Under 2 ½ hours

2 large red onions, thinly sliced	¼ cup honey
2 tablespoons vegetable or canola oil	¼ cup ketchup
1 large red cabbage (about 2 to 2 ½ pounds), shredded	2 tablespoons brown sugar
1 tablespoon kosher salt	¼ cup tomato sauce
4 apples (2 Granny Smith, 2 Cortland or	1 tomato, pureed or finely diced
Macintosh), peeled and sliced thin	Juice of 1 lemon

Heat the oil in a large sauté pan, cook and stir the onions, over medium heat, until just soft, about 10 minutes. While the onions cook, shred the cabbage. Add the shredded cabbage to the pan and sprinkle with the salt. Using a large pair of kitchen tongs, toss the cabbage and onions so the salt works its way into the dish. Continue cooking until the cabbage has cooked down and begun to release its liquid, about 10 minutes.

While the cabbage cooks, peel and slice the apples and prepare the remaining ingredients. Stir the apples into the pan and add the honey, ketchup, brown sugar, tomato sauce, tomato, and lemon juice. Cover the pan, reduce the heat to low and cook for 2 hours, stirring the cabbage every 30 minutes. Season to taste with salt and balance the sweet and sour to your liking. Serve hot as a side dish.

Regina Finer's Kluskies – Classic Potato Dumplings

Think of this recipe as the little black dress of potato dishes. It goes with everything and you can keep it basic or dress it up. Their firm but spongy consistency makes them perfect to soak up rich gravy or float happily in a bowl of soup. Regina likes to sauté some onions and spoon them over the dumplings for a variation of this popular side dish. When preparing the dumplings Regina suggests you have a schmatta (rag) handy to wring out the excess water from the grated potatoes. If you don't have a schmatta, no worries, a dishtowel or cheesecloth will do just fine.

Yields: About 30 dumplings; Start to Finish: Under 30 minutes

6 russet potatoes (about 2 pounds), peeled then grated	1 egg, beaten
	½ onion, grated (about ⅓ cup)
¾ cup of all-purpose flour, sifted	1 ½ teaspoons kosher salt
¼ cup matzo meal	6 turns of grated black pepper

Bring a large pot of salted water to boil. Grate the potatoes using a box grater or food processor fitted with the metal blade. Process in 3 batches and use the pulse feature to break up any chunks that do not finely grate. Place the grated potatoes in a towel and wring out the excess water.

Stir in the flour, matzo meal, beaten egg, onion, salt and pepper and mix thoroughly. Nothing works better than your hands, so get in there and knead the dough. You'll know it's ready when it is no longer sticky, adding a little extra matzo meal as needed. Roll the mixture in your hands and form small dumplings about the size of a walnut.

Drop the dumplings into the pot of salted boiling water. Do not over crowd the pot, as the dumplings will stick together; shake the pot while boiling to free those that cling to the bottom. Boil until they float to the top, about 5 minutes. Remove with a slotted spoon and allow them to drain. Serve while they are still nice and hot.

Nadzia Goldstein Bergson's Home Baked Challah

There is nothing as satisfying as baking your own challah. It is a feast for all the senses: the tactile sensation of kneading the dough, the welcoming aroma in your home, and the satisfying visual of braided bread with its golden, eggy crust. The recipe handwritten years ago by Nadzia is an authentic reminder that makes preparing this challah so meaningful. We've filled in some of the blanks, but Nadzia's recipe is the foundation. Her original notes were to make two loaves, which commemorates the double portion of manna that fell in the desert on Fridays when we wandered for 40 years after the exodus from Egypt. It is also traditional to cast off a small piece of challah into the oven as a nod to the ancient custom of providing a bit of challah as a tithe to the priests in the Temple in Jerusalem. For the home baker, two loaves can be hard to manage, so this recipe creates one large loaf. There are many braiding techniques, six strands being the most traditional, round for the New Year, and this version which has three strands, a good place for the home baker to start.

Yields: 1 large loaf; Start to Finish: Under 4 hours

1 ¼ cups warm water (yeast thermometer should read between 105 to 115 degrees)
1 ½ teaspoons active dry yeast
½ cup sugar
2 tablespoons vegetable oil

1 egg
4 cups bread flour
1 teaspoon salt
egg wash glaze:
1 egg plus 1 tablespoon water, beaten

In the bowl of a standing mixer, combine the yeast, water and sugar and allow the yeast to bubble, about 10 minutes. Add the oil and egg, beat on low speed with the flat paddle until combined. Slowly begin adding the flour and mix until all 4 cups have been incorporated. You can then turn the mixer to medium and mix for several minutes. Replace the beater with the dough hook and knead for 10 minutes longer, adding more flour if needed to create a smooth, firm, elastic, non-sticky dough. Turn the dough out onto a lightly floured surface and knead for a minute or two so you can judge if the dough is right. This is more about feel than exact measure. Pour a drop of oil into a bowl and then place the dough in the bowl rolling it around so all sides are covered with oil; this will help prevent a crust from forming while the dough rises. Cover the bowl with plastic wrap and then drape with a towel. Let it rise in a warm place for at least 1 hour, or until it has doubled in size. If baking the dough at a later time, you can refrigerate the dough overnight and proceed to the next step.

Turn the dough out onto a lightly floured surface and punch down several times. So that all the air is released from the dough. Return the dough to the greased bowl and cover in the same manner as before. Let the dough rise an additional hour.

Lightly flour a work surface, and turn the dough out. Punch down the dough and separate into three equal parts. Roll the dough sections in your hands to form three ropes, each about 12 inches long. Squeeze out the air as you roll and gently pull on the ends so the strand is thicker in the middle and narrower at the ends.

Place the three ropes on a lightly greased baking sheet. Pinch the ends together at one end and begin braiding the bread just like you would a ponytail, by moving the far right piece over the middle piece, taking the far left piece and bringing it over the middle piece. When done braiding, pinch the remaining ends together, and then tuck them underneath to create a neat finish. Cover with a plastic wrap and a towel and let the dough rise one more time, about 30 minutes. Preheat the oven to 350 degrees.

Prepare the egg wash and using a pastry brush, coat the challah. Bake at 350 degrees for 40 minutes, or until the top is nicely golden brown. When you tap the bread you should hear a hollow sound. Let the bread cool completely before slicing.

Frania Faywlowicz' Meat and Potato Cholent

Cholent is considered a special dish by observant Jews who needed to prepare Saturday's midday meal, before Friday at sundown.

The combination of ingredients are as varied as the families who prepared them, but traditionally included meat, potatoes, beans and barley. The common factor is the slow baking, up to 24 hours, at a very low temperature. The stew would be assembled at home and then the pot would be brought to a local bakery Friday before Shabbos began, to bake overnight.

Almost a ritual itself was retrieving the pot from the bakery and eating the dish Saturday afternoon. Frania's version has two textures of potato, melding into beef flanken and creating a satisfying, comforting, full-bodied meal.

Yields: 4 to 6 servings; Start to Finish: 15 minutes prep, then slow roasted for up to 15 hours

2 russet potatoes, peeled and very thinly sliced, plus 1 russet potato, peeled and grated	fresh cracked black pepper, to taste
2 teaspoons kosher salt	2 pounds beef flanken

Preheat the oven to 225 degrees and line the bottom of a heavy lidded pot with wax paper.

Slice 2 of the potatoes paper-thin. Cover the wax paper with half the sliced potatoes. Sprinkle the potatoes with 1 teaspoon of salt and a few turns of cracked black pepper. Lay the flanken on top of the potatoes and surround the flanken with the grated potato. Season with the remaining salt and additional pepper. Pour 2 cups of water into the pot, and then spread the remaining sliced potatoes on top. Cover with a piece of wax paper, which seals the ingredients and helps retain moisture while the dish bakes. Cover the pot and bake at 225 degrees, overnight. Do not stir the dish or disturb the ingredients while baking.

Take the cholent out of the oven, remove the wax paper and dab a paper towel on top of the sauce to absorb any oil that has collected on the surface. Be sure when serving that you do not scoop up the wax paper from the bottom of the pot.

Carrot and Prune Tsimmes

In Yiddish, a tsimmes is a big deal, but when it comes to cooking one, it's pretty easy. The idea of a tsimmes is to combine root vegetables, which were plentiful with a few sweet elements. This recipe which features prunes lightly sautéed with onions melds perfectly with carrots, apricots and raisins to make a unexpectedly hearty tsimmes.

Yields: About 10 servings (6 cups); Start to Finish: Under 1 ½ hours

10 to 12 carrots, peeled and sliced into ½ inch thick rounds

4 sweet potatoes, peeled and quartered, then quartered again

2 tablespoons vegetable oil

1 medium onion, chopped (about ¾ cup)

1 pound pitted prunes

½ cup golden raisins

½ cup dried apricots or ½ cup apricot preserves

1 ½ cups orange juice

¼ teaspoon ground cinnamon

½ cup honey

¼ cup brown sugar

¼ cup granulated white sugar

Preheat the oven to 350 degrees.

Bring a pot of salted water to boil, and cook the carrots and sweet potatoes, until just tender, about 15 minutes. Drain and reserve. Heat the oil in a skillet, cook and stir the onions, over medium heat, until lightly browned, about 10 minutes. Stir in the prunes and apricots

280

(if using preserves add them later, along with the orange juice); and continue cooking for 10 minutes longer. Stir in 1 cup of orange juice (preserves), cinnamon, honey, brown sugar, granulated sugar and raisins.

Place the carrots and sweet potatoes in a 13x9x2 inch Pyrex baking dish. Stir in the prune mixture. Bake at 350 degrees for 30 minutes. After 30 minutes, add the remaining ½ cup orange juice. Continue baking until the potatoes and carrots are tender, but not mushy, about 15 minutes longer.

Fira Stukelman's Summer Borscht

While hot borscht with vegetables and flanken warmed the cold nights, Fira's blazing red cold borscht turned vibrant fuchsia from a dollop of swirled sour cream, cooled the hot summer days. Fira skips the middleman and boils the potatoes with the beets so they not only pick up the sweet flavor, but they become a colorful addition when served.

Yields: 8 to 10 servings; Start to Finish: Under 2 hours, then time to chill in the refrigerator

3 to 4 large beets (about 2 pounds) washed and scrubbed clean

2 medium red bliss potatoes, peeled and cut into eighths

3 carrots, peeled and grated on the large hole of a box grater

2 teaspoons kosher salt

½ teaspoon black pepper

2 tablespoons sugar (more or less to taste)

½ teaspoon sour salt or 3 tablespoons lemon juice (more or less to taste)

Suggested garnish:
sour cream, fresh chopped dill leaves, hard boiled eggs, chopped garlic, chopped sour pickles, grated carrot fried in a little butter

In a large pot bring 8 cups of water to boil and cook the scrubbed beets, over medium heat, for 45 minutes. Remove the beets with a slotted spoon and allow them to cool for 30 minutes, do not discard the water. While they cool, cook the potatoes and grated carrots, in the beet water. When the beets are cool enough to handle, trim the ends and peel the beets using a paper towel to gently rub off the outer skin. Hold the end of the beet with the towel (or a tined gripper) and grate the beets, on the largest hole of a box grater, directly into the soup pot. Cook, uncovered, over low heat for 1 hour. Stir in the sugar and sour salt or lemon juice and additional salt and pepper, adjusting to your taste. Transfer the soup to a large container and chill in the refrigerator until nice and cold.

Top the borscht with any or all of the suggested garnishes. If you prefer to serve the potatoes as a side dish, prepare the soup as directed above and boil the potatoes separately before serving.

Chana Wiesenfeld's Ukrainian Winter Borscht

Chana makes this wonderfully colorful and flavorful soup, chock-full of beets, vegetables and beef to warm even the coldest night. While long considered peasant food by many, beets have been rediscovered for their amazing nutritional quality and sweet buttery taste. Beets have a high sugar content yet surprisingly low caloric count. They are rich in nutrients and vitamins and can be eaten cold in a salad or hot as in this authentic Ukrainian soup. Be sure to follow Chana's advice, "a good cook is the one that watches the pot."

Yields: 12 cups; Start to Finish: Under 2 ½ hours

1 pound beef flanken

4 large purple-red beets (about 2 ½ pounds), washed, peeled and halved

1 pound carrots (about 5 to 6), peeled and grated

1 small green cabbage (about 1 pound), shredded in long strips

1 whole onion, peeled

4 (8 ounce) cans tomato sauce

Kosher salt and pepper

2 garlic cloves, chopped

4 ½ cups freshly chopped dill leaves

2 tablespoons telma chicken flavor powder (optional)

boiled new potatoes, for garnish (optional)

In a very large pot, bring 6 cups of water to boil and cook the flanken, skimming off and discarding any foam that rises to the surface. While the flanken cooks, prepare the vegetables for the soup. Take a spoon or small melon baller and scoop out the center of each cleaned and peeled beet half. The centers can be tough and sometimes bitter, discard them. Using a large box grater, grate the beets and carrots on the largest hole. Shred the cabbage into long strips and peel the onion, but leave it whole. By this time, the flanken should be cooked.

Remove the flanken from the pot, rinse and pat dry. You can remove the meat from the bone and cut it into small chunks, or leave it on the bone. Rinse out the pot and fill it with 8 cups of fresh water or broth. Stir in the beets, carrots, cabbage, onion, tomato sauce and flanken. Cover and cook on medium heat for about 1 ½ hours, skimming off and discarding any foam that rises to the surface. After 1 ½ hours, stir in the Telma powder (if needed to boost the flavor), garlic and dill and season to taste with salt and plenty of pepper. Cook an additional 5 to 10 minutes. Serve the soup hot with the boiled potatoes.

Berta Kiesler Vaisman's Barenikes – Pierogis

Every culture has their version of a pierogi. The Eastern European variety are usually filled with a flavorful potato and onion mixture that wants to burst out of its sealed pocket and dive right into a bowl of cold sour cream. You can finish them in the oven topped with fried onions or toss them into a hot skillet and brown them on the stove. Either way, make plenty, they disappear quickly.

Yields: About 30 pierogi; Start to Finish: Under 1 ½ hours

For the filling:
3 large Yukon gold potatoes, peeled and quartered
5 medium onions, chopped (about 2 ¼ cups)
½ cup (8 tablespoons) vegetable, canola or olive oil
Kosher salt and pepper

For the dough:
3 cups all-purpose flour
1 stick (½ cup butter or margarine at room temperature
6 cups of the reserved potato water
1 teaspoon salt
1 egg plus 1 egg yolk

For the filling:

Bring 3 quarts of salted water to boil and cook the potatoes until very tender, about 20 minutes. While the potatoes boil, heat 4 tablespoons of oil in a large skillet, cook and stir the onions, over medium heat, until lightly browned, about 15 minutes. Reserve the onions. Remove the cooked potatoes from the pot and reserve ½ cup of the potato liquid. Drain and reserve the potatoes.

Mash the potatoes and stir in half of the browned onions and 2 tablespoons oil. Season to taste with salt and pepper. Reserve the remaining onions and the remaining 2 tablespoons of oil for baking.

Preheat the oven to 325 degrees and bring a fresh large pot of salted water to boil.

For the dough:

In a large mixing bowl, or the bowl of a food processor, fitted with the metal blade, combine the flour, butter, egg, egg yolk, salt and reserved potato water. When a ball forms, remove the dough from the bowl and knead with your hands for a couple of minutes. The dough should be smooth and elastic.

Divide the dough into two halves. Flour a work surface, and roll the dough to a little less than ¼ inch thick (don't try to stretch, it will only tug back). Cut the dough into rounds using a 3 inch cookie cutter or the rim of a glass. Have a glass of water standing by to dip your fingers into. Place 1 teaspoon of filling in each round and seal by dipping your fingers in the water, running them along the rim of the dough, folding the circle into a half moon and pinching the edges closed. Drop the pierogis, one at a time into the boiling water and boil for about 5 minutes, do not overcrowd the pot, they will float to the surface when they are done. Drain on paper towels. Repeat with the remaining pierogis.

When all the pierogis have been boiled, place them in a large Pyrex dish and cover them with the remaining onions and oil. Bake at 325 degrees for 30 minutes. If you prefer a crisper pierogi, do not bake them. Fry them in a large skillet, heated with the remaining olive oil. Drain on paper towels, and serve with the remaining onions.

CPSIA information can be obtained
at www.ICGtesting.com
Printed in the USA
BVHW022335140722
642221BV00020B/443